JASON BAHBAK MOHAGHEGH

Omnicide

MANIA, FATALITY, AND THE FUTURE-IN-DELIRIUM

sequence

For the mother of the many changing names, places, languages.

Published in 2019 by

URBANOMIC MEDIA LTD
THE OLD LEMONADE FACTORY
WINDSOR QUARRY
FALMOUTH TR11 3EX
UNITED KINGDOM

SEQUENCE PRESS
88 ELDRIDGE STREET
NEW YORK
NY 10002
UNITED STATES

Second edition 2025

US Library of Congress Control Number: 2019933719

BRITISH LIBRARY CATALOGUING-IN-PUBLICATION DATA

A full catalogue record of this book is available
from the British Library
ISBN 978-0-9975674-6-5

Printed and bound in the UK by
Short Run Press

Distributed by the MIT Press,
Cambridge, Massachusetts and London, England

www.urbanomic.com
www.sequencepress.com

CONTENTS

Mania Tabula

Part 1
Augomania (light)
Heliomania (sun)
Selenomania (moon)

Part 2
Selamania (light flashes)
Neuromania (nerves)
Tremomania (trembling)
Ataxomania (disorder)
Eruptiomania (explosions)

Part 3
Uranomania (heaven, divinity)
Vatomania (prophecies)
Apeiromania (infinity)
Zeusomania (fate)
Hademania/Stygiomania (hell)
Daimonomania (demons)

Part 4
Pyromania (fire)
Fumimania/Capnomania (smoke)
Pyrexiomania (fever)
Frigomania/Cheimatomania (coldness)
Crystallomania (crystals)

Part 5
Dromomania (travelling)
Ecdemomania (wandering)
Cartogramania (maps)
Kinetomania (continual movement)
Dinomania (dizziness, whirlpools)
Labyrintomania (labyrinths)

Part 6
Graphomania (writing)
Linguomania (language)
Bibliomania (books)

Part 7
Chromatomania (colour)
Leukomania (whiteness)
Melanomania (blackness)

Part 8
Ombromania/Pluviomania (rain)
Antlomania (floods)
Thalassomania (oceans)
Bathymania (deep water)
Aquamania (drowning)
Kymomania (waves)
Ablutomania (washing, bathing)

Part 9
Dysmorphomania (physical deformity)
Decapomania (headlessness)
Teratomania (monstrosity)

Part 10
Eremiomania (stillness)
Clinomania (staying bedridden)
Somnemania (sleep)
Insomnemania (sleeplessness)

Part 11
Typhlomania (blindness)
Achluomania (darkness)

Part 12
Aeromania (air)
Animania (soul)
Respiromania (breath)
Anemomania (winds, drafts)
Etheromania (sky)
Nephomania (clouds)
Aviomania (flight)
Basimania (falling)
Trypomania (holes)

Part 13
Phonomania/Acousticomania (sounds, voices, noise)
Questiomania/Erotetomania (questions)
Silentomania (silence)

Part 14
Gymnomania (nakedness)
Ommatomania (sight, eyes)
Faciemania (faces)
Iconomania (images, icons)
Idolomania (idols)

Part 15
Praecidomania (mutilation)
Tomomania
(surgical operations)
Stauromania (crucifixion)
Xyromania (razors, knives)
Trypanomania (needles)
Cicatromania (scars)

Part 16
Agromania (open spaces, abysses)
Clithromania (confined spaces)
Claustromania (enclosure)
Anginomania
(extreme tightness)

Part 17
Atelomania (imperfection)
Peccatomania (sins, crimes)
Subteromania (undergrounds)

Part 18
Algomania (pain)
Pathomania (disease)
Molysmomania (contamination)
Narcomania (drugs)
Iomania (poison)

Part 19
Necromania (death)
Thanatomania (death-magic)
Coimetromania (cemeteries)
Klaiomania (weeping)

Part 20
Monomania (aloneness)
Isolomania (isolation)
Megalomania (self)
Catoptromania/Eisoptromania
(mirrors)
Colossomania (giants)

Part 21
Choreomania (dancing)
Melomania (music)

Part 22
Dendromania (forests)
Nebulamania (fog, mist)
Brontomania (storm, thunder)
Spectromania (ghosts)

Part 23
Chronomania (time)
Atemania (ruins)
Petramania (ancient monuments)
Geomania (stones)
Osmomania (smells, odours)

Part 24
Politicomania
(power structures)
Misomania (hatred)
Haematomania (blood)
Phobomania (fear)
Polemomania (war)

Part 25
Geumomania (taste, the mouth)
Aceromania (sour things)
Limomania (hunger, thirst)
Geliomania (laughter)
Zoomania (animality)

Part 26
Haphemania/Chiraptomania
(touch)
Dermatomania (skin)
Amychomania (claws, fangs)
Mechanomania (machines)
Ergomania (work)

Part 27
Nihilomania (nothingness)
Eremomania (the desert)
Taphemania (being buried alive)
Athazagoramania (forgetting)

Foreword: In Praise of Abnormal Persistence

Robin Mackay

By what signs shall we recognise the maniac? In the works of Emil Kraepelin, foundational for twentieth-century psychiatry, we encounter a figure whose implacable 'busyness' makes him a 'stranger to fatigue', and in whom an intense 'pressure of activity' (origin unknown) impels a lavish 'flow' of ideas. This condensation of a specific symptomatology for mania (as opposed to its blanket meaning of 'madness') has recently been reformulated in DSM-5, according to which the maniac taps into inexhaustible reservoirs of energy to fuel an unchecked spiritual dilation. Here the condition is said to involve a 'distinct period of abnormally and persistently elevated, expansive, or irritable mood' and 'abnormally and persistently increased goal-directed activity or energy'.[1]

1 J.R. Calabrese, K. Gao, G. Sachs, 'Diagnosing Mania in the Age of DSM-5', *Am J Psychiatry* 171:1 (January 2017).

Indifference to the specific goal toward which such energy may be directed aligns this conception with the new hegemony of psychopharmacology and a return to the disease model of mental illness on the part of the DSM (itself aptly decried as a work of neo-Kraepelinian 'nosologomania'),[2] which now lists the condition only as a subsidiary instance of the bipolar.[3] This shift cancels both the singularity of mania and the plurality of *manias*, along with any existentially meaningful dimension that might be claimed for them. The situation was different when, in the early nineteenth century, Jean-Étienne Esquirol first appropriated the stamp of Greek *mania* to coin a plethora of neologisms, beginning with *lypemania* and *monomania* and fostering yet others including *pyromania*, *kleptomania*, and *megalomania*, in parallel with the *phobias*, *phrenias*, and *thymias* that entered into circulation during the same period.[4]

It is this multiform madness, this plurality of manias, that Jason Bahbak Mohaghegh embraces in *Omnicide*, a fragmentary catalogue of the thousand-and-one species of manic disposition. Indeed, the declension of these 'miniaturist enchantments' is so varied that the book,

---

2 S. Nassir Ghaemi, 'Nosologomania: DSM and Karl Jaspers' Critique of Kraepelin', *Philosophy, Ethics, and Humanities in Medicine* 4:10 (2009).

3 Also a return to Kraepelin's model. See J. Angst, 'Will Mania Survive DSM-5 and ICD-11?', *Int J Bipolar Disord* 3:24 (2015).

4 T. Haustgen, 'Les langues de la psychiatrie, de Pinel au DSM', *Psychiatrie, Sciences humaines, Neurosciences* 14 (2016), 45–57.

though itself abnormally persistent, presents only a partial archive of those listed in its (provisional) *Mania Tabula*. The DSM's mechanism-specific neglect of this variegation, of course, reflects psychiatry's ongoing mission to diagnose, classify, and expel mental infection. Mohaghegh instead asks that we enter into the logic of mania, explore the many forms of extremist compulsion, and even admit that some may already lurk within us awaiting ignition.

Indeed, the first question raised in each of the passages below is the same: *What ignites the mania?* What kind of circumstances provoke an obsessive focus on the most minute object or activity? But a more disturbing question immediately ensues: What could incite such mania to flare up into the lethal conviction that *everything must be annihilated*?

Many are the routes via which the maniac's autohypnosis may arrive at a juncture where they are unveiled to themselves as harbinger and instrument of a new world order, and set about all necessary preparations for a cleansing annihilation. In each case the delirious passage between mania and omnicide is levered open by the mutual reinforcement of a compulsion to clear the way (everything other than the manic object is an obstacle), and a renunciation of consensual reality (the subject sacrifices everything to the cause, including itself, becoming a mere vector of some hostile passion for the real). *Omnicide* examines the potential for every idea, without exception, to undergo this deadly extrapolation—to be wielded not as truth, but as a nascent compulsion which, at the limit, will command the razing of everything in its path.

In a suggestion rich with overtones of contemporary apocalypticism, Mohaghegh intimates that an alternative to the exhaustion of the West can only be found in such a 'practicum of mania', a practical apprenticeship in madness, a neomagical delirium that draws on the 'inexhaustible reservoirs of fanaticism', transmuting groundlessness from grey affectless postmodern haze into polychrome rapture, turning frustration at the collapse of truth and the proliferation of undecidable fictions into an opportunity to infuse the slightest inclination with the most intense commitment. In something like a kaleidoscopic serial refrain of Nietzsche's eternal return, *Omnicide* tests our ability to withstand resorption into extremes whose virulence we would exclude, but to which we can formulate no effective riposte. For if *nothing is true*, as the maxim of that 'order of free spirits par excellence' would have it, then the conclusion swiftly follows… and once *everything is permitted*, the tactics of willed illusion instigated by Hassan-i Sabbah lead us ineluctably to wonder how visionary unreality is converted into effective force.

It is undoubtedly to such enthusiasms, newly armed with modernity's technical arsenal, that we owe not only the barbarities of contemporary terrorism but the atrocities of war and the fanatical fervour of causes revolutionary and fascistic alike. The delirium of excess has also exerted a fascination upon many base-materialist students of the peculiar insanity of the West—Nietzsche, Artaud, Bataille—and has been flirted with by thinkers of unreasonable liberation such as Foucault and Deleuze, not to mention being incarnated in a fictional lineage that culminates in the Kurtz-gradient initiated by Conrad and intensified by Coppola. But Mohaghegh sets out to convince us that it is exampled more copiously, more dazzlingly, and with more force in those literary productions wherein the mythical and mystical traditions of the Middle East pass through the defile of global modernity and emerge transformed, still charged with their original fervour but equipped with ominous new armaments. *Omnicide* therefore instigates its discourse on obsession, entrancement, excess, and delirium by entering the chaotic imaginations of the most significant contemporary poetic talents of the region, joining manic trajectories more insinuating and twisted than that straight line into the heart of darkness that is the unrequited death wish of an undead West.[5]

Shaped by the experience of being neither the victor nor the vanquished of modernity, the writers Mohaghegh

---

5 See J.B. Mohaghegh, *Insurgent, Poet, Mystic, Sectarian: The Four Masks of an Eastern Postmodernism* (New York: SUNY Press, 2015), 238–39.

places in conversation here manifest a stance he has designated as the 'occluded alternative': they are those 'third ones' largely excised from the narrative of world history yet who, having never bowed to colonial subjectivity, persist in developing modes of thought and speech that lie beyond the dialectic of master and slave, the West and its Other. It is in studying this 'zero-world literature' that we encounter, rather than delirium fetishized as fantastic spectacle or limit case, a studious cultivation of mania as pain, pleasure, discipline, and an egress to untold futures.

Following impassioned calls for an appropriate reception of these literary currents still largely alien to the Western critical canon,[6] in this work Mohaghegh uses the question of mania to confront us directly with the singular sensibilities of their greatest proponents. Between these texts he then excavates an elaborate network of subterranean concepts and interpretive chambers in order to discover the byways and burrows by which mania communicates with fatality—like secret passages leading from one of the multitudinous details of a bustling Persian miniature to the blank burning immanence of the desert.

Accordingly, *Omnicide* involves itself deeply with a certain landscape. Or, as Mohaghegh has written, '*moodscapes*, untrustworthy epistemic climates'[7] each with its own 'kind

6 See ibid., and J.B. Mohaghegh, *New Literature and Philosophy of the Middle East: The Chaotic Imagination* (New York: Palgrave Macmillan, 2010).

7 Mohaghegh, *Insurgent, Poet, Mystic, Sectarian*, 39.

of temperature, ambience, weather, and mesosphere of the mind/body'.[8] Saturated with poetic images of the blinding sun and its intolerable heat, the coolness of desert nights and their lucid constellations, full of fragmentary stories of restless wandering, trade routes, dusty cities, mud tracks, caves and tunnels, peculiar topographies and cartographies, unexpected passages between one space and another and between the inside and the outside, here we find ourselves in the 'nightmaze' of which Joyce (through Shahrzad) spoke.[9] These are perilous physical and psychic climates in the sense of *klima*, convoluted slopes or dubious inclinations that invite successive slidings toward extinction.[10]

Foremost among these catastrophic protocols is the 'profound Saharan code' of a climate that does not even meet the requirements of being a 'place', a site of possible dwelling or settlement.[11] The desert is where the soul shines, burnished by the body's confrontation with encroaching death, which renders existence luminous for as long as its frail vehicle can withstand. A featureless invitation to

8 Ibid.

9 See L.B. Jamili, 'Shahrzad and the Persian Culture in James Joyce's *Finnegans Wake*: A Chaotic "Nightmaze"', *International Journal of Humanities and Social Science* 3:19 (November 2013).

10 See the discussions of *klima* in R. Negarestani, 'The Militarization of Peace' and 'Solar Inferno and Earthbound Abyss', in *Abducting the Outside* (Falmouth and New York: Urbanomic/Sequence Press, 2019).

11 See *In the Desert We Visit Death*, interview with Ibrahim al-Koni by Anders Hastrup (Louisiana Channel, produced by Louisiana Museum of Modern Art, 2014).

abyssal contemplation, it has long been a geographical, metaphysical, mythical, and spiritual topos for the Middle East, its emptiness, its cruelty, and the plenitude of its promise glimpsed only dimly through the colourful caravanserais of the Orientalist canon and the desert islands to which European and American robinsonades chronically return.

The West has generally been more prudent about where it deigns to wander. It was only in later times that the terror of the unnamed wilds, the badlands where indifferent nature reigns supreme and where the logos has no purchase, was supplemented in Judaeo-Christian theology by the idea of wilderness as a space of contemplation and purification outside of the fallen world, a conception that comes to us in diluted form in the romantic landscape. In Middle Eastern thought, an unbroken tradition dedicates itself to contemplation of the desert as an appropriate locus for both fear and exaltation—and as a climate that perpetually ungrounds political life. Fourteenth-century thinker Ibn Khaldun tells of how great dynasties form and cities rise from the sand only for their ways of life to slowly lapse into decadence—upon which nomadic incursions will again overrun sedentary civilisation, closing a cycle traversed in more recent times by Ibrahim al-Koni's 'oasis trilogy'. In other words, what both underlies and undermines (state) history is the desert and its wandering peoples, united in their indifference to all that seeks to remain and endure, to write itself indelibly in sloping sands.

The protocols of certain strains of Middle-Eastern mysticism seek to engender this same vitalizing chaotic indifference within the soul. Chaos is unbound not only through mental ascesis (spiritual exercises) but by the practice of wandering, an errancy that helps unanchor the spirit. Becoming madmen or outcasts, mystics profess invented religions and doctrines, experimenting with the wildest new beliefs and practices in order to cleanse themselves of all attachment to belief. Geographical and social dislocation, states of exhaustion, exile, solitude, and evacuation serve to loosen the bolts of the mental scaffold.[12] A deserting of others and of oneself, an existential vagrancy, a renunciation of the search for meaning, ground, and home,[13] open up more intense prospects for a desert soul denuded of all that is worldly.

Mohaghegh honours the claim of those modern writers who rediscover such methods, those who 'live apart from the rest, in houses of ruin that mirror their own estrangement from the rigidified cities and their decadent trances'.[14] If the city is the place of man, along with all of the relations and self-relations that keep him woven into

---

12 Mohaghegh, *New Literature and Philosophy of the Middle East*, 28.

13 In the interview cited above Ibrahim al-Koni recalls that the Tuareg peoples use the same word for 'house' as for 'grave'.

14 Mohaghegh, *New Literature and Philosophy of the Middle East*, xiv.

the fabric of convention, present to himself and others, then these distressed domiciles herald its imminent return to the desert, an apparent void whose plenitude is there to be discovered by those willing to face its cruelty—or who find themselves with no other existential option. And since these writers and their characters have been born into and shaped by modernity only to inexorably fall through the cracks of its grid, each will have their own particular perversion, forming, like those venerable wandering mystics, a solitary sectarianism, a cult of one.

Yet the maniac is never alone for long; their mad intransigence is liable to corrode the sound minds of those around them, as in the case of the mystic whose arbomania is the subject of a Persian tale of the late Middle Ages. Insistent that he is a tree, 'planting' himself in the middle of the desert and refusing to speak, this maniac is discovered by a pair of soldiers who at first ridicule his absurd fancy but then, as all of their provocations meet with no response, begin to doubt their own sanity, ending up in an escalating quarrel that eventually turns violent. Only once they have killed one another does the tree-man leap out of the ground, dancing and singing.... Such epidemic effects can only further fuel the errant maniac's omnicidal design: to fully realise their virtual desertification at any cost.[15]

---

15 See Negarestani, 'The Militarization of Peace' on desertification and 'die-back'.

With the reader thus fully forewarned of the risk they take when entering such a maniacal multiverse, then *how* are we to read this book (that is, if it's not one of those necronomical tomes which, through its mere presence in a library, triggers the most eldritch inclinations in the casual browser...)? Its author uses theory and word-image to conjure states of the soul, corporeal states of being, and the geopoetical environments to which they belong. In a work that eschews mainstream critical postcolonialist narratives that bemoan and critique orientalist tropes and imaginaries of the Middle East, Mohaghegh's deep knowledge of the region's culture and literature seem paradoxically to intensify their effects, casting the unfamiliar reader into a climate that is far more alien than expected, beyond all exoticist affordances.[16] As he describes in his introduction, each selected fragment is extended and distended using a formidable armamentarium of different techniques; he pulls at the threads of the citations until they come loose, become unrecognisable, form new knots; he compounds their errancies with his own. Not a word is wasted in these divagations, though, even if many strike a note that is puzzling or gnomic. In its exacting yet uncompromisingly torsional relationship to major language, this is a writing that must be attended to with full alertness; it requires an intense concentration while

---

16 On affordance, see Negarestani, *Abducting the Outside*, passim.

at the same time exerting a hypnotic effect, working by means of ritual incantation and repetition, in an insidious rhythmic poetics that demands submission and elicits abnormal persistence.

Eschewing summary and generalisation, this book plunges us into one unique inhospitable climate after another, each attesting to the omnipresent possibility that even the most whimsical thought, the most fleeting desire, may incubate annihilative spores. A warning, a pleasure, and a discipline, *Omnicide* absorbs the reader into unfamiliar and estranging landscapes whose every minute detail threatens to become an irresistible invitation to all-encompassing oblivion.

Introduction:
Movement of the Lost Cause

I

On one night among many, a man sets ablaze a random building or village, and then dances. What persuaded this implausible design into incarnated possibility, to become the exclusive signature of his touch? Another convenes a militia or occult legion, donning long robes of self-deification. What folkloric principle or totemic theology could have drawn this otherwise unfathomable streak to the surface of his mind-body? A woman declares herself the enemy of certain archaic gods, and stabs her forearm upwards with sacred weapon in hand. What gives her warrant to pierce the skies? These questions must be answered, for everyone's sake; they must be approached through a detailed practicum of mania then willed toward inflection, gestation, and incision.

Omnicide: The killing of everything. What kind of miniaturist enchantment would lead someone to end the world?

In the wake of 'catastrophic' actions initiated by some obscure figure (rebel, mystic, insurgent, felon, artist...), the ensuing social-discursive panic serves only to cloak the more pressing question of *how* they were ever capable of this thing—*how* not in the scandalized moral sense, but in the predestinarian sense of an accomplished inevitability: What words or impulses effectuated the vital task at hand?

We must therefore start by compiling an inventory of incandescent delusions—the personal derangements, myths, stories, and legends one must tell oneself in order to become a dangerous phenomenon (mania baseline). What would suffice is nothing less than a catalogue of insane reinventions of subjectivity in an always already insane world, transpiring under the guidance of the self-misguided: namely, those who claim alternative titles, missions, lineages, and stakes in creation. Here must converge all the most perilous narrations and genealogies of self that would transform a man or woman into an armament, an improvised explosive device, all the careful manipulations of consciousness that furnish the precise basis for a philosophical license to violate. Thus the lie becomes a nether-methodology or wicked calculus, a formula of manifestation, execution, and concretion; exponential twistedness; the exact semblance that occasions the wound, wrenching the undeniable across our backs. Whatever justification works, whatever hypnotic turn gets things done. For this, we must learn to make fluid the otherwise rigid metrics of the indisputable. You can't argue with results, as the old saying goes.

In essence, we seek an archive to aid us in examining how one convinces oneself to assume otherwise, to study the deceptive architecture of thought that one must build around one's self-image in order to become a deviant or threatening grain of sand. Hypocrite, charlatan: identity surrendered to the most powerful untruths. The mesmerizing costume that perception must wear in order to overthrow the regime of an inherited existence (individual fiction versus universal fiction)...half-sorcery, half-ironwork. We might call this process a 'becoming-unreal'.

Modernity itself, upon entering the age of simulation, has seemingly opened the Pandora's Box, laying us prone to being devoured, as it were, by humans-become-visions (figments of the twice-unthinkable). As a consequence, aerial cosmologies alone will suffice hereafter (those of breath, wind, or pale smoke). This is the new theatre of war, amidst the fabrication of malicious sublimities: no longer the warlord who becomes a nightmare, but rather the nightmare that becomes a warlord. Wrath of abstraction; millenarian gasp. The right fable is enough to place all in jeopardy.

That most ancient Aramaic incantation—*Abra Cadabra* ('I create what I speak')—could be adopted as a moniker for that which radically distinguishes the omnicidal subject (practitioner of the spellbinding) whose tongue-becomes-hand-becomes-world, from the all-too-human subject of the current epoch who sinks ever further toward the middle-degree of affect. This distinction is nothing short of a seismic confrontation between the enslaved ones of an old world-historical order of the real and the enlivened ones of this will to illusion, and the conceptual scaffoldings that each rabidly constructs for themselves: that of disappeared emergence versus emergent disappearance, nihilistic paralysis versus nihilistic rapture, ironic seriousness versus artificial severity, democratized conformity versus apocalyptic aristocracy, sublimation versus pretending, banalized extremity versus extremified banality.

The fear of the former (apologists of the postmodern haze) is that the thematising of a phenomenon bears witness to the obsolescence of the phenomenon itself, so that a notion can only be enunciated once its death warrant has already been signed. In this context, the advent of thought marks the irreversible vanishing of possibility: revolution only became a concept once true revolutions had ceased to exist, the unconscious became plausible only once the unconscious was dwindling from the psychic strata, and the future became susceptible to theory only once there was no future left in store.

On the other side we have the omnicidal conviction (that of the compulsive and the aroused) that every new idea signals the approach, ominous hovering, and onslaught of an exception that will thrust into our midst the inconsumable—that which can never be accepted, for to do so would mean the very extinction of our race. In this second context, thought would seal some unwanted potentiality into the befallenness of all things: for these certain paragons and images would appear only once the terrible horizon of the event's dawning had already begun to flame.

What this leads to, in effect, is the performative engagement of the neo-magical, though devoid of its former affiliations: the prophetic without transcendence (for no higher power must intervene), the miraculous without belief (for no great leap of faith is required), the sacred without law (for no dogmatic structure can tame its ecstatic arc). Just the leanest mixtures of anomaly, revelation, and disaster.

And where might we seek tangible illustrations with which to navigate this labyrinth of omnicidal dynamism?

There are already countless mappings of this fatalistic eventuality (quest for ruin) in the history of modern world literature, and in almost every instance to be found where the striations of mania and cruelty meet. The arrival of a minor fixation (a luring of the fascinated gaze toward some object, image, sensation, or whim) increasingly expands and mutates into a lethal articulation, such that desire falls into instantaneous collusion with death-dealing.

In the Iranian Sadeq Hedayat's masterpiece *The Blind Owl*, the most blood-red strains of iomania (obsession with poison) trickle down a path to amicide (the killing of a lover). In the Japanese Kobo Abe's *The Woman in the Dunes*, the descent into ammomania (obsession with sand) fulfills itself in a kind of hospiticide (the killing of a host). In the Cuban Reinaldo Arenas's *The Color of Summer*, the author's heightening thalassomania (obsession with the sea) leads to a highly restless type of nosticide (the killing of the homeland). Moreover, within every one of the contemporary Iraqi writer Hassan Blasim's short stories, we can locate the many crossroads between a peculiar aggravation or curiosity and the escalating pulse of a decision to annihilate everything outside it: in one tale, an old man's melomania (obsession with music) culminates in patricide (the killing of a father); in another tale, an editor's bibliomania (obsession with books) comes to necessitate an act of xenocide (the killing of a stranger); in a third tale, an ambulance driver's iconomania (obsession with portraits, in this case virtual images) builds in him an otherwise forbidden motion toward dominicide (the killing of a master) and vaticide (the killing of a prophet); lastly, the fourth tale in the collection tracks a young madman's automatonomania (obsession with human-like statues) into a vast condition of urbicide (the killing of a city). The list goes on as if across an infinite continuum: Franz Kafka's dendromania (forests); Samuel

Beckett's dueling agromania (open spaces) and clithromania (closed spaces); Antonin Artaud's uranomania (heaven, divinity); Yasunari Kawabata's somnemania (sleep); Yukio Mishima's petramania (ancient monuments); Sargon Boulus's xyromania (razors); Unica Zürn's teratomania (monstrosity); Fernando Pessoa's fumomania (smoke); Clarice Lispector's crystallomania (crystals); Laszlo Kraznahorkai's nihilomania (nothingness). These are focused reckonings, without doubt; these are inexhaustible reservoirs of fanaticism, which nevertheless conceal the edge of an impending chasm or abyss. Beware crevasses beneath the waters.

The equation of each textual vanguard: on the one side, entrancement, seduction, drunkenness; on the other side, extinction, breathlessness, murder. No stronghold remains; no tyranny or right to permanence.

But why must each fugitive trajectory of devotion fall under the influence of a predatory drive? Is this the only model of apotheosis—the sumptuous, the necrotic? If we follow Nietzsche's warning that the artist 'forgets most things so as to do one thing, unjust to what lies behind him',[1] then we can begin to comprehend the tremulous balance, the dark commerce, between a thirst for the exactingly particular and the compulsion to extinguish.

---

1 F. Nietzsche, 'The Uses and Disadvantages of History for Life', in *Untimely Meditations*, tr. R.J. Hollingdale (Cambridge: Cambridge University Press, 1997), 64.

From this inescapable standpoint, there are many conceivable motives for omnicide: (1) to make of the deadened world a gift to one's manic object (mortal offering); (2) to clear all obstacles to one's manic object (vigilant protection); (3) to deprive the world of one's manic object (spiteful hoarding); (4) to elevate the manic object to final exclusivity (incomparable solitude).

And so, each of the aforementioned examples provides us with an inhalation-exhalation reflex: more specifically, together they chart the ever-contorted yet viable channels between some attractive universe (of adoration, worship, intoxication, or astonishment) and the overarching instinct to engender oblivion beyond that universe (through hatred, envy, indifference, rage, or forgetting). Such is the singular, imaginative link between madness and vengeance, a prospective explanation for the origins of both terrorism and poetry. In any case, there is no turning away from the imperative to study this riddle in all its mystifying complexity—to walk the tightrope across which a lone state of delirium might form a hidden route to world-erasure.

Movement of the lost cause.

II

Something must be craved, and something must then pay the price (a bridge to what the Stoics called *ekpyrosis*: the burning of all)....

To embark across this odd pendulum, beyond even eros and thanatos, one must seek the very heart of a logic of exalted penalty (the reckoning, the test). And this will require more than mere symptomatology. Of course, the affective topography and implications of mania are clear enough according to the 'authorities': accelerated speed (racing thoughts); elevation of mood (expansiveness, insatiability, playfulness, energetic gesturing, agitation); hyper-sensitivity (arousal, provocation, immanent triggers); hyper-expressiveness (overflowing language); strictest intentionality and orientation (maximum rigidity, precise targets); sleeplessness (ultra-vigilance, concentration, temporal imbalance); triumphalism (theatrical self-projection, immense valorization of purpose); risk (impulsiveness, recklessness, destructive pleasure-seeking); psychic gatewaying (linked to schizophrenia, bipolarity, obsessive-compulsive disorder, and delusions of grandeur and persecution). Fair enough, but entirely insufficient. No, one must be willing to decipher the ultimatum on its own terms.

When attempting his ingenious psychoanalysis of fire, Gaston Bachelard set out from the poetic verses of great pyromaniacs (obsession with fire), just as when he sought the secret pathologies of rain and thunder he enlisted the calamitous voices of literary brontomaniacs (obsession with storms). Only these textual rantings could provide the necessary entry-points into a domain of interiority that itself forges a radical outside. And where did it all lead? To the obliteration of the psyche itself at the hands of a new paradigm of the night-dream: 'The night dream does not belong to us. It is not our possession. With regard to us, it is an abductor, the most disconcerting of abductors: it abducts our being from us. Nights, nights have no history.'[2] Intrigue, theft, defeat of mind.

A far cry from Bachelard's Parisian reveries, we find the Libyan novelist Ibrahim al-Koni carving out his own definitions of otherworldliness in his meditations on the desert. As he stares upon the arid region before him—its excess, its waste, its many barren natures—a fine line is drawn between ambulomania (the obsession with walking) and androcide (the extermination of the human species). What appear at first glance to be mere allegories populated by soothsayers, tribal elders, herdsmen, and Bedouins are in fact anthems to a more profound Saharan code. Within an entire mausoleum of writing, two cryptic passages from the hands of the old storyteller are enough

2 G. Bachelard, *The Poetics of Reverie*, tr. D. Russell (Boston: Beacon Press, 1960), 145.

to show the way. First the desire (for roaming, drifting, aimless digression) must be inscribed:

> The desert is a paradise. Civilization, a city without a soul, is hell [...] The human community early on was split into two tribes. They were so completely different, as if they came from two different worlds. This evolved through time, and resulted in the nomadic tribe and the settled tribe. The nomadic tribe's capital was freedom. They had no ties to a certain area, so they turned to contemplation...The settled peoples' capital was ownership, and all the disasters ownership entails of course [...] That is why the spirit among settled people is dead.[3]

And now the perishing (through betrayal, beheading, hysterical violence):

> Then Cain climbed the rock from the flatter side, and, laughing wildly into the face of the sun, bent over the herdsman's head where it hung bowed. Taking hold of the beard, he passed the knife over [his] neck in the manner of one well used to slaughter, one who'd slaughtered all the herds of gazelles in

3 I. al-Koni, *Ibrahim al-Koni Interview: In the Desert We Visit Death*, interviewed by Anders Hastrup (Louisiana Channel, produced by Louisiana Museum of Modern Art, 2014).

> the Red Hamada [...] The jinni maidens in the caves responded with their lamentations, and the mountain was rent. The face of the sun turned dark, and the banks of the wadi vanished in the eternal desert. The murderer flung the head down on a flat stone there in front of the rock [...] The head, severed from the body, murmured: 'Only through dust will the son of Adam be filled.'[4]

We listen closely to each line, for the author is careful to note that, amid this slow visceral assassination, there are many shrieks and howls from the peripheral onlookers, though no scream or moan or even half-sigh escapes the lips of the dying one. No lexicon, no emanation of resistance whatsoever, for the necessity and sacrificial cost of the event is understood. Euphoric silence of the martyr.

In this instance, we must qualify the director's near-perfect injunction to 'become immortal, and then die'.[5] Or rather, we must allow it to sound out an even greater severity: 'To make die, and thus make immortal.' This is what one is prepared to do for the final item of passion: intensity-torrent, supervention, that intimate transfer or bestowing achieved through the gallows alone. This is

---

4 I. al-Koni, *The Bleeding of the Stone*, tr. M. Jayyusi and C. Tingley (Northampton, NY: Interlink, 2002), 135.

5 Dialogue from *Breathless* (dir. J.-L. Godard, 1960).

how the 'one true thing' (always itself a conjuration) wins its eternality.

Even children's stories reveal the ever-present intersection of the beautiful and the grotesque that leads to omnicidal destinations. When lost in the woods or plunging down the rabbit hole into wonderland, these are no longer moral categories of appearance (the villain may be ravishing, the hero hideous and deformed) but rather intimidating vectors of conspiracy and combat. They seem at times to form dichotomies of good and evil, but in fact work together on behalf of the surrounding formlessness. First rule of the imaginary: runaway children are at once frightened and riveted by shapes unlike anything seen before, chasing them across the desolate and into the beyond that is actually here and now. Second rule of the imaginary: runaway children recognize the tendency for all charms to become potentially game-ending, for all fascination to turn omnicidal, if given sufficient time and opportunity.

So it is that this archaeological inquiry into a certain fragile strand of thought positions us at a point where one departs from the world, and then takes the world down alongside oneself, in the name of the infinitesimal. The particular will forever menace the universal. The last conflagration spreads from the flares of a lone ember, or a match struck one night amid the metaphysical freefall of a lover (of staircases, mirrors, diagrams, clocks, ghosts, gold, etc.). Anything might serve to undo the everything, any seemingly innocent sliver of a wish that, having reached its highest elevation, then slides inexorably to the zero-degree where no one dwells—or *the Someone who has become No One*. For make no mistake, It lives here, feeds here, delights and dies here; It holds the ring of keys, and falls beneath their weight. Perhaps the maniac is the only true keeper of the promise.

III 10:10 (METHOD INTO MADNESS)

The proper approach to a book of mania is to show willingness to enter manic straits and apply maniacal styles, to borrow mania's own harsh rhythm and to drink from its dangerous wells of inspiration (one risks in order to survive).

The first element of the procedure is to station ten highly distinct authors before every manic trajectory, and to each time extract from these ten recurring voices the crystal of a single literary passage that might win us some necessary ground in that isolated zone. Thus the ratio is simple though fractally disturbing: one manic category; ten authors; ten selected quotes that hang like puzzle pieces or hieroglyphic clues to be deciphered, misjudged, or invented. The ten writers that form this configuration are, not accidentally, drawn straight from the turbulence of contemporary Middle-Eastern literature:

Sadeq Hedayat (Iran), Réda Bensmaia (Algeria), Adonis (Syria), Joyce Mansour (Egypt), Forugh Farrokhzad (Iran), Ibrahim al-Koni (Libya), Ahmad Shamlu (Iran), Ghada Samman (Lebanon), Mahmoud Darwish (Palestine), and Hassan Blasim (Iraq). A vanguard whose hearts beat in manic syncopation. For each round, then, the ritual renews itself: to chase ten different shadows down their respective corridor walls; to swallow ten different elixirs; to jump from ten different rooftops of speculation. Their mastery (of cruel wisdom) is perhaps unrivaled, and so we meet these same ten faces, we call them forward again and again, at every mad turn.

The second element of the procedure is to fashion an interpretive machinery or martial art with many tactics at its disposal: in some instances, we follow a passage with a *neo-phenomenological* touch (noting descriptive, sensorial contours above all else); in other places, we take a *narrative* route (moving with a storyteller's attentiveness to situational shifts, actional arcs, and the crucial play of atmospheres and objects); still elsewhere, the method follows *conceptual* threads (tracing the implications of a single idea toward its strangest outer edges), or rather focuses on a *conceptual figure* (the thief, the beggar, the prophet) itself a personification of a precise technique or outlook; similarly, when loaded with counterintuitive significance, the critical gaze pursues a *poetic* register, tracing a selected word or phrase back into its richest etymologies or forward into its most devious maledictions, watching the minute inflections of language, tone, and utterance; and lastly, there are times when thought here must grow bizarrely *associative*, detouring into seemingly trivial, adjacent backdrops and forging unique connections with whatever other philosophies, mythologies, theologies, cosmologies, numerologies, fairy tales, mysticisms, occult archives, aesthetic paradigms, symbolic systems, scientific happenings, superstitions, and magical practices can be scavenged across such experiential landscapes. This is how one gains speed and dimensional complexity. This is how one establishes the correct mood (function of the ringleader, the conspirator, the visionary), so that thought might become a project's arsenal.

Part 1

Augomania (Light)
Heliomania (Sun)
Selenomania (Moon)

It is a persistent error for thinkers to envision the first human beings. For in their misguided dreams of 'the primitive', they often assume a consciousness based strictly in immediate material experience (eating, drinking, sleeping, hunting, sensual gratification). In this way, they deprive their hypothetical ancients of the capacity for abstract imagination, leading us to believe that when such half-naked figures stared at the sun and moon, they beheld them solely in their most visceral manifestations. But what if they were instead the most abstract speculators, able to envision bizarre metaphysical conspiracies in the shapes of night and day? What if the celestial spheres were anything but mere physical proportions to them, their illumination and evanescence part of a more devious cycle, a more dire rhythm that extended into wild creative cadences beyond the empirical realm? What if they were not 'pure body', responsive only to the sensorial impact of heat and light? What if instead they exploited the visual overlords of sun and moon in order to hallucinate something otherworldly, using the ignitions above to guide an ascent into the most complicated territories of thought? What if the first maniacal dreams belong to the barbarian?

Augomania (Light)

1

> *In this mean world of wretchedness and misery, I thought that for once a ray of sunlight had broken upon my life. Alas, it was not sunlight, but a passing gleam, a falling star, which flashed upon me* [...] *In its light, in the course of a second, of a single moment, I beheld all the wretchedness of my existence and apprehended the glory and splendor of the star. After, that brightness disappeared again in the whirlpool of darkness in which it was bound inevitably to disappear. I was unable to retain that passing gleam.*
>
> SADEQ HEDAYAT[6]

We encounter our first augomaniac facing the robbed sublimity of a light which is no longer a universal constant but rather an atypical tinge of counter-universal experience (something that should never have happened). Light appears as a sudden infiltration of the continuous, an emergent force that violates the supposed essence of world. Our narrator, in turn, is a creature removed—a 'blind owl', in his own words—ultimately displaced amid the four bare walls of a faraway shelter, gnawed at by internal and external solitude, and yet awaiting (against all odds) the invasion of some incredible glow.

---

6 S. Hedayat, *The Blind Owl*, tr. D.P. Costello (New York: Grove Press, 1957), 4.

This affords us a significant insight into the manic disposition: although the latter is invariably oriented toward excessive dealings, this excess can take the form of an overwhelming focus on the miniscule or the indistinct, the slenderest of turns, the slightest phenomenon rising over the hills, a breath of fugitive light that should not even be there.

From the first bitter lines of the passage we recognize our augomaniacal narrator as one of uncompromising nihilistic outlook, indicting the 'mean world of wretchedness and misery'. And yet these are in actuality three separate, loaded accusations: the world is *mean*, as in callous (insensitive) or tight-fisted (withholding what ought to be given freely), whether through colourless indifference or spite; it is *wretched*, fallen into degradation (an inferior or abject standing), wallowing in the lowest register of self-hatred; and it is *miserable*, prone to impositions of abstract pain (the reservoir of intangible sorrows or distress). Hardness, shame, emotional destitution: these are the apparent parameters of our continuum of being, the reigning order against which light will appear as a minor violation, a lone contrasting streak that wagers on turning around these otherwise repeatedly vile principles. This self-sufficient ray of ecstatic peculiarity, this flicker-in-haste. And yet it is crucial to note the author's insistence upon the transience of such shining alternatives: he clarifies that it 'was not sunlight' (still too monolithic a concept) but rather 'a passing gleam, a falling star, which flashed'—for to fall beneath the dominion of a flash means simply that we are doomed on arrival, our perceptual attraction drawing us toward an ever-waning current, a telescopic intoxication that begins its exit upon entrance, begins dying as soon as it lives, but which, in its rapid procession/dissolution, may perhaps also serve to dislodge its spectator from the tired world to which he was previously beholden. This is the liberating abrasiveness of ephemerality itself, according to which, as the blind owl rightly notes, this 'brightness [that] disappeared again in the whirlpool of darkness' was 'bound inevitably to disappear': its mysterious power of intrusion and unsettling rests precisely in its propensity to vanish, and this fatal sparkling is the very precondition of the terms 'glory' and 'splendor' to which it will subsequently be entitled (elevations that always exact a tragic payment, for they occur only as an aftermath, the rich rewards of a defeated romanticism). So what are we to conclude from this bold augomaniacal touch which immediately plummets back into the cavities below? Perhaps the more drastic implication is to be extracted from the word 'apprehension', in the semi-veiled middle sentence of the excerpt above, for it suggests a type of knowledge akin to a state of capture: an enlightenment that binds one to some kind of anti-destiny, that makes beholden the beholder, transfixed by its own abductive writing on the wall. Beyond this, it attunes the unlikeliest of believers to an attitude of adoration, only to relinquish him to peril as the amorous stare gives way to prior drained states once more, the viewer-turned-lover (though of a depleted eros). And yet what does it mean to become obligated to a lost glimmer, neither a futural ideology of permanence nor a god-structure of infinity but rather a come-and-gone ethereality, the mania of the 'passing gleam'? Perhaps it restores his consciousness to an even more violent stratum of discontent than the normal one of vacuity, despair, hopelessness, and absurdity; perhaps it introduces some further acrimony into the blood; for this was not quite an experience of pure nothingness, but rather one of temporarily interrupted nothingness, the nothing that for a brief second became something, an exception which then had to drown again beneath the former inescapable weight of futility—a dispossession which then leaves us (still clutching after the fleeing light) only one conceivable recourse for the rest of time: *to seek revenge*. This is how the deepest nihilist becomes the most profound maniac, a convert with a vendetta, determined to retaliate for the transpired, for the already-fleeting, the already-fled, for what cannot return, can never return, having been reclaimed by the all-seeping darkness that rules; yet who still pursues with redressing arms that same elapsed wrong which cannot be made right again: the extinguishing of the one fallen star.

Light and wretchedness; misery; passing; falling; flash; moment; apprehension; glory; splendor; disappearance; inevitability

2

Compare man to an instrument panel with a thousand light bulbs; some go out before others turn on.

An extreme fatigue after a long agony, but an abundance of light, a fear of the northern lights...

RÉDA BENSMAIA[7]

We encounter our second augomaniac as one who documents the trials of withstanding light's many fluctuations (both synthetic and elemental). If our preceding figure was marked by a vindictive reaction to the transitory nature of his one longed-for spark, our current author interprets this volatility in different terms, for here we are introduced to two duelling images of brightness: the first an apparatus of myriad artificial lucidities that somehow forms the inner logic of human becoming, the second an interplay of simultaneous exhaustion and panic caused by displays of the polar magnetosphere.

We are first dared to 'compare man to an instrument panel with a thousand light bulbs', a comparison that alters our conventional impression of affect or influence. For here, becoming is no longer an intrinsic matter of nature but rather one of mechanically-induced bad

---

7 R. Bensmaia, *The Year of Passages*, tr. T. Conley (Minneapolis: University of Minnesota Press, 1995), 2, 75.

habit, a tele-operational switchboard or systematic row of dimmers that regulate the rise and fall of thought/experience itself. A careful stratagem of reversals (chiastic plot), of intricate activation and deactivation that renders functional every transformative conspiracy. But even more fearful is the second half of the articulation: namely, that 'some [light bulbs] go out before others turn on', reminding us somehow of those mystics who warn that one must die many times in life (though here the warning takes on a more industrial contortion). The light switch must therefore be accompanied by the kill switch. But how does one determine the correct nodes of exchange between levers? What decides which dials are to be animated and which others disconnected at any given instant, and what repercussions arise from an attempted figuration if certain other facets are not shut down in time? Where is the technical manual that explains this existential-scientific balance, the fine line between mastery and mishandling, and its arcane trade-off between origination and extinction?

The second line resumes an augomaniacal posture, though this time facing the 'extreme fatigue' and 'long agony' that precedes a 'fear of the northern lights'. Indeed, there is some terror in the auroral zone, itself named after the goddess of the dawn: optical fireworks of a fluorescent green vault; charged particles of solar wind and plasma; accelerated dance of protons and electrons along unthinkable latitudes. But why this culmination in astral dread? Maybe the answer lies in the reference to its 'abundance', as if consciousness suffered from an outpouring of cosmological clarity (the pandemonium of seeing all too well), and awe itself were just the awful price of sidereal vision. Maybe the augomaniac alone can access this intuition: for is the dread of the universe not the same as the dread of the machine writ large?

Building upon this last insight, it is the interaction of these two lines about northern lights and light bulbs that interests us most pressingly. For perhaps it suggests a special conjoinment whereby the primordial and the futuristic follow an identical method of delirium, that of sheer contrivance, both manufactured across a platform of rotating pedals, discs, syphons, and harnesses. This would mean that the reflective glint of metropolis and sky are at the mercy of the same paradigm of contraption, like the ordinances of cylinder and gear, the pipes of a cathedral organ, or the wooden reeds of a loom. What if the will itself could be reconsidered, then, as nothing less than the elaborate drive to technical manipulation, but a *techne* of rampant illumination without revelation, poetics, or truth, with neither instrumentality nor epistemology, just the craftsman's arm upon the wheel...or better yet, just the wheel itself, propelled forward by its own manic velocity, chaotically uncoupled and unguided by any driver? Thus the great weariness associated with the radial bands of light ('extreme fatigue'), often known as *magnetic midnight*, with vectors cast toward the *nightside of earth*, for tedium is always the enervating symptom of automaticity; and yet from a collapsed clockwork cosmos of semblances-without-depth, its patterns and sequences unstrung, its minute-hands and second-hands becoming mere ticks of symbiotic composure and temperamentalism. Ageless wisdom thus amounts to both a foreman's oversight of the chambers and a madwoman's mixture of genius/lunacy at the helm, fingering the puppet-strings of both causation and accident in search of more ornate calibrations of luminescence. To run the lights—whether human or stellar—is to enter the spatial parameters of the workshop, to follow its codes of fabrication and imprinting, and to know specifically which districts of being must be shut down and which electrified in order to induce a certain event (deranged arrangement).

Light and instrumentality; the panel; going-out; fatigue; agony; abundance; fear

3

Light uproots the desert and the universe, fastened with a rope of angels / Do you see the relics of a star?
I gallop in the voice of the victims, alone on the brink of death, like a grave walking in a sphere of light.

ADONIS[8]

We encounter our third augomaniac as a skeletal combatant, a figure of both militaristic deathliness and deathly militarism for whom light is equated with both downfall and war. Once again, light is here construed not as an inherent property of the living world but rather as the enemy of all worldly currents, and thus requires someone who will swear oaths and fight on behalf of its cause (whether as guardian, footsoldier, or crusader).

The poet embarks upon these verses with aggression, reciting their first words—'Light uproots the desert and the universe'—as a kind of oppositional rallying cry, both war-declaration and boast. It is a triumphant statement that draws the proper differentiating line between parties, between the players of this lethal game, now relegated to their respective corners, with light occupying one side and desert/universe the other. And yet light seems to

8 Adonis, *A Time Between Ashes and Roses*, tr. S. Toorawa (Syracuse, NY: Syracuse University Press, 2004), 37, 93.

strike its own alliance with the sacrosanct, for the next clause tells us that it is 'fastened with a rope of angels', although one should be cautious of such benevolent readings when dealing with an author of notoriously iconoclastic tendencies—it could just as likely be a hangman's noose, from which the broken necks of angels are strung helplessly. No, we must embellish the backdrop of this augomaniacal struggle with further detail: in surrounding stanzas we are told that we find ourselves 'in the murderous age', one wherein 'a child stammers', where 'the night pushes away the mountains', 'the Earth jeers', and 'the revolutionary fell'. An upside-down era for which only the inverse rites of antagonism, riot, and mutiny would prove honorable, and whose infamy is compounded by two further worsening details: 'We did not feel it / Spent blood'; 'We divulged our secrets'. These fragments speak to even some fouler betrayal whereby: (1) the people of this damaged place never sensed the atrocity that bled their wounds dry (imperceptible decimation); (2) before being scattered to the four winds, they sold their most intimate portions to the same world that demanded their execution (whether voluntarily or under coercion). Ambush, disclosure: this is the unworthy scene onto which our poetic subject launches his tirade, across a terrain of civilizational pyres, aligning himself only with a half-inscrutable light born not of any purity but from 'the stains of our tears'. Blemish, imperfection:

these form the dye and tint of disgrace from which our light-drenched reproach is born.

And the angels, again? There is an answer to this riddle, given to us in the next line: we are asked whether we 'see the relics of a star'. The sacred light did not survive the pollution at hand; it goes unsaved, whatever light remains being precisely one generated across the threshold of the former's horrendous dissolution, the divine orders reduced to foregone status, now just obsolete emblems and insignias of a heaven failed. The maniac of this newer elegiac light therefore wears such archaic forms (the rope of angels) as a mere necklace into battle, their once-iridescent bodies persisting only as remnant, superseded artifact, token of the surrendered halos that could rescue nothing any longer (not even themselves).

Menace of the horseman. In the second passage, we are told that the augomaniacal one 'gallops in the voice of the victims', thus placing us in a highly acute triumvirate: (1) the light-bearer has a steed at his disposal, and rides at frenetic pace across some field of engagement (the war is urgent); (2) the light-bearer's conflict is waged within the (perhaps slit) throats of those abandoned by desert/universe (the war is an echoing effect of a certain screaming or wailing voice); (3) the light-bearer defines the dispersed peoples before him as victims, which connotes a demise sealed by either criminal force, deception, or sacrifice (the war coalesces in the wake of those who have become prey, unwitting casualty, or burnt offerings to history). Moreover, we learn that the augomaniacal author goes 'alone on the brink of death, like a grave walking in a sphere of light', thus impersonating something unhealthier than the victims themselves by epitomizing the dead-already, the dead-too-soon, the dead-before-their-time, perhaps even paralleling the undead, escaping the collective massacre but drawn now into a different solitary march, a procession of the aggrieved, becoming what is at once most dead and yet cannot die (overdosed on finality). He thereafter takes on the ghostly demeanor of one who haunts/torments the prior scene of brutality, makes his headquarters in the graveyard, and conveys not the pristine white light of a consecrated world (there is nothing blessed left) but instead the eeriness of that pale blue light given off from a spirit unforgiving, a spirit that does not let go, a spirit that wrings itself amid the faulted reputation of all.

Light and uprooting; the desert; the universe; fastening; the angelic; the relic; galloping; voice; the victim; the brink; death; the grave; the sphere

4

Last night I saw your corpse.
You were damp and naked in my arms.
I saw your shiny skull
I saw your bones kicked up by the morning sea.
On the white sand under a hesitant sun
Crabs fought over your flesh.
Nothing remained of your plump breasts
And yet that's the way I liked you
My flower.

JOYCE MANSOUR[9]

We encounter our fourth augomaniac using light to make sensual connections between the most distant experience (the vanishing point of death) and the most intimate (the lover's body). A bizarre philosophical treatise on beauty is in play here: even dismemberment, if wrought in utter transparency, if bathed in light all the while, retains the original beauty of the form...or perhaps even enhances it.

She is enthralled by deformity, warping, amputation (for it passes the test of endurance), so long as light coats the scene. She opens the question of how one can bear the sight of the lover's mutilation, asking whether one can still compose words of irresistible attraction in the face of

9 J. Mansour, *Screams*, tr. S. Gavronsky (Sausalito, CA: Post Apollo, 1995), 21.

presumed repulsion (would this not be the most authentic lyricism?). Thus we meet this augomaniacal figure at the moment of her most graphic seeing, confessing the words 'Last night I saw your corpse' in a miraculous anti-psychological turn whereby she accentuates the violently evident (moving toward ghastliness) rather than seeking some repressed depth. From here we follow her minute descriptive inventory—archiving his dampness, his bones, the nothingness now left in his once-full chest cavity, his skull (the unrecognizable armature of faciality, bereft of identity)—but of even greater significance perhaps are the continual terms of luminosity that accompany (and then somehow retrieve) each misshapen appendage: 'naked', 'shiny', everything displayed 'on the white sand under a hesitant sun'. It is the ever-present light that allows for an abnormal poetic idealization of the spoilt and the crooked, that turns the otherwise macabre toward elegance, to the extent of the most refined affirmation in the final line: 'that's the way I liked you / My flower.' An axial component is at work in perception here, one that enables a spotlight effect to entwine seamlessly with horror, like a magnifying glass that lends actual magnificence to what it frames, and thus courts the sickening, drawing it toward shimmering states of delight.

Light and the corpse; dampness; nakedness; shine; skull; bone; hesitation; the flesh; the flower

5

a city on the shore of that roaring river
with chaotic palms and nights full of light
...which for years
has opened its arms to him and me.

FORUGH FARROKHZAD[10]

We encounter our fifth augomaniac on fertile ground, amid the lushness of rich climates where people gather at night to avoid the sweltering texture of the environment. Here, then, light refers to an emancipatory instant of exemption, the chance to dwell outside again, moving in open air and along the cooler waters, though it also welcomes another, more devious potentiality: lights that guide one into the folds of infraction, lapse, and disobedience.

Since we are dealing with a dissenting poetic figure who once wrote that her 'body exudes green shoots of light',[11] we must start from the ministered connection between sensuality, wildness, and an especially disruptive kind of luminescence. Thus she tells us of the 'roaring river' (soundscape of naturalistic defiance), and mentions that the city itself borders 'the shore' (right on the verge

10 F. Farrokhzad, *A Lonely Woman: Forugh Farrokhzad and Her Poetry*, tr. M. Hillmann (New York: Three Continents Press, 1987), 13.

11 Ibid., 128.

of radical openness). Specifically, what we find here is a movement against the pictographic theological light of halos and heavenly beings; instead she returns to an adopted dream of savage liberation, of the body restored to its jungle-properties, and to an accompanying discourse of ripeness in which light is equated (if anything) with impurity over purity. For the vines of the rough country are those of interloping and entangling forms, losing themselves in the vegetal lattice of a certain unruliness, 'chaotic palms' that showcase the vivid turmoil of living and growing energies. They drape, wrap, and clasp themselves together in a kind of all-contaminating mess, forming the model by which human desire might then be encouraged to its most wilful and seditious plans. Hence the sly transition by means of which this same tropical outpost then 'opened its arms to him and me', a looser form of being-held that hangs wholly in the balance of these sliding evening states, permitting her to exit the concrete grip of the city for the caressing modalities of trees, leaves, and lovers. And again it is light that makes this seasonal-spatial-experiential shift viable, a light that invites anti-authoritarian escape and plant-like embrace, for it alone can construct a smooth conceptual bridge between disloyalty and devotion: to favor one possibility, she must betray the other (must become uncontrolled). Call this an ancient rule of the strife between being and becoming, stasis and flow, cement and fire, between the tyranny of daylight (harrowing order of everydayness) and the insubordinate shafts of the nightlights that traffic one's (un)earthly wants beneath the curtained state of exception.

Light and the city; the shore; the river; chaos; night; fullness; opening

6

The sun vanished behind the mountain, but still poured itself on the plain opposite. At sunset it pleased the sun to clothe the desert in the red mantle of its rays.

IBRAHIM AL-KONI[12]

We encounter our sixth augomaniac in contemplation of a remarkable paradox: that certain phenomena (here the Saharan sunlight) do not surrender force as they vanish, but inflame by retrocession, maintaining their stranglehold throughout processes of vast self-distancing. In fact, the logic of power here might even hinge upon this backdoor relation, such that the receding sun grows somehow more vicious with each incremental dwindling. Perhaps not in the immediate physical reality of its effects—for certainly this ebbing grants the desert a momentary reprieve—but rather precisely in the indecency of this ritual delay, and in the perceptual dread of its promise to soon return and blaze over the entirety again (intermittency within the unremitting).

What we are dealing with here is a system of intimidation: by day, the sunlight is the warden of a terrible craft (making all dismal); it litters the dunes, it beats down with unheard-of viscosity, forcing the desert-goer to drink

12 Al-Koni, *The Bleeding of the Stone*, 11.

back great draughts of its obviousness. No doubt this is the leaden portion of what light dispenses; for the claustrophobia of the desert is an odd thing, built upon an affect-composite of compression, oppression, and depression (the tiresome nature of the tireless) as the sun 'still pour[s] itself on the plain opposite'. But then by night it crosses oceans of time; it ceases its harassments and enters a period of critical fallback: 'the sun vanished behind the mountain'. Is this a defensive posture, though, or even a humiliating retreat before the onset of darkness—or just another dimension of the ploy?

The answer is far worse than one could imagine, for we are told that it is precisely in its evacuation that the light experiences its own highest satisfaction: 'At sunset it pleased the sun to clothe the desert in the red mantle of its rays'. And what does it mean to say that 'it pleased the sun'? Philosophical courage would demand that, rather than taking the easiest path and anthropomorphising this pleasure-principle, we instead confront the dire possibility that there exists some other demarcation that we might call *elemental pleasure* (and what fantastic or extra-sadistic laws sustain this class of experience?). No, from the lines above we can at least discern that this is no passive recoil. The brisk shift from blinding white light to blanketing redness is just another facet of the star's cruel trade. This augomaniacal source is the undisputed owner of everything out there in the sands, the behind-everything, and itself calls forth the dusk's shade only in order to fortify its dominion. Its faintness is therefore just the vessel of a new exacerbation, a glass bottle that will slam itself back against the hanging mouth of our narrator the next morning, again reducing his speech to unaffordable mutterings (the plea for no-light). It drops low in the sky, tucks itself away in contempt, gone for the brief meanwhile, only to renew its otherwise chronic goal: the ruthless comeback, another tomorrow, the end of stamina, an all-slackening, all-encroaching arche-shallowness. Indeed, this light's departure is actually the keystone of its regime of overall abduction (the abduction of ourselves from ourselves), an oscillating cord that relaxes and constricts around being in its most pointless hours...to make us altogether something else. The abomination; the flatliner.

Light and vanishing; the behind; pouring; the plain; pleasure; cloth; the mantle; the rays

7

Throughout the entire night, there is no light
Throughout the entire city,
there is not a single scream.
Oh fearsome, night-allied, darkness-craving gods!
Wait until I hang the devil's lantern
from the porch of every hidden torture-chamber
of this oppressive paradise

AHMAD SHAMLU[13]

We encounter our seventh augomaniac in a state of cosmic rebellion, but one where the typical scales of justice are reversed and the political morality of the 'good' is mysteriously traded out for a deal with the devil. This gives us pause to wonder: What would cause the revolutionary will to shake hands with the demonic will, what hard decision had to be reached in the rebel consciousness in order for it to fathom an alliance with the malevolent one? Is it simply a matter of having crossed the struggle's threshold of desperation, beyond which one entertains all necessary means to winning (or ending things), or is it that this devil figure actually holds a specific weapon of political-ethical necessity, an illumination that would

13 A. Shamlu, *Born Upon the Dark Spear*, tr. J.B. Mohaghegh (New York: Contra Mundum Press, 2015), 13.

make victory possible, an illumination harboured by evil alone?

The devil's lantern (for this is what we are told is at stake), the only item that could possibly counteract the fact that 'throughout the entire night, there is no light'. Now, it is easy enough to trace a certain monotheistic genealogy of evil through which Lucifer is inextricably tied to light (his very name means the 'light-bearer' or 'morning star') and of course to hellfire (negative source of eternal light), and then also to the most nascent doctrine of rebellion (he is the one who first refused to bow, the fallen angel, splitting heaven in half and thus forever outcast). He also fuels the subversive fires of other players of the sacred history, whispering into the curious ears of the Edenic couple and possibly even offering suggestive advice to their child Cain, harvesting bad temperaments and pushing them toward the limits of their vexation. But this standard biography would miss the greater point of this literary verse, for here the author has carefully distorted several fundamental premises of the cosmic order: (1) the god-force is not considered one but many (note that the conventional almighty is absolutely unified and evil always perceived as legion/multiplicity, whereas here the devil alone boasts individualistic singularity, and his enemies appear as a sky-horde); (2) these gods are 'night-allied' and 'darkness-craving' (note that the conventional almighty requires no structure of 'alliance' since it rules unconditionally, and also rarely operates within the kind of framework of personal desire that the word 'craving' implies). This single line, then, places us into a new theo-poetic genre of the accusation, for if Satan is the first provocateur, then our rebel poet puts himself forward as the first great accuser. Accusing the Creator of what exactly, though? Of hypocrisy, deception, or fraud, of concealing that the one true God is in fact a fractured band of many conspiring gods, or of the fact that creation itself is nothing more than the hosts' own aberrant lust for darkness? Or even more, that 'throughout the entire city, there is not a single scream'—meaning that this false paradise has so numbed its many detained souls that they have even forgotten how to cry out?

Whichever this most severe infraction may be, it is enough to drive our cosmic rebel to an augomaniacal quest: to seek out the devil's lair and to acquire evil's lantern (whether it is confiscated by request or force remains unsettled). More importantly for the question of maniacal writing, though, it is upon his gaining possession of this artifact that we then witness the lightning-quick transition of the poem from a phase of accusation into one that effectively combines two other oratorical modes: the threat and the taunt. Indeed, a composition entitled 'Curse' and which cites gods and devils might lead one to assume that all damnations would descend from above or below; but here it is the poetic figure who condemns the gods themselves, hurling omens of defeat and promising their imminent overthrow at the nearest turn. Thus he issues the alarming threat: 'Wait until I hang the devil's lantern from the porch of every hidden torture-chamber of this oppressive paradise.' This baleful nod to futurity, to a shame-ridden future in which the old gods' trickery will be universally exposed, already required the light of the infernal to accomplish itself. The lantern therefore reveals the hollow deceit of revelation itself: there is no overarching truth beyond the dark-sick whims of a ring of petty gods, a clique that forged this existence in the likeness of a 'torture-chamber' so as to serve their voyeuristic fixations.

But what is the cost of taking hold of the devil's lantern, and does it not somehow mangle one's constitution irreversibly? Without doubt, the answer is luridly apparent in the passage's changing tone, for we notice that the poet has long foregone the grave, sombre resonance of the rebel (figure of focus and righteous preoccupation) and since taken on the scornful, jeering resonance of the devil (figure of sardonic and contemptuous hissing). Thus a crucial mimicry accompanies the purchase of hell's lamp, one that changes the revolutionary into the deviant, who does not wish to heal or save the world, but only to uncover its duplicity and aimlessness (laying bare, unmasking, or denuding the pretence). More precisely, it is in this state of deviant consciousness alone that one turns to catcalling existence, and stages this theatre of insult based upon a crazed imitation of the gods themselves...speaking in tones of wrath and punishment as if to drag the absolute into pathetic superficiality.

Yes, there are ill-born nights when one crosses paths with the figure of 'the saboteur', not an authentic double but rather a devious performer, a sinister actor who simply plays at one's identity, simulates one's movements, inhabits one's appearance like a diabolical costume, a being of perilous frivolity who wears one's face as its disguise or visor. This saboteur has paid an unspeakable price to attain such merriment, such mean humour and such eeriness, and will undercut everything in a light-show born of perdition itself.

Light and entirety; alliance; craving; gods; the devil; the lantern; hiddenness; the torture-chamber; oppression; paradise

8

She ran in, only to be met by a sight which was beyond belief. Her crystal ball was aglow with lights that grew alternately brighter and dimmer, and inside it she saw a series of explosions go off in splashes of red, blue, green and grey [...] *She tried to flee but the glass ball was emitting what seemed like electrically charged particles that fixed her glance right where it was, preventing her from looking away. It was as if the ball were a powerful magnet that had emerged from the depths of myth and legend.*

GHADA SAMMAN[14]

We encounter our eighth augomaniac in the studio of a fortune-teller, sitting across the table from a crystal ball erupting with constellations of coloured light. We are told that this clairvoyant had just left the room for a while (always beware the meanwhile), pulled away for some convenient duration, running back in only to be struck with amazement at the spectacle of her globe churning with pyrotechnic streaks. One wonders, though, whether this is the shock of pure instantaneity (something unseen; the unprecedented) or the defenseless dread of an event once witnessed long ago and which she prayed would never recur (something recognized; the unabating sporadic).

14 G. Samman, *Beirut Nightmares*, tr. N. Roberts (London: Quartet Books, 1976), 346.

Does she in fact understand what this vulgar overproduction of light entails, or is it a unique affair that escapes the scope of her expertise, ability, mastery? More than this, what are the implications of a loss of confidence in the oracle or sage? What are we to suppose when the priestess staggers across the room in pure astonishment or the seer trips into a confession of non-knowledge and doubt?

We might start from the expression 'beyond belief'—not as some dead-end precept of the unacceptable, but rather as the gauge of an overwhelming fullness of meaning (nonsense as that which grasps/pronounces too much), the blinding clarity of an untruth experienced as fitful moment, harangue, and turbulence. This is the marker of its profuse nature, its instability and insatiability; it bursts with lights that grow 'alternately brighter and dimmer' so as to remain without pattern or continuum (inundation, cascade). Note also that, although 'she tried to flee', the light-emissions 'fixed her glance right where it was, preventing her from looking away'; for here we come upon a truly serious point of argumentation surrounding the inescapable. There are two kinds of arrestedness, the first belonging to forces of order (law, power, truth, society, morality, reality) that paralyze subjectivity through constrictive fear, the second belonging to forces of chaos (intensity, movement, speed, blurring, image, pulse, visionary speculation) that suspend subjectivity in the gaping doorway of admiration, wonder, and awe. We can also understand this as a war over the definition of 'the limit': on the one side, an impossible stoppage or barricade sustained by discourses of total subservience, on the other an ocean horizon or cliff's edge that tempts self-overcoming through the will to breathlessness/fallenness (to careen through free space). Thus she tells us that '[i]t was as if the ball were a powerful magnet', and yet this magnetism drags the trapped gaze not inward or even toward itself, but further outward, into the furthermost terrain where one drops from the face of earth, into the weird flecks of the orb's light-games, into the vapours that she describes as 'the depths of myth and legend'.

And yet myths and legends are forms of patchwork storytelling or missive-delivery; they transmit and dispatch partial echoes; under the right circumstances, their fragments can be intricately deciphered, and so the fortune-teller's stunned expression before the crystal ball may indeed have been a learned practice of engagement with this arousal, one of ceremonial respect or tribute or marvel that would grant her access to its significance. For sure, the performance of surprise (the cannot-look-away) may simply be a necessary endowment toward this eventuality, the ritual offering to unlock intuitive potencies and with it the correct affective approach to fatalistic turmoil. For there is a special kind of language, one that strays closer to the age-old logic of incantations, in which communication is superseded by rhythm, tonality, and trance-like immersion. This is what the early mystics in their chanting called the passage to bewilderment, as words became vital passcodes to the other side of reason. Strangely enough for our current topic of augomania, this perplexity is precisely what certain mystical strands would deem 'illumination' or 'enlightenment': that is, the hour of thickest obscurity and confusion.

Light and disbelief; glow; alternation; dimness; explosion; fleeing; the particle; looking-away; magnetism; emergence; depth; myth; legend

CONCEPTUAL DETOUR

Having introduced the fortune-teller into our textual midst, let us note the multifarious and long-held traditions of divination (future-reading) that have existed across different epochs and subcultures. Some have heard of stroking tea leaves or palms, have seen the tarot cards spread out by carnival women in their tents and along run-down boardwalks, or have sought the wise yet amoral counsel of the scarved ones in gypsy camps, or even studied how the ancients would spatter the blood of a sacrificial animal's entrails across the wall in order to discern its tricklings. Note that, above all else, each inflection is tied less to the inner identity of the fortune-teller than to the hyper-specificity of an object or phenomenon in play, for indeed the key to the medium's translation/enunciation rests more in the ability to summon a certain manic bond with the thing itself. A short list is included below, with many forms intentionally deleted, and ending abruptly at a certain letter, in order to just suggest an esoteric link between mania, the future, and the unknown:

> acultomancy (divination by using needles); aeromancy (divination by means of the weather); ailuromancy (watching cats' movements); alectormancy (sacrificing a rooster); alomancy (using salt); alveromancy (using sounds); ambulomancy (taking a

walk); amniomancy (examining afterbirth); anthomancy (using flowers); anthracomancy (using burning coals); anthropomancy (using human intestines); apantomancy (using objects at hand); arithmancy (using numbers); armomancy (exam ining one's shoulders); aspidomancy (sitting and chanting within a circle); astragalomancy (using knucklebones); astromancy (using stars); austromancy (using wind); axinomancy (using an axe or hatchet); batraquomancy (using frogs); belomancy (shooting arrows); bibliomancy (opening a book at random); botanomancy (using burning branches or plants); brontomancy (using thunder); capnomancy (blowing smoke); cartomancy (using playing cards); catoptromancy (examining mirrors placed underwater); causimancy (starting fires); ceneromancy (using ashes); cephalonomancy (heating a donkey or goat's skull); ceraunomancy (using thunderbolts); ceromancy (wax drippings); chaomancy (examining phenomena of the air); chiromancy (studying the hands/palms); chronomancy (by means of time); cleidomancy (using keys); cleromancy (using dice); conchomancy (using shells); coscinomancy (using a sieve and a pair of shears); critomancy (using cakes); cromnyomancy (using onions); crystallomancy (using clear objects); crystalomancy (using a crystal globe); cubomancy (by throwing dice); dactyliomancy (by means of a finger); dactylomancy (using rings); daphnomancy (using a laurel); demonomancy (using demons); dririmancy (observing dripping blood); eromancy (using water vessels); gastromancy (hearing sounds from the belly); geomancy (casting earth onto a surface); graptomancy (studying handwriting); gyromancy (falling from dizziness); hieromancy (studying objects offered in sacrifice); hippomancy (using horses); hydromancy (using water); hypnomancy (using sleep); ichnomancy (using footprints); ichthyomancy (inspecting fish bowels); iconomancy (using icons); idolomancy (using idols); knissomancy (burning incense); labiomancy (lip reading); lampadomancy (divination by flame); lithomancy (divination by stones or meteorites); logarithmancy (divination by algorithms); logomancy (divination using words); thumomancy (divination using one's own soul); xenomancy (divination using strangers).[15]

15 Various segments of this list have been circulated in several places, including on pages 22–27 of Michael Berman's *Divination and the Shamanic Story* (Newcastle: Cambridge Scholars Publishing, 2008), but its original compilation can be traced to S. Chrisomalis, 'The Phrontistery', <http://phrontistery.info/divine.html>.

9

You will light up the tunnel of the unthinkable questions about this existence and about the brief wall of time.

MAHMOUD DARWISH[16]

We encounter our ninth augomaniac amid the guesswork incited by a spatial clash: being-in-the-tunnel versus being-against-the-wall. This is a concise yet thorned statement on the tension intrinsic to existential experience itself, one for which there is no avoidance or cure: the discordant sensation of living within the wide-open and the crashing-down-around. To complicate matters further, we are then handed another detail of this quarrel of spatial-ontological conditions, with 'the tunnel' being associated with 'questions' and 'the wall' with 'time'; further, we are warned that the questions are 'unthinkable', the time allotted 'brief'. Hence this situation hauls us before the hourglass, in a countdown-effect which forces us to scale the most nebulous reaches of mind and test the fissures of a cavernous inquisition (What are we asking, though?). A dispute without procrastination; a racing of thought against impermanence...for the light goes out soon enough.

16 M. Darwish, *Unfortunately, It Was Paradise*, tr. M. Akash, C. Forche, S. Antoon, and A. El-Zein (Berkeley, CA: University of California Press, 2003), 44.

This same poet declares elsewhere that '[w]e are of fire and we are of light',[17] both of which must regress and die out. There is a gradual downward tide here, one that reaches its nadir in the expiration of all dawns (thus the 'brief wall of time'). But this is common knowledge, the inevitability of our parting ways, so it is the tunnel that intrigues us and invites us to pursue matters further. For how can we begin to contemplate this cylindrical zone, this underpass (is it impenetrable or can the language of the unthinkable question alone burrow through)? Is it a snare through which all oxygen steadily seeps out, or does the flare set off by such relentless inquiries afford us something (an extension, resolution, proud defeat)? To advance, let us adopt a scattered migratory lens instead of a fixed theoretical one, and reconsider the tunnel now as four other separate dwelling-places:

> Axiom 1: *Nowhere.* What if the tunnel is the nowhere? There have been many names for this nowhere over time (the abyss, the chasm, the valley, the forest, the cave, the underground, the badlands, the outside). The names have differed but the design remains the same: to seek out sites of intimate unfamiliarity, the shadow-places where one can walk without history or self and thus experience a critical freefall (the will to

---

17 Ibid., 45.

become lost). One could even call it a kind of chaos ladder, near the house of non-belonging, at the edge of a certain essential oblivion.

Axiom 2: *Maze*. What if the tunnel is a maze? If architecture began as a conspiracy to somehow transcend death, to cheat the game of mortality's jowls and hide in some delusion of infinite metaphysical height, then we must return to the disorienting hallways and floors once more, to the awful torsion of the maze... its insanity, its futility, its ceaselessness. Only there can we invent a more impure architectonics, a diagrammatics of stealth or a criminal cartography that seeks no centres or destinations but only points of exit and escape, sites of skulking and imperceptibility.

Axiom 3: *Shipwreck*. What if the tunnel is a shipwreck? In its wooden carcass, we would reimagine ourselves as a vessel crashed along the rocks—to create as shipwreck, write as shipwreck, dream as shipwreck—such that thought itself becomes nothing more than a series of fractured beams and mossy particles of the unsailing thing. A 'disappearance at sea', as one used to say.

Axiom 4: *Bedchamber*. What if the tunnel is a bedchamber? Here we must allow for the birth of a new prototype of thought: that of the philosopher-anaesthetist.

This figure would follow the correct anaesthetic stages (induction, analgesia, amnesia, paralysis, recovery), prompt the correct anaesthetic effects (delirium, hypnosis, involuntary excitement, automatic breathing, immobilized motor reflexes, swallowing reflex cessation, eyeball movement cessation, light reflex cessation, pupil dilation, muscular-skeletal relaxation), and thereby fashion ideas according to their agonistic-antagonistic nocturnality: that is, the ability to put others to sleep (those who listen, read, or inhale).

Are these the light-borne questions we might at long last deem unthinkable (because they corrupt thought itself): those that lead into the no-man's-land, or that corner us in ever-curling networks, or that maroon us along uneven banks, or that sing themselves like fatal lullabies of a sleeper already drifting away?

Light and the tunnel; the unthinkable; the question; briefness; the wall; time

10

> *The neighbourhood was dazzled by the aura of light which radiated from the young men [...] Their silence added to the mystery of them. They were well-mannered and dignified, but with a light touch of good humour. The people of the neighbourhood fell in love with the two young men and grew accustomed to their radiant appearance every morning.*
>
> HASSAN BLASIM[18]

We encounter our tenth augomaniac recounting the story of two foreigners known as 'the blondes', identical twins of fair hair and complexion who come each morning (their place of origin and purpose unknown) to roam down the main street of a neighborhood called the 'Darkness District'. This quarter of the capital city is thus named for being the only sector still lacking electricity, and our narrator describes the residents there as physically gaunt and existentially worn down. This is an unwell place, and so the sudden arrival of the blondes represents a contrast, a radical anomaly and an enchantment-in-waiting for a zone that otherwise wants nothing more than to lay down and give up forever. We are told that the ambiguity of their

---

18 H. Blasim, *The Madman of Freedom Square*, tr. J. Wright (Manchester: Carcanet Press, 2010), 39.

circadian walk has an immediate transformative effect on the district; though these figures never speak, they cast gentle glances upon the inhabitants on either side of the street, and this courtesy soon bears miraculous fruit as the wishes of each person, young and old, man and woman, find themselves granted. By day and by night, the Darkness District escapes its former wretchedness to become an increasingly scenic area, with the government finally bringing electrical power and the locals planting flowers and showing acts of kindness to one another...all in honour of their two strange visitors (with whom we read that everyone has grown enamoured). They even build a stone monument in veneration to these silent newcomers. But then one morning the blondes do not materialize, as a violent coup is underway that sets the district on fire with bombs and missiles; amid the fighting, our narrator is flung against a wall, his life then saved by one of the blondes (their statue since demolished), and awakens in a mental asylum railing about the speechless aliens who rescued him (and the others)—only to find that no one has any memory of such beings or any trust in his recollections of them; he later finds himself strapped with a detonative suicide vest (the final light-bracketed image).

We start with two terms of immense difficulty strewn finely across these pages: *Inspiration* (to breathe or blow into) and *Adoration* (to beseech or worship). If these are the two dominant axes along which the foreigners' lightness is experienced, then we must acknowledge that: (1) their light is an invasive procedure, a subtle possession of the lungs; (2) their light arises as the response to something implored, a muted pleading that brings the outsiders forth. We must then reconcile this inspiration-adoration dynamic with the macro-setting and micro-setting of the story itself: that is, the light of burning oil fields in the distance, and the immediate gaslight-effect upon the psyche of the engrossed narrator and upon his entire district.

We are told that these saintly brothers 'dazzled by the aura of light which radiated' from them, but dazzled comes from the more sinister word 'dazed' (meaning to baffle or cloud judgment, to confound and cause misperception), and furthermore is linked disconcertingly to weariness (Old Norse *dasathr*, meaning 'weary'), as if reducing one to a state of stupor (the people grow 'accustomed'). Beyond this, there is the matter of their 'aura' (actually meaning 'breath or breeze' in ancient Greek). But the aura is most often sensed as circular light, thereby leading us to consider how this dangerous thought of the circle somehow always brings us closer to the winds of forgetting, disappearance, and grim alteration. Is the lit circle a gesture of breathing toward oblivion or excess, drawing us toward the pale sigh of the nothing or toward the hyperventilation of the unbearable?

The brothers are holders of some privileged information; they are entities of distinction ('well-mannered and dignified'). And yet they are wraiths; they have no faculties, and are equipped only with the slightest trace of 'humour' (At what are they smiling all the time?). No, their light is neither heroic nor wicked, but rather the third-party light of neutrality itself: in the end, they do nothing, allocate nothing, intervene in no form, make contact with no grand event, they just glide coolly across the avenue of appearances in the early hours and glide away from it each afternoon. It is as if they realize something at once unburdening and devastating: that there remains a purpose for this world, that existence is not pure senseless void but rather does lead somewhere in the final stride… and yet that it has nothing to do with us. What despair or freedom might this bring, to imagine that, across the vague horizon, there awaits some destiny or hope of which we (the human) are neither the inheritors nor even the central players? What would it mean to inhabit a state of universal irrelevance? The light of pure carelessness.

Light and the dazzled; aura; radiation; silence; mystery; humour; love; custom; appearance

Heliomania (Sun)

1

> *The sun, like a golden knife, was steadily paring away the edge of the shade beside the walls... The sun, sucking with a thousand mouths, was drawing the sweat of my body.*
>
> SADEQ HEDAYAT[19]

We encounter our first heliomaniac before a creature of almost tentacular orifices/fangs (vampiric sun), a resilience-sapping organism that gradually laps and tears at the narrator's energy, referred to both as a 'golden knife' and as a 'thousand mouths'. Nevertheless, what intrigues here is the fact that this depletion occurs through two different mechanisms: (1) the shaving away of the human shadow along the wall (why does it strike indirectly, assaulting from the edges, targeting the phantasmic projection over the authentic being?); (2) the continual tapping of sweat from the body (what victory does it claim in drawing the inside outward, causing slickened interiority to spill over the solid border between self and world?).

Sun and the knife; paring-away; the edge; the shade; the mouth; sweat

---

19 Hedayat, *The Blind Owl*, 73.

2

> *The sun that kept beating down on my head, I was drowning in a pool of ashes, the memory of the whole business was torturing me, and it was literature that refused to let me down! SSCML! Sun, Skull, Cinders, Memory, and Literature.*
>
> RÉDA BENSMAIA[20]

We encounter our second heliomaniac in a haggard vortex powered by the union of solarity and literature (torturous sun), a joining of the forces of intense heat with those of the writing-act that hounds an author already spending too much time in self-shearing mental loops. Nevertheless, what intrigues here is the phenomenological conjunction of the two into a synchronous strain of obligation, a double-horned burden/compulsion that leaves him simultaneously 'drowning in a pool of ashes' (the sun's melting effect on the head) and punished by 'the memory of the whole business' (writing's affliction of the temples). Together they form a vice of absolute fire closing in on him from all sides, its tightening influence necessitating the formulation of a desperate neologism, an abbreviation of the compounding powers of 'Sun, Skull, Cinders, Memory, and Literature.' This leaves us to wonder after

20 Bensmaia, *The Year of Passages*, 22.3.

the vested interest of elemental matter in the games of language, expression, artifice, imagination. Do originary creation (born of Nature) and aesthetic creation (born of human nature) share some underhanded agreement, one sealed in pain rather than beauty, a partnership between the most ancient form and a craft devoted to formed remembering, and does this mirroring-pact serve a mutual outcome of some kind?

Sun and drowning; ashes; memory; torture; literature

3

> *The sun resides inside me. Night, offer me your shadows now.*
>
> ADONIS[21]

We encounter our third heliomaniac in the grip of a frightful paradigm-reversal (integral sun), a rapid folding from science to conscience for which the exploding star is no longer beheld as the most distant or outlying event but rather as the most native, intrinsic property of sheer being. It lives too near the self, rooted perilously into consciousness; for all we know, it might actually *elicit* consciousness itself, and this perceptual-ontological teleportation of the astral fire to a focused point within, knotting itself in the embryonic, into what 'resides inside me', into the core of nascent experience, is simply too much to withstand. Not transcendent omniscience (that which discovers later), but intimate omniscience (that which already knows what one knows). The poetic figure therefore seeks an escape from such heliomaniacal nakedness, seeks to flee the eternal witness, this watcher/judge forever within, and pleads with Night for its protective offering (shadow-sanctuary). A call to diurnal self-betrayal; intervention or shielding

21 Adonis, *The Pages of Day and Night*, tr. S. Hazo (Evanston: Northwestern University Press, 2000), 283.

against sun-essence: no choice left but to develop scotopic vision/adaptation, to align with anything not of oneself (that which lives separately), and thus to favor the extrinsic safety of the 'early black' or the 'after dark'.

Sun and residence; the inside; offering; shadow

4

During the day I'm a serpent
I sleep and then I listen
To the sun's clanging on the green water of your eyes.

JOYCE MANSOUR[22]

We encounter our fourth heliomaniac describing herself as a serpent scheming with the scarlet orb above (reptilian sun), as if the latter conveyed its true intentions only to the coldblooded, the bellycrawlers, the slithering ones. We are reminded of those calendars of Aztec civilizations that feature snake deities against the backdrop of fully-manifest suns, pondering the coiling conceptual link that allows one to sneak into grass or under stone '[d]uring the day', at once a sleeper and a listener with ears attuned to 'the sun's clanging on the green water of your eyes'. The sun sounds a silent alarm, disclosing the position of the serpent-poet's chosen prey; it guides the hunt of this ectothermic being, accomplice to its camouflage and its incisors, confidentially signalling the whereabouts of all vulnerable things—those fit to be squeezed, swallowed, poisoned, or bitten.

But how do the forked-tongued ones know this secret dialect of the sun above others? Here we turn our attention

22 J. Mansour, *Essential Poems and Writings*, tr. S. Gavronsky (Boston: Black Widow Press, 2008), 189.

to a parallel species, another carrier of elongated scales and shedding skin, sister to snake and sea-serpent, that also slinks beneath the tentpoles of ancient human fear: the dragon. The Viking and Chinese mythologies of the dragon similarly assume it to be avowed to the nuclear sky, supposedly the source of its fiery breath. But there is something else about this winged prototype worth noting, an overlooked dimension: its obsession with gold. The image is preserved in both fairy tales and sacred texts: combining radical patience with radical greed, the dragon supposedly rests in caves for thousands of years atop piles of treasure, hoarding coins, necklaces, and other gilded wares. So is its heliomania caused by its endless appetite for gold, or is it the other way around (gold as microcosmic symbol of the solar source), and which of these poises itself at such extreme levels of desire that it makes the beast carnivorous and deadly?

Note: The first alchemists, whose guilds stretched from China to India to Arabia to the Mediterranean, would share their proto-technic findings and philosophical affinities in baroque decorative graphs, equations, recipes, hieroglyphs, and illustrations, from which we can ascertain the three following imperatives:

First imperative: *transmutation*. Many are familiar with the most common image of the alchemists as those who strove to turn base metals into gold, but in actuality this was just a middle platform from which they aimed for something far more impressive: the ability to distort destiny. Thus gold as material fortune stood for the larger puzzle of altering Fortune itself, meaning the power to invade, subvert, and twist the foundations of existential reality, to malform or reform essences and thereby allocate futures at will.

Second imperative: *exoticism*. Many have interpreted alchemists as being dedicated to rituals of purification, but in fact deeper study reveals an unslaked interest in contamination above all else, in the study of contagions and rigorous processes of corruption so as to mislead things into their most unbecoming states. The alchemists' methods are therefore definitively more criminal than scientific, seeking not inner truth but rather extraneousness-by-extortion, looking for the fastest way to turn forces against themselves, to make them affront their originary properties and rush outwards, torn away from their oppressive naturalism and into the anarchic beyond (alien freedom). Thus some orders perceived gold itself as the most outlandish foreign substance, such that to turn objects into gold represented no less than an insolent ability to make worldly things unworldly.

Third Imperative: *immortality*. If the alchemists did not respect the elemental laws and structures of being but rather always sought the escape-route, the defect, or the deviation, then the same principle holds even for the utmost boundaries of life itself (the way out). The alchemists' most glamorous quest was for the uncovering of what they called *the alkahest* (later known as the 'philosopher's stone'), a hypothetical universal solvent that would supposedly dissolve all other substances including gold. They risked body, sight, and health to test the combustible limits of mercury, sulfur, and caustic limes in search of this liquid, which was also said to harbour the crucial combination of ingredients needed to outlast death and to summon doubles (though awful in nature), faculties they argued could alone facilitate soul-fulfillment. Indeed, the search for this everlasting fluid consumed entire lifespans of certain alchemical masters, across many continents, revealing their third premise: that true power, and with it the secret traits of invincibility, would stem from the ability to both infinitely disappear and multiply the living world...including even their exalted golden idol (the alchemical ultimate as takeover or replication of the ultimate itself).

Sun and the serpent; listening; sleeping; clanging; gold

5

> *The sun*
> *the sun grew cold*
> *and blessing left the land.*
> *...The sun had died,*
> *the sun had died, and tomorrow*
> *came to have a mute lost meaning*
> *in children's minds.*
> *They illustrated the strangeness*
> *of this old word*
> *in their notebooks*
> *with a large black dot.*
>
> FORUGH FARROKHZAD[23]

We encounter our fifth heliomaniac in an era of crepuscular death (frozen sun), a time of fossilized dawns, of the muted and the unblessed, in which the once-swirling disk has taken on a defunct quality. The sun seeps into ubiquitous gray (the nowhere-to-be-found), and a new post-apex generation emerges whose children, knowing nothing of the former ways, are instructed to 'illustrate the strangeness of this old world in their notebooks', documenting the iced-over form in charcoal tracings with an air of bleak misunderstanding. Consequently, what is left behind is a mere heliomaniacal lingering

---

23 Farrokhzad, *A Lonely Woman*, 48–49.

for which the object loses its three-dimensionality and persists only as barest linear drawing, as codex or sketch, preserved abstractly as a now-extinct inkling, a lesson in ahistoricality (tomorrowlessness). The record; the outline; the 'large black dot' whose dwarfing subsumes the surrounding planets in pitch-black tiers; thus we are left to wonder what happens when Universe is reduced to a mere representational universe, to symbolic or metaphorical gesture, irreversibly long-gone and banished to the pages of lifeless mimicry, seminar, or allegory.

Sun and coldness; non-blessing; dying; mutedness; meaninglessness; tomorrow; strangeness; the dot

6

> *On his way back from the wasteland, after the stranger had disappeared, he had almost perceived a secret truth. He had almost bagged an illumination about governance. Yet he had to acknowledge now that this enlightenment had also faded away* [...] *The houses' roofs and walls were illuminated by a disorienting, dawn-colored firebrand.*
>
> IBRAHIM AL-KONI[24]

We encounter our sixth heliomaniac returning from a wasteland sojourn, during which he nearly stumbled upon an esoteric principle (cryptic sun), for these badlands apparently serve as a holding-chamber for some exclusive wisdom. From this account we gather that the sun-caped places are themselves warehouses of the most impenetrable doctrines, hiding 'a secret truth' in their broad daylight and hyper-transparent blaze. We are reminded of the telling aphorism of that greatest of Western philosophical figures who warned that 'Night too is a sun', for here, in perfect Eastern contrast, we face the alter-possibility that 'Sun too is a night'. This counterpoint suggests simply that the sun's torridity is its own modality of concealment, covering, or occlusion; it is a fever-dream that buries

---

24 I. al-Koni, *The Puppet*, tr. W. M. Hutchins (Austin, TX: Center for Middle Eastern Studies, University of Texas, 2010), 38.

illumination within illumination, pretending at clarity but all the while spawning a 'disorientation' that leaves one always 'almost perceiving' the enlightenment that had 'also faded away' (veiling through pyrexia). The only further clues we are given in this tale of puppets and puppet-mastery, as indicated in the title itself, is that this solar credo has something to do with 'governance', and that it perhaps only offers its code of supremacy to 'the stranger', a sun-stricken emperor who gains entitlement to rule humans by enduring inhumane calefactions? For what would it mean to envision a sociopolitical arena wherein the sovereigns must always be chosen unfamiliars, presiding over the lives of populations with whom they remain unacquainted, perhaps never even learning their names (estranged authority)? Would it imply a monarchical order of 'the firebrand'—note this last word in the passage, signalling a stirrer of some agitation, one who lays waste—as if imposed across roofs and walls by a forceful yet disaffected philosophy of searing (at the hands of the troublemaker-become-king)?

Sun and wasteland; the stranger; secret truth; governance; disorientation; the firebrand

7

The sun is alive!
In this pitch-black night (whose black-surfaced obsidian
has turned its entire spirit head-to-toe into a mouth
so that it can chew on hatred's rubber)
I have heard
the hardened song of the sun's heartbeat
clearer
madder
with harsher blows than ever before...

AHMAD SHAMLU[25]

We encounter our seventh heliomaniac in mid-exclamation, crying out an anthem of revival (resurrected sun) that will challenge a time of the obsidian. Here we learn that an unusual transmutation has taken place: night has somehow warped itself into a totalized jaw that gnaws upon hate-as-textile. This grinding motion is its own hegemony, and thus the speaker uses his poetic faculties to create ardor once more, as if climbing the stairs of a pedestal, tablets in hand, to unfold hymns of solar backlash before the soul-weakened crowds (restoration through over-delivery). He swears to them that what was presumed forever beaten will resume, and makes reference

25 Shamlu, *Born Upon the Dark Spear*, 24.

to its continued throbbing. Thus the heliomaniacal figure here becomes a kind of circus ringleader whose task is the ultra-enunciation and glorification of the coming attraction. Language here becomes intentionally emphatic, to the point of gaining contagious or vicarious status, a diacritics of accentuation and marvel, if not revelation, by turns singsong and tonally grim, moving between hype and solemnity, as the prodigy waves his hand, tongue, and body in frantic circumflexions. He brandishes radioactive strains of orality/aurality, he coalesces fresh hysteria around the image of the still-immovable, the unthrashed thing that bangs and salutes again, becoming furious ('madder'), becoming pitiless ('harsher'), set to bring its heavy bars crashing down upon all opponents as never before (the daring revivified).

Sun and aliveness; heartbeat; madness; harshness; the blow

8

> *Consequently, ultimate annihilation looks like a foregone conclusion—that is, unless the inhabitants of planet Earth join forces to head off the tragedy of the sun's death by migrating to some other planet whose sun is still in the prime of life...*
>
> GHADA SAMMAN[26]

We encounter our eighth heliomaniac at the critical height of solar dissolution, a state of emergency necessitating flight to another system (replacement sun). This image resembles the scientific prediction whereby it is projected that the sun will in several billion years become a 'red giant', coming to the end of its main sequence and swelling to proportions that contravene our own orbit, levelling us to an oven-like broiled-earth state, making oceans dry and land uninhabitable (no water, no harvest), and then depleting its own helium and hydrogen particles to the extent that the known world becomes nothing but molten lava. We meet our narrator at the eleventh hour, as this thermogenic failure closes in; the hour of desperate searching and moving-apart (toward the untried zone), of space travel and universal evacuation, for which 'ultimate annihilation looks like

26 Samman, *Beirut Nightmares*, 156.

a foregone conclusion' unless all leave at the speed of light. And what happens to consciousness when forced to operate under the appalling logic of the foregone, when obliged to stare into the fabric of consequence itself, that unflinching confrontation for which doom and insistence collide beneath a now-languishing gas sphere? Coruscation in atrophy; the gyre in entropy. We are speaking of the moment of necessary disloyalty, of justified infidelity to the origin or the source, trust in which must now be channelled into a vision of some alternative guardian or binary star. But are they to be faulted for not staying with their dying sun, for exiting the scene before reaching coronal finality, declining together in sheer overlapping proximity, cheating the experience of the absolute end and thus the option to attain heliomaniacal martyrdom? The minatory; the absention. Does this helical leaping of our reality's imperfection signal cowardice or a species defect, bartering for other fountainheads, for less-tragic patrons still 'in the prime of life'—or is there no cosmic postulate that would mandate our remaining in the heart of our own terrible exigency (to be broken along with our idols)?

Sun and annihilation; the foregone; tragedy; migration; the prime

9

> *Three o'clock. Daybreak riding on fire. A nightmare coming from the sea. Roosters made of metal. Smoke. Metal preparing a feast for metal the master, and a dawn that flares up in all the senses before it breaks.*
>
> MAHMOUD DARWISH[27]

We encounter our ninth heliomaniac throwing out an assortment of short raving clauses, a stuttering filament whose terseness signals a lack of spare time, for the elements have themselves swung into serrated attack (irate sun). This crisis compels him to talk in spiked micro-assertions, elocution of a thousand small cuts, together reading like compressed telegraphic messages, for the sun has come to devastate all things (such is the predicament). And yet our attention is above all drawn to the unique conceptual arrangements that occur as a result of this machine-gun-fire speech act, as thematic territories begin to coincide in ways previously unforeseen, wired together by panic before ambient catastrophe—an intersection of terms and visual paradigms, each noted on some roasting afternoon when we find '[d]aybreak riding on fire' (state of incitement).

---

27 Darwish, *Unfortunately, It Was Paradise*, 4.

To begin with, this association invites us for the first time to perceive the sun itself as rider, a conceptual persona of complex lineage who belongs on racetracks or battlefields (and why would the sun take up arms?). More than this, though, that it strides while itself on fire is an incredible masochistic understanding of the solar will as both outwardly destructive and self-inflicting—as if it subjected itself to the same punishment and desecration as its intended victim, pouring kerosene on its own body to ensure the combustion of all else within its path. Nevertheless, another irregular conceptual component is then flung our way, as we are told that the roosters (heralds of emergent day) are 'made of metal' and that likewise 'metal [is] preparing a feast for metal the master', for this now correlates the sun with a tautological machinic destiny (environment turned iron), also a self-fulfilling procedure (laying out its own banquet), partaking of and nourished by robotic/programmatic spreads, just as the rapidity of our author's language above begins to mimic nothing more than the reflex-reaction of a joint being struck (thoughtless twitch, spasm, or shudder). Is this somehow the answer, then? And does this in some way speak to the reason for such a 'nightmare coming from the sea', namely, that the catastrophic occurs precisely at that nexus where nature becomes sheer mechanism, where dawn takes on the steel, copper, or titanium disposition of a simple killing machine? The catapult; the guillotine; the electric chair; the drone (blood made technical).

In another poem by the same author many years later, we find a further outbreak of heliomania: 'when the sun falls from white poplars, we are overwhelmed by a desire to cry for one who has died for nothing.'[28] Does perishing at the hands of a sun-turned-metal, then, somehow make all subsequent death an inadequate category of experience? And note that there is only a supposed *desire to cry*, but no actual crying: the machine-sun has apparently erased all capacity for tears (retuned to an unfeeling world).

Sun and the rider; the nightmare; the rooster;
smoke; metal; the feast; the master; the breaking

28 Ibid., 62.

10

Day by day people became more and more attached to the two handsome youths, and their coming and going became like the rising and the setting of the sun. The children were the first to grow attached to them: they would gather early in the morning on the edge of the quarter to wait for the young men to appear from across the wasteland. They would bet Sinbad cards on which lane the men would come down today.

HASSAN BLASIM[29]

We encounter our tenth heliomaniac back in the same story of the two light-skinned foreigners whose daily visitation brings grace upon the tainted and mortified space of the Darkness District (xenophiliac sun). We thus recall that our narrator, now named the Madman of Freedom Square after an explosion has permanently damaged his mind, remains the only one to authenticate their benevolent intrusion; he alone still wants to behold their presence, longing for those footsteps whose 'coming and going' is 'like the rising and setting of the sun'. We have already seen how the people of this derelict zone fell into some temporary infatuation; the way they developed an ever-growing attachment to these otherworldly figures,

29 Blasim, *The Madman of Freedom Square*, 39.

waiting idly each morning for their appearance, is all part of an important conceptual connection between mania, desire, and anticipation. But what intrigues us here is the makeshift ritual of the children who begin betting cards 'on which lane the men would come down today', since this takes us into a thematic coincidence between mania and the wager, a whole relation to chance that deserves further consideration. For the children reveal that theirs is a dual gamble, a speculation on both cyclicity and trajectivity (and simultaneously both repetition and difference): they hazard their prizes at once on the uncertain likelihood of return and also on the random orientation or angle of that return. Thus the expectant one is placed into exhilarating jeopardy; against an anxious absolutism (that must know time and place), they bring the object of ultimate desire (its continuance, its locus) into the circle of the game, the stake, and the guess.

This notwithstanding, what perhaps gives us the most unorthodox point of departure for the question of heliomaniacal experience is the detail of the specific type of playing cards exchanged by the children: namely, those depicting Sinbad, character of classical Arabian literature, figure of the seven voyages, the wayfarer/seafarer, both rogue and star-crossed, whom the sun calls to embark on adventures, perpetually chasing horizons, yet whose sails always find an ill-spraying wind: soon separated from his shipmates, craft torn asunder, left adrift on cracked rafts in the middle of the ocean, stranded on islands alone and dying of exposure or thirst. The recounting of these travails afford us incalculable resources: valley of the diamonds and the giant snakes, nests of the devil bird-men, man-eating beings of coal-shaped eyes and hideously long nails, insanity-causing herbs and plants, entombment among dead lovers and being sold into slavery, starvation amid tall cliffs, imprisonment by the Old Man of the Sea, hostage of the city of apes and the Elephant King's graveyard, consorting with caliphs and scavenging lands for precious gems. No doubt this mediaeval persona is the truest master of eluding certain death (always finding the outlet), equipped with some rare antenna for concealed rivulets and serpentines that grant him nick-of-time passage; his is not a heroic portrait then, for he is at once the most harassed and the most advantaged, addicted to razor-thin survival, to pressing his luck further, lord of countless doomed vessels and near-fatal escapes; nor is his erratic saga that of the conqueror, for he constantly steals but never plunders, keeping his pockets relatively light, pillaging opportunity itself, an individualistic rover, jovial and generous and cutthroat, disinterested in totality, content to bring back only the one most valued thing, to lift the invaluable, returning home rich beyond measure and yet restless beyond control, giving away the gifts of faraway kings to vagrants (becoming stir crazy, squandering fortunes). The sun therefore provides a perfect excuse, itself emblematic of that which wins everything by day and loses everything by night again, to take to the scimitar waters once more (the heliomaniacal dream as one of perpetual floating).

Sun and attachment; gathering; appearance; the bet; the lane; the card

Selenomania (Moon)

1

> *A deep silence fell upon the tower. The moon was slowly rising and its cold glimmer gradually outlined the inside of the sanctuary. Shiny white bones glistened in the moonlight—skulls, limbs, shinbones, broken ribs, jaws with locked teeth, fists clenched in spasm...*
>
> SADEQ HEDAYAT[30]

We encounter our first selenomaniac in the afterlife, although this is more just a tedious and underserving afterwards, for which the moon serves each night as rising overlord (establishing the practice of utter futility). It marks the gathering-hour of the purgatorial, this empty twilight that sits above the ceramic domes of a mausoleum, and beneath which the long-dead and recently-dead emerge to wander and murmur among themselves in pure listlessness. Their enervation causes them to spend forever in languid rituals (the useless eternal), somehow trapped within the crescent's 'deep silence' and 'cold glimmer', moving spiritlessly between tower and sanctuary (more bonepit than refuge, since it protects nothing but only circumscribes). They themselves are nothing more than

30 S. Hedayat, 'The Benedictions', in E. Yarshater (ed.), *Sadeq Hedayat: An Anthology* (Boulder, CO: Westview Press, 1979), 78.

the 'outline' cast by a moonlight that governs the middle-ground, the gap of inaction, one that compartmentalizes the human form into separate dismal appendages and organs...a mass grave stealing all traces of sensation or endeavour, leaving just the memory of 'locked teeth' and 'fists clenched in spasm'.

It seems an unsuitable place for a manic trigger of some kind to emerge, and yet a single element within the stale nightly routine strikes at our interpretive curiosity and signals this possibility amid the very dreariness: namely, the story later reveals that these apparitions are sometimes allowed to teleport themselves to visit old family or sites among the living. Thus the drowsy interactions of these dead, their every conversation soured by half-nihilistic condemnations of an existence that promised more than it could deliver, a cosmological order that did indeed bother to construct an afterlife but one of such inane quality, entrusting perpetuity to inertia, without judgment or revelation or impending heaven (this is all there is), are nevertheless punctuated by wandering returns to the scene of past longings and associations. They stare, they take note, and then find their way back to the cemetery tower with no greater intention, without dispensing horror or sadness or blessing, for these are not proper hauntings, the dead being too far divested from whatever developments they observe to make contact or seek influence. It is not necessarily impossible, but they appear affectively stripped of the very impulse for crossover, never grasping outward, never reconnecting, making us wonder what potential event could inspire them to move across the breach...and we are given a small track, near the story's conclusion, where we learn of the mildest pleasure that they take in hearing their names still spoken on occasion (across breathing lips), and that the old word soothes their bareness, their monophonic void, enough to endure the cheerless moon and its permanent meanwhile.

Note: We are here reminded of the Watchers (Aramaic *iryn*; Greek *egregoroi*), the race of angels presumably sent by God to look over humans since exiled from paradise, but with strict commands never to intervene or make direct contact with those who had broken covenants and thereby failed the pages of Genesis. And yet after years of absolute neutrality, remaining adjacent, keeping them silent company in their daily struggles and screechings, the Watchers' gaze began to accumulate interest; *scopos* became kaleidoscopic passion, and an increasing attraction to these humans damned. They could no longer withstand their continued disengagement, this state of the almost-touchable (excruciating proximity), and began aiding and reproducing with the garden exiles. Thus the Watcher angels inevitably broke their code: according to apocryphal writings from the Book of Enoch, grandfather of Noah, they taught men the heavenly art of war (making knives, swords, spears) and women the equally heavenly art of seduction (makeup, dance, adornment), and they took lovers among them at night beneath the moon, creating tainted offspring, a bastard species of giants (half-divine, half-mortal) called the *nephilim* who would terrorize the land with exceptional strength and rage. It is this supposed perversion (in some readings) that causes a now angered God to cast out the Watchers, who are then rooted forever in a cursed valley, and to call forth the great flood, thereby allowing us to entertain the following premise: that a lone selenomaniacal compulsion to touch from beyond, removing the cleft between ethereal and living, sky and earthly surface, is what brings forth the first catastrophe (the all-drowning).

Moon and silence; the tower; the sanctuary; coldness; spasm

2

> *The last time we closed our schoolbook Gagarin was making his first excursion on the way to the moon. The moon! The moon! Think of that! The moon! We still dream about it. For us it's pure havoc, a shambles of the worst kind.*
>
> RÉDA BENSMAIA[31]

We encounter our second selenomaniac amid a recurring dream of the first moon travel, a dream that turns nightmare and then ultimate fiasco (disarray of mind). It is this final-limit disaster, that of the riling image of the moonwalker—'a shambles of the worst kind'—that reminds us of the original etymology of the word *lunatic* itself: namely, one drawn into madness by the intermittent cycles of the moon (the blameless ailment; the outwardly-deranged head). Thus we can focus on two elements in circulation here: firstly, the reference to a foreign cosmonaut, the first to reach outer space, to orbit the Earth, to experience weightlessness and the farther echelons, master of concave and convex flight patterns, yet who also died years later while piloting a craft in a downward tailspin, as if connecting the inner thread between galactic victory and fatality; and secondly, the conjuring of the term 'pure havoc' to describe this unwanted return of the moon-vision, for havoc (related to the words *seize*, *clutch*, and *hook*)

31 Bensmaia, *The Year of Passages*, 26.7.

arises from the older war-signal *to cry havoc*, as in to call armies to looting, raiding, and burning. Given this origin in post-battle vandalism, what does it mean for us here to enter a selenomaniacal imaginary wherein the moon is recognized as a vicious marauder, an agent of ransacking, of imperial scouring, of raking and despoiling homes, of the sacking of cities, making peaceful citizens into slaves, the subjugation of thought and dream?

Moon and excursion; the dream; havoc; shambles

3

In the beginning the moon
was a single eye, and heaven—
the forehead of a viper.

...I murder
that charlatan, the moon.

ADONIS[32]

We encounter our third selenomaniac amid three transmogrifying classifications, referring to the moon at once as an eye, a viper, and a charlatan. Certainly, each attribution provides us myriad conceptual routes: the single eye, an image tied to the oculus, to the third eye as receiver of wisdom or gnosis, the evil eye as purveyor of spite, eliciting interpretations of omniscience or voyeurism (the scowl versus the leer); the viper, an image tied to the primaeval human fear of the jungle, of brutal wildness, to hemotoxic venom and the striking of the bite-mechanism (suddenness, injection, immobilization); the charlatan, an image tied to pleasurable deception, to the great temptations of the mask, to fanciful word-play, expression, or gesture, gaining confidence among the innocent, manipulating closeness in quick time, herself a combination of fictive techniques, learned

32 Adonis, *The Pages of Day and Night*, 33, 41.

skills of the trickster, the liar, the storyteller, the demagogue, and the fantasist. Indeed, these are the three identities that the author hurls in accusatory form at the moon—the eye, the viper, the charlatan—a tripartite wrongness extending back to 'the beginning', to an original crime somehow severe enough to warrant death penalty, thus bringing us into contact with a fourth figuration: the murderer, an image tied to transgressive foul-play, to a making-final by unnatural causes, over-personalized, without perceived right or authority, an air of vigilantism and lawlessness, of acts committed either in cold blood (premeditation of the diabolical mind) or in the heat of the moment (outburst of the uncontrollable heart/psyche), though always dwelling at the detested height of self-indulgence.

Note: We are rightly taught to fear beings of the single eye, from the three storm-driving brothers of Cyclopean awareness (named thunderbolt, lightning, and thunder) to the three sisters of thread-cutting Fates (named the spinner, the allotter, and the unturnable), from the Egyptian eye of Horus and Ra (one represented as cobra, the other as falcon, both etched upon funerary amulets or ancient boat-sails for safe passage) to the one-eyed Norse god Odin (old man with cloak and spear, associated with charms, warfare, alphabets, knowledge, and healing). Primogenital tool of malice; bad promise harboured in a lone all-seeing socket.

Moon and the beginning; the single eye; the viper; the charlatan; the murderer

4

Where I rest every night
My mouth full my hands covered
Sea sleepwalker salted by the moon

Then, on a night of the full moon, both of them left with their rusty chains around their necks, and years of deprivation in their hearts; on the mountain, behind the chalet, in the pines with their trembling heads and grayish stones, nature's wisdom teeth smiling.

JOYCE MANSOUR[33]

We encounter our fourth selenomaniac amid rhapsodies to two figures, each boasting an exclusive relation to the moon: the sleepwalker and the fugitive. For sure, there are many characteristics that bind these conceptual personae, mostly related to the fact that both enter acutely altered states of awareness or movement at the wrong time of day (prospering while others descend into syncope). And yet their experiences at once intersect and contrast along different axes: to begin with, the solitary sleepwalker is able to 'rest every night', finding comfort in her becoming-somnambular, whereas the fugitives, 'rusty chains around their necks', seem like a group of runaway

33 Mansour, *Essential Poems and Writings*, 209, 393.

slaves or escaped criminals who must make urgent use of the moon, exploiting every second of its momentary support. These are antithetical postures, the first one of slackened ligaments, the second one of tensed musculature, the first horizontal-slipping-vertical (levitation), the second vertical-sprinting-horizontal (sidestepping). Furthermore, the sleepwalker has her 'mouth full' while the fugitives carry 'years of deprivation in their hearts', again indicating a marked distinction along the lines of well-being and ill-being, security and danger, solace and maltreatment. Similarly, the sleepwalker's hands are 'covered' against cold and hardness, and she makes her bed on the quaint white sands of a seashore, while the fugitives are compelled to retreat through frigid windswept regions of 'pines with [...] trembling heads' and across the jaggedness of 'grayish stones'. But although the sleepwalker murmurs softly to herself in coasting incomprehensible half-sentences whereas the fugitives hum desperate spirituals while huddled beneath the full moon, they are finally drawn together again in the same poetic reference to the night's mouth. Strangely, the former's identity is brought into the sensory realm of taste through the word 'salted', just as the latter make their difficult crossing amid 'nature's wisdom teeth smiling'—as if both sleepwalker and fugitive must ultimately traverse the moon as decadent oral crater, each one a perverse delicacy held fast between its teeth (the luxury, the speciality).

Moon and rest; fullness; covering; the sleepwalker;
salt; rust; chains; deprivation; teeth

5

The road passes through the capillaries of life.
The quality of the environment
in the biosphere of the uterus of the moon
will kill the corrupt cells.

FORUGH FARROKHZAD[34]

We encounter our fifth selenomaniac establishing a complex spatial-biological lattice, one of compromised anatomical coatings, for which the moon takes on a simultaneously medicinal and viral logic. Against this conceptual backdrop, we learn of a supposed road (though there is no word as to where it begins) that winds through 'the capillaries of life', carving a channel across miniscule branching vessels and microcirculatory networks to reach the inner lining of its true terminus: 'the biosphere of the uterus of the moon'. This obscure triangulation of images and functions (biosphere, uterus, moon) is itself a three-strand braiding of spatial territories of growth (ecological, reproductive, and celestial) into the theoretical crux of the road. Nevertheless, while all three preceding references (that of the vivarium, the womb, and the lunar sphere) are types of rounded enclosures, in this instance what compels their unification more

34 Farrokhzad, *A Lonely Woman*, 161.

importantly is an immediate epidemiological and ecological threat from nearby 'corrupt cells'. No doubt there is a feminine exclusivity to this state of intimate siege, and perhaps an unnamed child to be defended here as well (the disparate potentialities of the unborn, the newborn, and the stillborn), the 'killing' of which (in the form of a purging), we now realize, is precisely what conjoins the many aforementioned terms, each with its own internal mechanism of warlike disinfection: the environment with its millennial extinctions and ice ages; the uterus with its smooth layers of obstructive tissue; the moon with its tidal waves. All are capable of sanitizing, rinsing, and decontaminating toxic or carcinogenic forms, all are prone to the sudden flushing of systems, evacuations of the rancid, conversions of enemy substances into mere superfluous discharge (keeping the veins spotless), thus giving the lunar experience here a vital foetal content, and with it a different kind of immaculate conception: namely, one of immaculate procreative violence (the barricading of the incipient).

Moon and the road; the capillaries; the biosphere; the uterus; corruption; killing; the cell

6

> *His father concluded his tales of animals that night with the melancholy muwwal on gazelles, which he never tired of repeating whenever the moon rose a few paces higher than the ground, covering the wilderness with its pale silver beams and turning it to a place of magic and mystery.*
>
> IBRAHIM AL-KONI[35]

We encounter our sixth selenomaniac amid the night-songs of his father, each one a suppliant vocal arrangement (Entreating what, though?) that reflects the moon's potential relation to music, poetry, narrative, and grieving. Thus we are told of the 'melancholy' refrain that accompanies every moonrise, intoned by a figure at once hunter and shepherd, tracker and caretaker, of the same creatures to whom the elegant cry is dedicated (thereby also making him their mourner). But what is the nature of this heartrending 'magic and mystery' brought forth by the selenomaniacal state, one that commands human aesthetic energy to moan beautifully, to recognize its fallen animal counterparts and to shed tears for their victimhood, their sacrifice, or for something even far more inchoate?

35 Al-Koni, *The Bleeding of the Stone*, 45.

Note: There is a strain of existentialist thought that considers madness the sole authentic response to Being, as if to stare into the condition of radical meaninglessness could lead only to pure despair (and later absurd freedom). But what if there is an equally correct reaction in the form of sorrow? Pantheistic sadness; sadness of the pre-archetypal desert moon; sadness of pagan shapes that precede subjectivity. Thus we can fathom an affect unsheathed and in full provision before ever tilting into human consciousness, this first agony that wafts and ripples like a histrionic air, only later settling itself like a fine dust upon the individual identity of the herdsman, drawing lamentations from his larynx one after another and attaching them to the ancillary stand-in object of the gazelle. No, artistic subject and object are mere proxies here, secondary attendants to some other playhouse, strumming on behalf of another's pain, another's offering. Even the moon itself serves as mere timekeeper/courier to this more far-reaching release: it amplifies the sound of anguish for world, not the human being's anguish before their unruly circumstance, but rather the world's own suffering for itself, for which human imagination is then set in motion as mere mouthpiece, virtuoso, corroborator ('he never tired')...made to play and countersign this cosmic torment over and again.

Note: We are here reminded of a lineal origin story derived from the biblical Hagar, mother of the Islamic peoples, former slave-mistress of Abraham, knight of faith, but then flung eastward with her young son into parched lands, their throats dehydrated and on the brink of starvation, her orphan boy the forbear of a faith led millennia later by an orphan prophet, a creed not coincidentally symbolized by the shape of the crescent moon, and who curiously is known for two distinct qualities among her hardships: (1) that she became a madwoman (the seething one), skin bronzed but eyes paled, tearing at her hair and cheeks in nightly fulminations; (2) that she would repeat inconceivable lines of thought to herself, talking circles in darkness, becoming known as the Reciter, with only the unsympathetic moon to bear witness and listen (from the sacred word to the unanointed noise). Another interpretation of melancholic surplus; another woefulness brought forth beneath the lunar pallor.

Moon and melancholy; the tale; repetition; magic; mystery

7

To rekindle the moon
I climbed to the roof
with agate stone and grass and mirror.
A cold scythe passed across the sky
that banned the flight of doves.
The pines said something in a whisper
and the night watchmen frantically drew swords
upon the birds
The moon
did not rise.

AHMAD SHAMLU[36]

We encounter our seventh selenomaniac in the midst of an esoteric ritual, preparing certain occult ingredients for an invocation to recover lost moonlight. He carefully places these formal articles into a black satchel and smuggles them to the rooftop where some combination of potions, tonics, and sorcerer's words will come together to reawaken a past lunar twinkling. However, it is also evident from the worried description above that we find ourselves in a deeply totalitarian interlude, an age of perpetual unglittering midnight masterminded by those who 'banned the flight of doves' and 'drew swords upon

36 Shamlu, *Born Upon the Dark Spear*, 88.

the birds', meaning that the selenomaniac's rite represents an outlawed act (aligned with the old expunged ways). Clearly he is a figure of great cunning, someone who understands artful secrecy and stealth, evading the many gluttons and traitors roundabout, evading the night watchmen that stand like reapers and continuing undeterred by their 'cold scythe pass[ing] across the sky' and by the conspiratorial informing of the pines that say 'something in a whisper'. He goes about mixing his mortars and pastes swiftly yet calmly, arranging his necromantic accessories upon an outlaid blanket (forming an unassailable parlor). It is a time of colluding factions, each with their own cryptic idiolect, their ranks of accomplices, a time in which one must operate beneath ever-present guile and peering eyes, forever schemed against and scheming counter-gradations in turn, risking all to tip the balancing scales back in favor of a forbidden luster. And yet what do we make of the fact that the practitioner's rekindling spell ultimately fails, that the moon remains unrisen in spite of the cautious ceremony of quartz, earth, and glass? Be warned, lest one misread the tactical logic of magicality itself: this does not mean absolute defeat; rather, this abortive séance serves as testament to the essential unpredictability and necessary repetitiousness of all magical practice (forever attempting again), which is never a one-shot affair but rather a patient, ongoing process of experimentation and partial gains (contra finitude)... There will be another night, another rooftop, and another set of delicate conductive objects to ransom back whatever eclipsed forces from their incomplete obliteration.

Note: This is not the only time this poetic figure references drawing blades on the moon, for elsewhere he warns the reader to '[u]nfold your tent beside the night, but if the moon rises draw your sword from its sheath and set it beside you'. This type of maniacal thought reminds us of Xerxes the Great, Emperor of Persia and builder of the Hall of a Hundred Columns, who struck the Greek city-states with a convoy allegedly carrying a million soldiers (and led by an elite scale-armoured band of fighters known as the Immortals), but who, most tellingly in the present connection, commanded his generals after a storm to lash a strait three hundred times and cast chains into its waters as punishment for thwarting his efforts to cross it with his fleet. Thus the question is set before us: What is it exactly that occurs when one punishes an ocean channel with whips and manacles, or takes a steel weapon to the moon? Are the psychoanalysts right to pore over such dreams only to yield reductive interpretations of paranoia, or is there a grander cosmological tremor in play here, some magnificent determination known only to mad emperors and sorcerer poets, a megalomaniacal gesticulation that actually makes viable for a split second what was otherwise foolish? Must not the will, in its most daring hours, aspire toward this fabulous extent, closer to fairy tale than reality principle, blending extreme reservation (it might fail) with extreme arrogance (it might succeed), for which certain hidden procedures and blatant confrontations might sometimes wrest the most outlying phenomena into the closest quarters?

Moon and rekindling; the rooftop; the scythe;
the sword; the watchmen; the unrisen

8

'Pleased to meet you,' they replied, 'Where's your ID?'
Pointing skyward with his gnarled hand towards a gaunt-looking moon, he said: 'That's my ID.'
They didn't even lift their heads, since apparently they'd got out of the habit of using them for anything but hunting. Then one of them took aim at the moon and fired, shattering the delicate crescent and bringing its corpse tumbling to the ground in a heap of ashes. That got a laugh from his cronies....

GHADA SAMMAN[37]

We encounter our eighth selenomaniac at the asphyxiating nucleus of the checkpoint, arms strung out to sides in the fashion of the scarecrow or the crucified, and with this a further act of humiliation: slaying of the teacher (moon) in plain view of its most elder disciple. This is the ultimate experience of Unlikelihood, as young armed guards overstep their bounds, desecrating sacred ground, infantilizing a senior visitor, filled with improper conceit, these weak sentries, and funnelling sadistic laughter through their rifle-sights (concatenated vanity). These severed offspring, with no memory of traditional powers, dare bring down the once-unblended moon, shot into a

37 Samman, *Beirut Nightmares*, 158.

mound of black soap and powder, thus calcifying an age of pathetic authority (the offense). But they have crossed a being of awesome singularity here (the one of 'gnarled hand'), at once enchanting and bloodcurdling precursor, covered in both algae and eye shadow, for whom this dehumanization of the already-inhuman brings about a subtle transformation of the face, which now emulates the 'delicate crescent's' own gauntness. The slight is at first met with apparent restraint, as if the old man is unmoved by such dishonour, the astral ripped apart by projectiles and emptied cartridges. Formerly 'pointing skyward', soon thereafter he begins to resemble the very slaughtered icon at his feet: his angularity; his agedness; the profuse jutting of features; the continual sharpening of chalk-like bones. Make no mistake about it, this gradual chiseling-down of the aspect is the façade of highest outrage; to claim the look of exterminated moons.

Moon and identity; gauntness; shattering; the corpse; the ashes

9

> *We cleanse the moonlight. Your road is long, so dream of*
> *seven women to bear this long journey on your shoulders.*
>
> *I walk on the lip of the well: I have two moons,*
> *one in the sky, the other swimming in the water.*
> *I have two moons.*
>
> MAHMOUD DARWISH[38]

We encounter our ninth selenomaniac with two compartments of radical thought at his disposal—that of the visionary and of the schizophrenic—for which moons become imbued with the madman's singular logic of survival. In the first instance, a task of ablution (ritual washing) occupies the author's mind, and yet this lunar bathing is itself an overwhelming strain of obligation, a 'long journey' of such improbable percentages that one must invent some ecstatic distraction, a pastime, to remain unthrottled by longevity. Such is the cunning of the visionary: to project hallucinogenic images before the mind's eye, never with the dialectical flaw of fantasy that remains conscious of the original reality-referent, never with the helpless economy of delusion in which the madman loses the capacity for creative intervention, but rather

38 Darwish, *Unfortunately, It Was Paradise*, 11, 59.

as a phantasmic dressing of the impossible core endeavour (to 'cleanse the moonlight') with a side-chimera (the 'dream of seven women'). This peripheral overlaying of illusion upon illusion, in turn, lightens the experiential load and makes the otherwise dank assignment into an avatar of excitational desire (rapture-diversion).

Note: This provides an important clarification to our understanding of mania, which is often reductively linked to an irresponsible pleasure-principle; for here, the author remains acutely aware of the fact that the manic object (the unclean moon) is itself the source of a potentially lethal burden.

In the second instance, we uncover an alternative perceptual ruse that contests all romantic, idealist, and metaphysical hierarchies of unity: the establishing of the object of manic passion as a concomitantly transcendent and immanent phenomenon. These two, usually conflicting principles of divinity are made to reinforce each other in the fractal mindscape of this author, as the moon is split into two lifeblood counterparts, one flung upwards into a remote unsullied sky, the other parachuted downward onto the moving surface of the water, one forever unreachable and the other immediately touchable, the never-there and the always-here, the unspeaking and the freely conversant, separated but joining to form the new recognition that 'I have two moons.' Once again, this is a tactic of subsistence exclusive to the madman's intelligence, one that opens onto a certain razor's edge of potentiality (to 'walk on the lip of the well'): namely, to leave the most precious item in riven state, torn into infinite grains and modicums (the iota, the speck), so as to hinder any conceivable appropriation/elimination, forsaking the fragile law of totality and instead breaking moons into immortal fragmentary slices stored both in the nearby and the faraway.

Note: This provides a further important clarification to our understanding of mania, which is often reductively linked to neurosis; for while the neurotic is guided by a compulsive preservation-instinct (hoarding, guarding, purifying) that allows neither transcendent nor immanent properties to gain strength, the manic figure here showcases a divisive technique of insurmountability-through-crumbling that steals the philosophical powers of both transcendence and immanence in one strike.

Moon and cleansing; the road; the dream; the journey; the lip; the well

10

> *The two friends lit cigarettes and set off towards the cemetery. The sky was clear and a moon as big as Ali's fear shed its light on the grave as the two friends dug it up. With a piece of orange cloth Ali cleaned his mother's bones, then put them in the old bag.*
>
> HASSAN BLASIM[39]

We encounter our tenth selenomaniac amidst a very upsetting trek, a refugee crossing entire barred nations to fulfill a promise that combines both pure intimacy and pure horror: the burial of his dead mother's bones, carried everywhere in a loose sack over his shoulder for miles and miles. Moreover, the moon here takes on an analogical effect, mirroring the protagonist's own elevated panic ('a moon as big as [his] fear') in the same way that classically monstrous beings (the vampire, the werewolf, the mummy) often have the full moon reflected in their blank or ravenous eyes. Thus the sheer urgency of the selenomaniacal parallel, for which the moon continually typifies this, the toughest of illegal passages, imitating its terrible enormity in a kind of sympathetic magical resemblance, makes traumatic experience itself obsolete: the refugee does not have the luxury of elapsed time in

39 Blasim, *The Madman of Freedom Square*, 65.

which the atrocity might finally congeal as a past event, to then return in involuntary flashbacks or uncanny visitations. Instead, the atrocity remains unfinished, freshly present in the backpack slung across one's own body, and also disallowing the subjective flailing associated with traumatic memory by virtue of our narrator's supra-subjective concern (he thinks never of himself, only of the bag). Rather, each lunar cycle marks an existential resetting-to-zero, for in this story the hereditary scraps make their own continual demands, the wrapped dead body controlling the refugee's live body in a kind of constant walking daze to which no repression-based automaton or psychological being could even aspire, for we are closer here to a theory of lucid waking (as opposed to lucid dreaming), the hyper-vigilant and yet vacant stare of the one who must stay alert in unthinkable, barbed-wire circumstances. Thus he 'clean[s] his mother's bones' each night while the other fellow migrants sleep, faultlessly loyal to wiping dirt from the remains of a matron damned to foreign soil, then using the skeletal relics as his own pillow, the moon swelling and shedding its grotesque light to pay tribute to the poor soul escaping beneath its nightly reign.

Note: This tale's conceptual combination of dismemberment, adversity, catatonia, and revulsion can be connected to the frightening figure of sleep paralysis that haunts countless folkloric-biological traditions. Much like the narrator above, for whom the bag holding his mother's bones becomes an object of increasing pressure, and the moon in turn a celestial looking glass of coercive density, this creature, described vividly in different forms by different peoples, during episodic sleep paralysis is said to sit upon the chest of the sleeper and disallow autonomous movement. Mind awakes while body remains immobile, resulting in a forecast image of someone or something perched upon the sternum in hideous delight (and the ensuing sensation of terror). To this end, Scandinavian tales abound of an *incubus* or *succubus* ('accursed woman') who crouches on the rib cages of unsuspecting sleepers to cause them nightmares, whereas the swampland/bayou folklore of the American South speaks of the *haint* ('old hag' or 'night hag') who constrains breath by straddling the victim's upper body, while Pacific Islanders refer to a possessive process called *kana tevoro* ('being eaten by a demon') through which one might obtain crucial answers from a dead relative's spirit in the midst of soul-feeding, and Mongolian shamans of the dark side have coined the notion *khar darakh* ('to be pressed by the Black') in which the polluted shadow-dimensions of the universe themselves are at work; the Turkish concept of *karabasan* ('the dark presser') asserts a specific demonic origin to this supernatural being (part of the *jinn* race) from whose stranglehold only the recitation of the Qur'anic Throne Verse will achieve release, and there exist numerous further versions such as the Bangladeshi idea of *boba* (the being inducing 'speechlessness'), the Nepalese *Khyaak* (a ghost living beneath the house's staircase), the Nigerian *ogun oru* ('nocturnal warfare'), or the Kurdish *Motakka* (attacker of children for reasons of jealousy, familial feuding, or moral punishment). This prolific assortment of rationales, derived from goblin lore, wraiths, scorned wives, etc. extends almost endlessly: as a further example, the creature of the German *Alptraum* ('elf dream') who parasitically drinks blood from male and female breasts and tangles sleepers' hair into elfknots, fearing only the sign of the Cross; or the Catalonian *Pesanta*, a massive dog with steel paws that bewitches reclining sleepers by laying astride their torsos; or the Brazilian *pisadeira* ('she who steps'), always taking the shape of an old woman characterized by white disheveled hair, bloodshot eyes, foul green nails, and cackling laughter, and who lies in wait on rooftops to jump onto the full stomachs of those abed below. Lastly, there is the old Persian naming of the sleep paralysis creature as *Bakhtak* (literally meaning 'small fortune'), a little being of distended stomach who amuses itself by blanketing, smothering, and dismantling nerve-endings (to bring about the Unfeeling), and yet whose spiritual-physical infiltration can be turned from a maleficent onus into a stroke of freakish luck. In one rendition, upon waking in the sleep paralysis condition one must somehow claw Bakhtak's nose from its face, revealing its loathsome deformity in the moonlight—its real nose was cut off as penance for drinking of the forbidden river of eternal life, replaced only by a frail clay stub to hide its shame—whereas another rendition encourages the waking sleeper to snatch Bakhtak's hat to expose its bald head, in either instance allowing one to enslave it to grant continual wishes or share treasure. One therefore wonders after the covert ties between lunarity, malice, stasis, and windfall, and furthermore one should observe the advice given, in such stories, of a critical anti-traumatic antidote: that one must fight against the feeling of Being's heaviness, the claim of Event/Reality to constrictive solidity and its subsequent choking-effect, through a gesture of lashing-out (the graze, the scrape, the weaponized hand), for wish-fulfillment is attained only through manic engagement with the broods of nocturnal oppression (gift of the nightmare).[40]

Moon and fear; the grave; the mother; the bones; the bag

---

40 Many of these cultural narratives and explanations can be found with full further references in various searches for the 'Night Hag', and also in T.A. Green (ed.), *Folklore: An Encyclopedia of Beliefs, Customs, Tales, Music, and Art*, vol. 1 (Santa Barbara, CA: ABC-CLIO, 1997), 588.

Part 5

Dromomania (Travelling)

Ecdemomania (Wandering)

Cartogramania (Maps)

Kinetomania (Continual Movement)

Dinomania (Dizziness, Whirlpools)

Labyrintomania (Labyrinths)

New theories of 'restlessness' are concealed within the silhouette of a neo-Bedouin. Through diligent tracking of the compulsions, desires, ideas, images, sensations, and subjective constitutions that emerge against the backdrop of this figure's futural desert paths, a singular existential prototype surfaces for which standard regimes of spatiality and movement fall by the wayside. For in drafting an acute profile of this neo-Bedouin consciousness, we gradually come to realize that, in fact, we are describing a great centrifuge of six manic inclinations: Dromomania (obsession with travelling); Ecdemomania (obsession with wandering); Cartogramania (obsession with maps); Kinetomania (obsession with continual motion); Dinomania (obsession with dizziness, whirlpools), and Labyrintomania (obsession with labyrinths). By inquiring into these various conditions and showcasing the typologies of excessive power manifest within each of them, we detect a certain will to frenzy, misanthropy, distance, and nonbelonging that supersedes our well-worn concepts of alienation and exile. The trajectories of estrangement or disturbance that take shape here amid the sand dunes of modernity—across their seemingly infinite landscapes of waste, heat, submersion, cruelty, delirium, and entrapment—afford us that rare glimpse into a universe of interminable agitation for which no oasis can furnish a redemptive destiny or destination; a vista whose recurring doomsday signals only the neo-Bedouin knows how to decipher—and to survive.

'I am the Bedouin that the deserts have emitted / that the palaces have rejected / that the suns have disavowed/ that the burning coals of the stars extinguished / in his eye sockets / I am the Bedouin who is made to carry the plagues.'[41] These are words taken from an iconic yet reclusive Iraqi poet stabbed to death by drifters in his old age during the country's occupation, selected from a relatively obscure work titled 'The Bedouin Whose Face No One Saw'. An intimidating configuration of the self is given immanent reign in this cosmological drift, a geoscape of the radical elsewhere-nowhere in which only a vagrant non-identity can persist, at once ominous and vigilant, accursed and ecstatic, yet whose own individual abandonment might lay claim to a greater,

41 M. al-Buraikan, 'The Bedouin Whose Face No One Saw', tr. A. Lawandow, from B. Al-Marabi (ed.), *Matahat Al-Farashah* (*Labyrinth of the Moth*) (Cologne: Kamel Verlag, 2003).

non-world-historical destiny. A becoming-farthest (and conviction of farness).

A dromo-methodology of sixty distinct passages follows, each installment carved out of the maniacal writings of our ten Middle-Eastern authors, to display the many curving masks of the neo-Bedouin (for whom every place is an invitation to desertion).

Dromomania (Travelling)

1

> *We had been travelling for a considerable time when the hearse stopped at the foot of a stony, arid hill on which there was no trace of greenery. I slid the suitcase off my chest and got out.*
>
> SADEQ HEDAYAT[42]

We encounter our first dromomaniac in the inner compartment of a hearse drawn by skeletal horses, its diabolical old driver charging toward some undisclosed burial ground. This first episode of travel, then, occurs in the aftermath of a murder, our narrator now resting paralyzed beneath the suitcase in which his lover's dissected limbs are stowed.

We are told that 'considerable time' passes on this journey. Under what specific conditions does travel incur a sense of temporal drag, and what new propensities arise in the mind of the one for whom duration is so protracted? It is a hearse that carries them to their terrible destination. What is the intimate relation between travel and death? In light of the 'arid hill', what kind of travel orients itself

42 Hedayat, *The Blind Owl*, 31.

toward the sheer drought of a wasteland or scorched earth, the dry outworlds of pure tracelessness? In light of the hearse's monotonous rolling and subsequent coming to a stop, what are the particular outlooks of the passenger (vehicular being), and what occurs in the dromomaniacal imagination when the apparatus abruptly halts its course to mark arrival? What does it mean to travel to the last stop, to the end of the line? In light of the suitcase positioned strangely on the narrator's chest, what link might we uncover between travelling and pressure (or compression)? How does free or careless travel differ from overloaded travel (the guilty)? Lastly, he then gets out of the hearse, suspending us at the critical moment of disembarkation. For what happens when the terminus' revelation compels one to throw anchor and ditch the transportive medium; what happens at the decisive point of breaking-away or disposal, the portside limit where such conduits can go no further and one walks alone thereafter? Is something indispensable left behind among the panting horses, some small fare forfeited to their thirst, or to the thirst of the apparatus itself?

Travel and death; temporal dragging; the hearse; the vehicle; the passenger; aridity; tracelessness; stopping (the last stop); pressure (the chest); disembarkation (the arrival)

2

> *It was only in the train from Marseilles to Nice that my sentences were going to start flowing again, sentences at high speed / slow and dull course of ideas, pain, the extreme pain of thinking / a flow unleashed: thought / disorder of sentences / ideas in slow motion, in constant struggle with the sentence*
>
> RÉDA BENSMAIA[43]

We encounter our second dromomaniac lurching down the narrow corridors of a train, a narrator attempting to synchronize his own literary expenditures with the rotation of the many wheels whirling beneath his feet. We are therefore compelled to wonder after some relational modality between travel and writing that would collapse the walls between interiority and exteriority, mind and body, self and world; in which movement through external space would become as one with movement in thought, the traversal of frontier and page conspiring under a unified dromomaniacal propulsion. (But would the patterns of inscription remain identical, or do they acquire new distortions when hitched to the railroad tracks?)

The word-streams 'start flowing again', but what kind of travel takes place in total fluidity (with no unevenness

---

43 Bensmaia, *The Year of Passages*, 48.9.

or interruption)? In light of the seemingly contradictory juxtaposition of 'sentences at high speed' and the 'slow and dull course of ideas', why does the author-traveler face such a contrast in pacing between an accelerated process of articulation and a decelerated process of contemplation? Why does the mind slacken while the creative instinct (in unison with the train itself) only increases the velocity of its eloquence, giving rise to a 'slow motion' effect? And then this 'extreme pain': What is the peculiar nature of the agony emanating from this experiment in orchestrating technological rhythm with the gushing propensities of poetic experience? Is this abrasion the effect of a once-human mentality now scraping against its metallic or machinic incarnation (the grinding and rusting of gears)? Moreover, in light of the reference to 'a flow unleashed', what are the particular means by which one exploits travel in order to enjoin a sort of crucial ejection? Is this radical discharge purely liberating or does it exact a fatal price of some kind? Once achieved, does it bring exaltation, or rather the complete annihilation of identity? And what valve allows this catapultian release of notions and energetic principles? Lastly, in light of the careful final references, what are the essential conceptual connections between dromos and 'disorder', dromos and 'struggle'?

Travel and flow; writing (the sentence); speed (acceleration, slowness); pain; unleashing; disorder; struggle

3

Thus we advance,
harvesting our caravans
in filth and tears,
bleeding the earth
with our own blood
until the green dam of the sea
alone
stops us.

ADONIS[44]

We encounter our third dromomaniac taking part in a mass exodus, though simultaneously composing an elegy for those banished and razed by historical disaster. These are condemned travellers, uniquely forced to retreat from some fruitless notion of homeland. Against a backdrop of parched dust, corpses, and fatigue, this disinherited legion draws itself outward in search of the ocean's current. Incremental, forsaken strides; the half-perished.

In light of the phrase 'Thus we advance', what are the acute differences between individual and collective travel? (Is there some accursed togetherness involved here?) And what does it mean to speak of 'advancement' in the wake of coerced departure? As for the expression 'harvesting

---

44 Adonis, *The Pages of Day and Night*, 46.

our caravans', what kind of dromomaniacal trajectory can be pictured as a reaping, especially one that continually wavers on the brink of starvation, so that famine and regeneration might be spoken of in the same breath? We have already in this same text found allusions to the hearse and the train, the first aiding a killer, the second an author; but what rare kind of intersubjective and anti-subjective prototypes are housed in the enclosure of the caravan? Is the caravan a mechanism of protection, concealment, or damned momentum? Perhaps an answer comes in the further thematic connection to 'filth and tears', which bind this mode of travel to the existential realms of wretchedness, abjection, profanity, and intense sorrow. Moreover, the mirroring act of 'bleeding the earth with our own blood' suggests a common destiny of haemorrhage and exsanguination, a mutual depletion of the particular (self) and the universal (soil). The remarkable blood-loss of the ages. Lastly, it is within the insane distress of those without sanctuary that we sense the swing of a utopian-dystopian pendulum: the very sea that once hinted at potential deliverance now rapidly converts into a traveler's dead end. They hang their heads; they strain for nothing. The horizon becomes the dam, daydream turns to nightmare, and we are left pressed hard against a realm of ultimate occlusion (the exhaustion-threshold; the broken promise).

Travel and banishment; advancement (collectivity, coercion); the harvest; the caravan; filth; sorrow (tears); bleeding; being-stopped (the dam)

4

Disemboweled
Sticking their mouths to its wounds
They pump the horse's blood and the knight's
So that they themselves can flow
Toward some obscure orifice?
A mad sailor tries to reach the open sea

JOYCE MANSOUR[45]

We encounter our fourth dromomaniac presenting an alternative vision of the sea, this time an open chasm that draws the traveller into gaping worlds. Here one finds oneself caught in an inescapable gravitational pull or siren's call that lures, misguides, and casts one into the vortex.

Are we being asked to consider an act of travelling that is equivalent to some form of mutilation, requiring the forfeiture of vital limbs or organs ('disemboweled')? Along the same lines, the initial idea of disfigurement is followed by the introduction of 'wounds', forging a conceptual bridge to the realms of purulence and close damage. More than this, the traveller's laceration is then *tasted*; the mouth is the organ of choice here, confirming the underlying suctional logic that seals this 'mad sailor's'

---

45 Mansour, *Essential Poems and Writings*, 305.

unkind fate. Affectionate destruction: the whole passage is nothing less than a desiring jaw. Moving on, we must juxtapose two facets of the next association, which tells us how 'they pump the horse's blood and the knight's': (1) this particular dromomaniacal arc is a matter of blood-pumping as opposed to bleeding-out, leaving us within a palpable arterial zone of hyper-circulatory excess; (2) the reference to knight and horse conjures up the ancient/mediaeval persona of the rider, in itself a complex profile that binds together certain affective codes of endurance, supremacy, balance, and fury. So is there a tormented nobility behind these haemophiliac plots of violation? Is there chivalry or even an ancestral valour to this non-clotting lesion? And where does this maimed champion go exactly, as he courses through veins and cellular walls? Toward an 'obscure orifice', she tells us. Taking each feature alone, the 'orifice' of course prompts us to recognize some seductive technique in play (falling-into-holes; wayward lust), whereas 'obscurity' can only confirm that this voyage is one of partial understanding (the glance; the sidelong impression). Bottomless and vague: unfathomable. Thus there is a strong connection between the traveller's passion and the mercurial blindness or mystification that takes hold of him: the ongoing odyssey is wanted, even though it is actually a plunging through inscrutable, throat-like depths. A connective tissue of obsession and bewilderment, obscene craving and total disorientation.

Futility of the fever-dream. Hence we are left eventually with nothing but the lost soul of the mad sailor who 'tries to reach' the waves in vain, confirming once and for all the great trickery through which this dromomaniacal impulse results only in a cyclone of lunatic striving.

Travel and disembowelment; the wound; the mouth; the horse, the knight (the rider); obscurity, the orifice; madness; the sailor; the open (striving)

5

The people,
the fallen group of people,
discouraged and downtrodden and dazed,
went from exile to exile
under the ominous burden of their corpses.

FORUGH FARROKHZAD[46]

We encounter our fifth dromomaniac as one of a platoon of corpsed travellers. The dead-already, one foot in the non-transcendent beyond, this drove holds nothing in store, merely lurching lifelessly from transposition to transposition. All that remains is their stupor: the stiffness, the murkiness of their halfway condition.

The poet begins by calling these cadaverous walkers a 'people', but then qualifies them as 'fallen', thereby suggesting that they no longer merit their former status as a populace—this is a people that was once a people, their folkhood dispersed or revoked. Furthermore, they are 'downtrodden', which reveals the bizarre sense of gravity that imposes itself upon them (as if trampled), the shoulder-crushing heft of those who remain only by dint of some technicality, those formally present but existentially evacuated (inhabiting no earth). We are also

46 Farrokhzad, *A Lonely Woman*, 49.

told that these travellers are 'discouraged' and 'dazed', conditions neither of which convey even the luxury of fear. The first term—'discouraged'—marks the total decrease of courage not from fear but in the face of its own effective irrelevance: for there is no prize here, nothing treasured, and thus no reason for bravery, as if they are caught underfoot of something stronger than history, memory, or even fate—this indistinguishable influence that has flung them below (note that their travel is always described in vertical, not horizontal terms). So it is that the second term—'dazed'—casts us necessarily into the dim ether of a sort of negative astonishment. There is a definition of travel, it seems, that cannot even apprehend itself, cannot grasp its own sheer happening, something made worse only by the fact of its incessant recurrence. But this is neither denial nor shock, for it is never a question of their not accepting this state; rather, the state itself embodies the unacceptable, its confusion purchased only on the other side of possibility. Thus we are confronted with the repetitive puzzlement of their weighed-down steps, sequence after sequence, physically difficult yet without emotive palpitation, 'from exile to exile', for the exilic here denotes that perfect combination of opacity, drainage, and semi-consciousness that alone could yield such purgatorial experience. Which is why they are the 'ominous', the people of the 'burden'. For they bring no good, and they will be known only by their dust-fastened stares and their general sunkenness; the paradoxical concurrence of heaviness and insubstantiality.

Travel and fallenness; discouragement;
the downtrodden; the dazed; the ominous; the corpse

6

> *The shadowy figures of travellers, who might bring either rain or harm to the community, always seemed portentous. So they consulted the diviner about the newcomer's intentions...*
>
> IBRAHIM AL-KONI[47]

We encounter our sixth dromomaniac as a being who inspires elaborate predictions of both dread and fortune in the collective imagination of the village. Hence they convene their night-counsels and begin a covert dialogue of dire speculation, circulating ill-born and idealized warnings into the morning hours. Some elders give heed of oncoming malice, some elders speak of a long-awaited end to suffering, for this rare species of traveller arrives only to resurrect or to ravage the sanctity of all things.

The passage above comprises the very first words of a lengthy novel, and already within these opening lines we are faced with a powerful conceptual intersection: that of the traveller and the shadow. That these approaching visitors are described as 'shadowy figures' places us in the domain of a certain imperceptibility (movements carrying many riddles): we are left wondering after their obscure

47 I. al-Koni, *The Seven Veils of Seth*, tr. W. M. Hutchins (Reading: Garnet Publishing, 2008), 5.

motivations, and no doubt the entire dromomaniacal equation changes when we are dealing with travellers who approach for unknown reasons. Their carefully guarded nature, and the stealth it requires, is nothing less than the sign of an all-or-nothing wager. That they can willfully invoke either 'rain or harm' upon those with whom they make contact is enough to reveal them as masters of a cosmic scale, an immense spectrum of providence held ready at their fingertips. They could quench thirst; they could just as easily condemn throats to desiccation. This is why the village's night congregation is a matter of the 'portentous', at once a beckoning and a foretelling, as it is extremely uncommon business to sit around the fire and discuss 'the newcomer's intentions'. Do they bring riches, affluence, the exquisite; or do they bring fiasco, calamity, the miscarriage? Thus the traveller's impending arrival calls for the entrance of another conceptual person: 'the diviner'. For the diviner is an expert reader of both prosperous and obliterating currents (interpreting winds, smoke, ash, flame, entrails, stars), able to draw on the same occulted sources as the traveller himself in order to determine which universal door will open (though still helpless to prevent this cataclysmic dromos).

Travel and the shadow; rain; harm; portent; the diviner; the newcomer's intention

7

I no longer crave a journey
I am no longer drawn to the air of a voyage
The train that passes in the middle of each night
groaning by my village
no longer constricts my sky.
And the road that extends beyond the loins of the bridge
no longer transports my wishes towards other horizons

AHMAD SHAMLU[48]

We encounter our seventh dromomaniac in the aftermath of all ideological quests. These are the words of a former rebel, political prisoner, and torture-chamber poet for whom the prospect of faraway professions no longer holds the slightest allure. Travel here refers to the procession of historical events themselves, and with them a once-formidable author of struggle now sets his world-historical hammer aside. This is a crucial moment, one that prompts us to ask what it means when the most legendary revolutionary actor chooses seclusion, indifference, and bitter immobility over the next venture?

The most obvious clue in the above passage is that this figure 'no longer crave[s] a journey', which implies

48 A. Shamlu, 'The Road Past the Bridge', tr. J.B. Mohaghegh, from *Majmu'eh-ye Asar-e Ahmad Shamlu* (*The Collected Works of Ahmad Shamlu*) (Tehran: Zamaneh Press, 1381/2002).

someone who once entertained great longing for such schemes but has now crossed an irrevocable threshold of battle-satiation. As such, the reference to such insurgent practice as a kind of craving and, further, an enterprise that requires one to be 'drawn' to 'the air of a voyage', places the radical's mission more in the domain of the magical than the political (aeriality over solidity), as if the revolutionary imagination were itself a kind of stratospheric spell or trance to which one must surrender all volition. Taking the connection between revolution and dromos further, we are then returned to the image of the train, this time one that 'passes in the middle of each night groaning by my village'. The expression 'in the middle' reveals the interminable suspension and deferral of the cause's accomplishment, as if it never arrives at its ultimate target but rather remains chronically in search of an improbable finality. Failed horizon, failed inevitability. The 'groaning' of the passing train illustrates how aged is this fanatical errand—something endeavoured a thousand times before and renewed 'each night' as if unaware of how old such dreams have grown (there is nothing unprecedented about this drive).

And yet it is the next line that definitively undermines the fundamental logic of ideological expeditions: despite all their claims to universal liberation, despite all glorious portrayals of progress and epochal radiancies to come, such utopian parades in fact do nothing more than to 'constrict my sky'. The poet's refusal to chase the next heaven is indeed a wholesale indictment of revolution itself as an archetype of suffocation masquerading as boundlessness, a verdict that leads our dromomaniacal fighter beyond entrapment in the vise of history's affairs (a hero grown incensed by the constraints of heroism). What is left in the place of revolution is something far more honest: anger, despair, intractable withdrawal, immanent disproof. The gunfire that once excited the veins now evokes only a sigh; the chest heaves in the opposite rhythm to the undulations of the historical crusade outside, each ambitious blast of the continuum now only heightening the exhausted traveller's counter-desire for solitude and distance. The boldness of walking-away and of ultimate weaponlessness consists in no longer lending credence to a stacked deck or rigged game (the fixed; the setup). And the humility of his last 'wish' (a term infinitesimally more modest than 'craving'): to 'no longer transport' himself beyond the ahistorical shack that encloses his tired, wartorn body. But this turning-away constitutes its own alter-dromos, a final dromomaniacal station subsisting on the outside of history's infertile perimeter, located somewhere 'beyond [...] the bridge' where revolutionary fantasy subsides (and toward remoteness).

Travel and craving; the middle; groaning; constriction; ideological sky; failed horizon; the wish

8

> *The night train came to a halt and its only passenger disembarked, stepping down on to a platform awash with blood. No sooner had the traveler arrived than he was accosted by a horde of creatures—birds of night, cats, mice—who gathered about and eyed him with curiosity. The newcomer's body was the trunk of an aged, gnarled olive tree and his hair was seaweed from the ocean depths. Whoever looked into his eyes would find himself lost in tortuous passageways with countless, mirror-lined walls and on his lips one could detect a half-innocent, half-bemused smile.*
>
> GHADA SAMMAN[49]

We encounter our eighth dromomaniac as a figure of simultaneous adoration and intimidation. He arrives at a twilight hour, with some rare charismatic power derived from suggestions of his otherworldliness, and an esoteric wisdom born of eternal standing. He is also a force of expansive multiplicity, able to coil between human, animal, and vegetal shapes—at once man, tree, and sea creature who aligns the magic of many territories. In fact, this hybridity is its own sacred geometry, one that gives him titanic sway wherever he appears, for one quickly deduces that he is both a saviour and curser of cities.

---

49 Samman, *Beirut Nightmares*, 157.

Is his tour upon the 'night train' a detail of major significance? What are the different implications of travel by night and by day? And then, in light of his first nocturnal footsteps, one wonders how to theorize the precise role of the 'platform' itself. Is it a mere banal middle-ground, or the stage for some sort of valuable transitional ritual, like a portal or a gateway? Does it aid in accomplishing a forthcoming rite or trial, a testing-ground before entrance into the commotion of the arena? The bloodstains on the platform suggest a grander violence in store, or a necessary cleansing, itself a point of departure for some warlike mission or sorcery. And yet the traveller here is greeted and revered, as demonstrated by the massive 'horde of creatures' that coagulates around him to stare with overwhelming 'curiosity'. What kind of traveller boasts such a magnetic effect? How is it that, despite his fundamental anonymity, walking among them as a stranger, all of the gathered beings demonstrate an intuitive recognition of his importance and exceptional, if not invincible, nature? An undeniable suspicion that he is someone to be venerated, and that his purpose there somehow commands their own future? Perhaps this peculiar fascination is linked to the paradoxical labelling of him as the 'newcomer' alongside the portrait of his body as 'the trunk of an aged, gnarled olive tree', framing the traveller as something at once novel and immemorial, a primeval breath of fresh air.

And yet he remains a harbinger of some archaic danger: his eyes are said to be 'tortuous passageways' in which one is preordained to become lost. What kind of perilous infinity is personified by this dromomaniacal glare? Why does this traveller's gaze escort the onlooker into a limitless hall of mirrors, and even more disturbingly, why does he oversee this optical entrapment with a 'half-innocent, half-bemused smile'? What lies on the other side of these incomplete equations? Are they yet further mergers of diametrical oppositions, coupling half-innocence with half-malevolence, half-bemusement with the half-revolted or half-enraged? But this is the severe lesson of all sage-like figures: their occasional frivolousness or humour is but a sign of their absurd realization of the impending doom of all things, and thus diminishes nothing of their devastating prophetic touch. Absolute disdain is worn lightly. If anything, the tranquil grin of this sightseer just off the night train is but a magnification of his sinister nature. Is it ultimately neither the look of compassion nor of wickedness but rather that of terrifying neutrality? Yes, a certain awful dominion is to be found within the relaxed posture of his visitation (appalling simplicity), which is itself the silent pronouncement of a ruling. It is the careless freedom gained from having seen/tread too much (beyond the full expiration of worlds).

Travel and night; the platform; the horde (gathering); curiosity; the newcomer; agedness; the eyes (becoming-lost); the passageway; the mirror; half-innocence; half-amusement

9

I will slog over this endless road to its end.
Until my heart stops, I will slog over this endless, endles road
with nothing to lose but the dust, what has died in me, and a row of palms.

MAHMOUD DARWISH[50]

We encounter our ninth dromomaniac as a figure of bleak persistence (traveller's spite). He strives in vicious recurrence, if only to deprive the surrounding enemies of their satisfaction, and thereby inflects exile from a paradigm of sadistic punishment toward a self-inflicted grind of masochistic defiance. Still what is most compelling here is the particular genre that such disfavoured movement brings forth (and the unique sound therein): namely, the cold musicality of a requiem. Dromos now gives rise to a striking melody of scorn, harmonizing the traveller's half-throbbing heart (always on the verge of stopping) with the tunes of a gray lullaby.

The stanza begins by selectively differentiating a kind of 'slogging', which underscores a certain weariness and cyclical aching of the 'endless road'. The enervated; the dismal; unvaried terrain. Moreover, this poetic

50 Darwish, *Unfortunately, It Was Paradise*, 3.

contradiction of seeking *an end to the endless* harbours a critical insight, for it suggests the sliver of an exit or an escape-hatch hidden in the folds of perpetuity itself, leading us to ask: What specific act or procedure could bring the eternal circle to a halt? And in fact, this poet elsewhere alludes to a special connection between the dromomaniacal figure and eternity, writing that 'Eternity opens its doors from afar to travellers at night.'[51] The duplicity of this gesture must not go unnoticed, for the same spatiotemporal logic—that of a doorway opening onto the eternal—can be harnessed to the opposite effect: a channel leading victoriously out of the eternal. But at what price (or through what necessary trickery) is one granted the ability to locate this egress, this lone conduit, vent, or fault line in the otherwise gruelling matrix of forever? Perhaps the answer lies not so much in the meaning as in the tonality of the poetic excerpt above; perhaps we ought to privilege hearing over sight/knowledge, recognising the verse's rapid ascent into a refrain. The lyrical repetition of the second line—'Until my heart stops, I will slog over this endless, endless road'—prefigures a kind of eerie drone, perhaps even a death march, yet it still carries a distinct acoustical eminence: that of the morbid sonority of a prison chain gang, or factory workers who sing in step with their hard labour. It holds an incantatory power,

51 Ibid., 66.

though it is more the chant of an anti-sacral ritual, one of worldly toil and over-exertion. And, like all incantatory techniques, the gradual rehearsal and pronunciation of the spell's words give way to a transformative process as we slingshot within a single line from nihilistic closure ('nothing to lose but the dust') to the flourishing of a 'row of palms'. This fatal frontier of the endless, then, once removed from the register of ontology ('what has died in me') and recomposed as a force of threnody, instrumentation, or voice, shows the way beyond its own dreary planes and toward other tropics. A lone aesthetic stands against the totality of messianic logic, teaching us that such graceless eternity can be evaded by charm, style, and song alone (dromos as intonation).

Travel and spite; slogging; endlessness; the requiem; eternity; intonation

10

> *More than once it has occurred to me that I will spend my life writing about the events and surreal happenings I have experienced along the routes taken by undocumented migrants. It's my cancer and I do not know how it can be cured.*
>
> HASSAN BLASIM[52]

We encounter our tenth dromomaniac in a forest of many runaways, thus casting us into the conceptual prism of the traveller-as-refugee. Hereafter we stand before a confederation of the unwelcomed, those who anticipate hostile nations and the shores of inhospitable vistas. They are well versed in the arts of circumvention, elusiveness, and the detour. They take deliberately crooked trails. They know only unforgiving landscapes (the marsh, the swamp, the mountain passes, the woodlands). They cultivate a temperament for cold nights, extended periods of hunger and thirst, sleeplessness, and perpetual discomfort. Such are the criteria for navigating the desolate.

In light of the expression 'surreal happenings', how does this traveller's experience collapse the once robust boundary between real and unreal? Is it the sensory extremity or the mortal risk that blurs perception into

52 Blasim, *The Madman of Freedom Square*, 62.

the realms of the surreal, leaving one stranded amid such ambiguous perplexity that the trek itself appears as an undefinable ordeal? In light of the 'routes taken', what strategy of travel is it that must seek only inaccessible pathways (forever off-grid), following the counter-maps of those who perfect invisibility? Trespass; slightness; unannounced entrance; forbidden border crossing. The excruciating tactical urgency of going undetected. Such are the basics of the intruder's choreography, stealth-endowed units who train in the practice of sneaking, crouching, and quiet infiltration.

The category of 'undocumented migrants' turns our focus toward the ever-hovering regimes of authority (fear of the patrols), self-appointed wardens of the official and the legitimate beneath whose radars our traveller-refugee must pass, continually avoiding the courts of stigma, intolerance, and harsh judgment. Moreover, the author's emphatic designation of this dromomaniacal legacy as a personal 'cancer', not to mention his pondering of its potential incurability, suggests a mode of travel that entails its own pathogenic share. Another conceptual transmission arises between dromos and affliction. And yet, doesn't criminal movement forge its own indelible bond between these hidden, uninvited ones? Is there not kinship among this temporary race, if only that of their common expectation and bareness? Does the shared misadventure and its extravagant cost (the life-and-death gamble; the unincluded countenance) allow for some untold level of proximity, one that runs counter to the disaffection of the metropolis and its oblivious crowds? The precinct versus the faction? Indeed, are we not motivated to invent an entirely new paradigm of 'dwelling' itself, just to accommodate those who slink and tiptoe in our midst? Agents of repudiation (at once discarding and discarded), of a compulsion-to-foreignness and a becoming-foreigner.

Travel and surreality; the forest; refugee; the happening; the route; the undocumented; the migrant; affliction (the cancer); kinship; foreignness

Ecdemomania (Wandering)

1

> *I began to walk and involuntarily followed the wheel-tracks of the hearse. When night came on I lost the tracks but continued to walk on in the profound darkness, slowly and aimlessly, with no conscious thought in my mind, like a man in a dream.*
>
> SADEQ HEDAYAT[53]

We encounter our first ecdemomaniac in a trance-like state, again staggering back from the burial-mound of his newly dismembered lover. He has just stared for one last time into the eyes of her severed head. Quite simply, then, this wandering marks the return from an ecstatic killing, itself a symptom of self-disbelief amid treachery, a heinous condensation that now destabilizes the traitor's legs as he stumbles along the road. Not fleeing from some random act of violence, but reeling from the drunken mixture of delight and guilt in betraying what was once closest: fatality's own adaptation of the Persian *siyah-mast* (literally 'black-drunk', the final stage of the intemperate drinker).

---

53 Hedayat, *The Blind Owl*, 35.

In light of the narrator's wandering 'involuntarily', what kind of automaticity follows highly intimate violence? Is it a counterbalance (feigning uncontrollability; losing track) to the overwhelming decision required in the preceding moment? In light of the fact that he 'continued to walk on', are we to recognize ecdemos as harbouring its own form of internal continuity? Against the stereotypical view of wandering as a loose, haphazard, or unsystematic gesture, can one discern within it a deeper texture of steadiness and regularity? Moreover, what does it mean to roam in 'profound darkness', and what of the claim to 'aimlessness' that follows this atmospheric rendering? Is it truly a pure submission of the will to the densifying incomprehensibility of the night, a casual admission of frailty and helplessness in a blinded world? For if all were mere triviality and guesswork, then why not just begin running headlong rather than treading 'slowly'? Aside from the practical rationale of avoiding unseen objects in one's path, the fear of hard unexpected impact, is it possible that these slow yet aimless paces speak to some mysterious ability to actually chart the darkness? Beyond empirical reason, is there a level of intuitive sensitivity that one might acquire, that would enable one to carve inroads through inexorable blackness, such that ecdemos here could constitute the sharpening of this same conjectural insight? The wanderer's mark of Cain, a sixth sense to steer through immeasurability? Perhaps this is the final secret behind the reference to an ultra-ambulatory narrator with 'no conscious thought in [...] mind, like a man in a dream', for it requires an exotic (i.e., extroverted) counter-awareness to pilot the immense unfamiliar. Nonsensical evenness; attunement to the thick outside; only a non-entity can manoeuvre through the indefinite. And the one most likely to entertain this necessary erasure? Precisely the depraved, the butcher, one who has slain every last conceivable particle of what is most precious. Atrocity (the unbearable, the unfathomable) thus wins this first ecdemomaniac a compass for the lair of nothingness. The most uncaring masters carelessness.

Wandering and involuntariness; losing-track; continuation; darkness; unconsciousness; the dream

CONCEPTUAL DETOUR

As the butcher enters into our textual midst, let us note the multifarious and long-held traditions of destruction (entity-killing) that have existed over time and across subcultures. Some killers are celebrated with heroic laurels for their violence (the warrior, the guardian), others lionized for overcoming great odds through militant aggression (the revolutionary, the guerrilla), and still others reviled for their hermetic plots to channel forbidden sources of hurt (the deviant, the loner, the woodsman). But how does one chart the fine supra-psychopathic line between the soldier, the vigilante, the mercenary, the shooter, the champion, the murderer, and the assassin? Note that, above all else, each inflection is tied less to the internal identity of the killer and more to the hyper-specificity of the external object to be killed. Indeed, the key to the killer's designs, methods, and capacities rests in this very ability to direct a certain manic-turned-fatal propensity against the thing itself. A short list is included below, with many forms intentionally deleted, and ending abruptly in a certain place, in order to give some suggestion of an esoteric link between mania and willed evisceration:

> suicide (the killing of self), patricide (the killing of the father), fratricide (the killing of the brother), matricide (the mother), homicide (the other), senicide

(the killing of the elder), infanticide (the child), amicicide (the friend), ecocide (the environment), floricide (flowers), genocide (a race or ethnos), populicide (the people), deicide (a god), hericide (a lord), dominicide (the master), episcopicide (a bishop), giganticide (a giant), regicide (the king), nepoticide (the favorite), philosophicide (the philosopher), prenticecide (the apprentice), hospiticide (the guest or host), hosticide (the enemy), tyrannicide (the tyrant), hereticide (the heretic), vaticide (the prophet), chronocide (time), famacide (reputation), urbicide (the city), linguicide (language), avicide (birds), cervicide (deer), felicide (cats), lupicide (wolves), microbicide (the micro-organism), serpenticide (serpents), ceticide (whales), herpecide (reptiles), tauricide (bulls), ursicide (bears), vulpicide (foxes), parasiticide (the parasite), monstricide (the monster), tomecide (books), logocide (words), ethnocide (a culture), petracide (monuments), fideicide (the killing of faith), menticide (the killing of the mind), legicide (the killing of the law).

2

> *The house saddens the dreamer: he leaves it.*
> *You know, we're all transients, people in passing;*
> *But who will follow us? No one who is worth being named...*
>
> RÉDA BENSMAIA[54]

We encounter our second ecdemomaniac as a figure of clear objection, one who disparages at every turn, a representative of anathema and censure, one who turns his back on birthright amid sentiments of disappointment and odium. The city has failed him, his wanderer status figuring as an extension of a more fundamental complaint or grievance, a flight born of aggravation, or even disgust.

The house 'saddens'; it is the bane of 'the dreamer'. This sadness is an insignia, the gnawing sign of the inconsolable for whom the idea of lineage itself has expired (beneath loathing and abhorrence). He lashes out for the anywhere-else; he makes anti-pilgrimages; his wandering becomes a negational tonic, and at the same time a gesture toward irreversibility, not nostalgic but rather vitriolic, the exorcism of a great dissatisfaction. Mania thereby facilitates at once a humiliation, purging-act, and shedding of the past; it hones the deracinated mind—the profession of no faith in context, title, or dust. It serves

54 Bensmaia, *The Year of Passages*, 50.1.

an anti-embryonic function, a tourniquet to clot regret and smash the crucible of being-among. Last principle of self-exclusion ('we're all transients'): to sell off any former ownership of an ethnos whatsoever, with no idealized origin (beyond all kingdoms), and declare oaths to impermanence alone.

Nevertheless, there is a subtle addition in the last line, in which we are prompted to consider some kind of following. 'But who will follow us?' he asks, seemingly harmlessly. And herein lies the attractive-repulsive turn, for it is inferred that this ecdomaniacal archetype is indeed a forerunner of some multitude-in-waiting, the leader of a looming zero-cadre of those not 'worth being named' yet who are stimulated by his own will to namelessness. His hatred will be a generational elixir, an enticement to existential dishonour (against the offenders remaining). It disseminates wanderlust among the impatient, perhaps tempting an era of those who would burn down their own houses. Only the most worthless prevail.

Wandering and sadness; the dreamer; leaving (taking-leave; leaving-behind); transience (people-in-passing); namelessness; the worthless (the follower)

3

A cloud crawled along: I surrendered my face to the flood and wandered in my debris...

ADONIS[55]

We encounter our third ecdemomaniac pursuing a theory we might call *decadent animism*: the presumption that all things possess life and thus the will to movement, but that, correlatively, they too (these inanimate-animated articles/forces) are caught in the descending game of mortal dissipation. More precisely, we must ask what it means when the objective portion of Being itself becomes sickened-of-world or cynically resigned to existence—as if stones and trees and dust now took on the base decadent qualities of morbidity, sloth, disease, indifference, and refined perversion. Thus we turn our critical attention to the word 'surrendered', for acquiescence is itself the first hallmark of the decadent slide, a subjectivity that has admitted defeat yet remains, since even suicide requires excessive effort—and wonder again what happens when nature itself begins to adopt this philosophical attitude of immaterial materiality, self-mockery, celebrated imperfection, and macabre elegance. The clue resides perhaps in the description of the cloud as something that 'crawled

55 Adonis, *A Time Between Ashes and Roses*, 93.

along' as if now reduced to lethargic earthliness, no longer feigning celestiality but instead inching its way lazily through gutters, back alleyways, opium dens, brothels, and absinthe taverns. Wastedness, rubble-composition: no epochal fulfillment, no utopian completion, only the residual deposits of a failed experiment and the filtrate identities left to 'wander in my debris'. Thus the ecdemomaniac takes his initial cue from the sluggish tempo of the weather itself, emulating the cloud's own casual approach to just going-along, its parodic outlook on surface, its farcical outlook on depth, sensing in each dilapidated corner only the fouled, the noxious, the charade, as if thereby stumbling upon a new brand of the mimetic faculty—a sort of apathetic mimesis—born of indolence alone (the universal barely-alive).

Wandering and crawling; surrender; face; flood; debris

4

For I must wander
On the deep sea bed
Showering pearls on dead men

JOYCE MANSOUR[56]

We encounter our fourth ecdemomaniac along the unique topography of the seabed, which includes the sub-topographical terminology of the oceanic floor, oceanic trench, or oceanic crust. The text thus places us within a paradoxical territoriality of watery jaggedness, combining further spatial notions of the ridge, the mantle, the shelf, basaltic magma, hydrothermal vents, continental drifting, plate tectonics, cascading sediment, and the lithosphere-asthenosphere boundary. But these details simply provide the atmospheric tableau for an even more imposing event: a woman strolls along the marine bottom (also known as the abyssal plain or abyssal zone) to 'shower pearls on dead men'. Our minds go immediately to the shipwreck (site of the wave-battered, the untimely death, the heap of toppled bodies), and we wonder why the former sailors' corpses are lavished with gems. What is the purpose behind this luxuriated catastrophe, crafting jewelry for those gone tragically overboard and

56 Mansour, *Essential Poems and Writings*, 183.

submerged underwater? Perhaps it is a funereal rite for the tide-stricken, but beyond solemnity and mourning we find an even more disturbing interpretation, one that suggests a somewhat paranormal theory of *covetousness*: that she (the seawoman) is in fact a childlike collector, and these saturated bodies (the seamen) are her many dolls, whom she dresses in garments and trinkets, staging phantom marriages and vignettes, reclaiming bloated forms in post-mortem play, arranging them in rows or audiences along the coral and deep valleys (to make them beautiful, objects of ultimate envy).

Wandering and the seabed; showering, pearls; the dead men

5

One dawn a woman reluctantly left
the city of light, love, pain and darkness.
It was a confused bird
who had lost her way
that weary and weeping headed nestward.

FORUGH FARROKHZAD[57]

We encounter our fifth ecdemomaniac astride an apparent contradiction that takes us beyond the architectonics of the conscious/unconscious: we are told of a woman who 'reluctantly left' but who also somehow 'lost her way', introducing a doubt as to whether she operates in the particular chambers of will, contingency, or repression. But this remains problematic only when we conceive this going-astray as a psychic matter, rather than as an anti-psychological alternative to the survival instinct (seceding so as to live). More precisely, here we can advance a theory of the *defective internal radar*, an anti-homing device or misbehaving antenna that inevitably sends one along errant paths (becoming-irrevocable), such that 'heading nestward' will always constitute the most misleading and maladjusted route to self-kidnapping. Rather than uphold the false value of going-home as an intrinsic existential

57 Farrokhzad, *A Lonely Woman*, 14.

need, we can instead suggest a counter-instinct toward the gone-missing, something within that remains devoted to the Old English etymology for wanderer (from *wandrian*, meaning 'wind') and its Persian equivalent (from *sargardan*, meaning 'head-turning'), an impulsive-abductive fleck that abides by prowling, looseness, crude and inexact positionality, off-balance steps, and a perpetually unsound relation to the supposed centre. The 'confused bird' is therefore not really confused at all, but rather given over to a supra-territorial catalyst that no longer recognizes shelter, habitat, colony, or hive, shattering the glass terrarium and its unqualified principles of adaptation and evolutionary teleology. Non-presidium: that which will no longer defend, protect, or preside over its own original domain.

Note: What of the increasingly reckless thought processes of those committed to extreme accuracy: the archer, the sniper, the racer, the mine-defuser? This is a matter rarely delved into but essential to study (willed volatility): for just like the manic personality, they too go awry of intentionality and the conscious-unconscious divide, as the once straight-shooting individual is evermore goaded (through intense repetitive visualization) into someday desiring the mistaken gesture, growing increasingly curious about the miscued result, picturing the boundless 'What if?' of the narrowly missed target (the anti-marksman). Consequently, such expert figures gradually begin to cheat themselves, subtly flinching the wrist, firing with hair-split bows or cracked arrows, brushing up against the wrong wires, hugging the deadly walls within fractionally-small measurements; they fabricate obstacles, they inject some extra complications or deterrences (making spurious), they forfeit their bearings and enter unsafe conditions (seeking gales), they shut their eyes at the decisive instant (praying for adulteration)—in short, anything that might take perfect aim down the valves of superb aimlessness.

Wandering and reluctance; confusion; losing the way; heading-nestward

6

Man betrayed the prophetic advice of his ancestors, who adopted the law of migration, believing that sedentary are the only dead ones, since they alone possess bodies that arouse the earth's greed. Nomadic people, who never stay anywhere or settle down on the earth, own nothing to provoke the earth or arouse its greed. The possess nothing: no gear, no walls, no bodies, not even dreams. All they possess is their voyage, nothing more. They possess a single riddle, over which the earth holds no sway and for which the lowlands can offer no explanation. This is deliverance.

IBRAHIM AL-KONI[58]

We encounter our sixth ecdemomaniac in recitation of a crucial lesson from the desert elders, one that links wandering to a defensive tactic against universal Being's own gluttony ('the earth's greed'), thereby compelling us to envision world as a voluminous throat in search of human sustenance. Nevertheless, this gastronomical mechanism is not indiscriminate, for we are advised that nomadic peoples more effectively evade the geo-stomach, their carefully-maintained customs of relocation/transplantation allowing them to throw off the hunting sensors of this Creation that devours creations (the runner versus

---

58 Al-Koni, *The Seven Veils of Seth*, 60–61.

the unscrupulous host). In a counterintuitive stroke, then, we must understand Bedouin wandering as a principle of focus, vigilance, and methodically-constructed movement, a warding off of the ever-detecting tongue of existence (born in avarice) through capricious, self-inflecting patterns (borne by zephyr). But even more compelling perhaps is the further articulation of the particular objects of 'provocation/arousal': existence rears angrily not just at the sight of 'gear' or 'walls', a logic of false possession and border-making that clearly offends the Open, but licks its lips most lasciviously at the thought of *bodies* and *dreams*. Thus the true ecdemomaniac bests terrestrial voracity by going bodiless and going dreamless, offsetting the earth's clench by grasping nothing, not even one's material self and abstract self, nestling lower than 'the lowlands', observing this 'single riddle' that alone provides 'deliverance', and therein yielding yet another reason why mania constitutes an antidote to the psychological prison-house: For what comes of a philosophical school (psychoanalysis) that locates almost the entirety of its diagnostic fury in body and dreams when it finally meets the one who willfully masters both bodilessness and dreamlessness?

Wandering and the prophetic; the ancestors; greed; provocation; dispossession; bodilessness; dreamlessness; the voyage; the single riddle; the lowlands; deliverance

7

To test the age-old faiths
he had ground his teeth
on the locks of ancient barriers.

Amidst the most far-flung paths
he roamed onward
an unanticipated journeyer
whose song was recognized by every grove and bridge.

Roads remain wakeful with the memory of your strides

AHMAD SHAMLU[59]

We encounter our seventh ecdemomaniac paying tribute to a figure of recent martyrdom, though here carving out a new panegyric or hagiographical mode wherein the voice is reserved for the most battered soul, the indecently dispatched wanderer, not he of unstained majestic rank but he of bruised skin, raising eyebrows to secret police, craning neck before executioner, until the final voyage toward immateriality. Here we are not meant to gape in pure veneration but to wince in non-empathic pangs (for we can never be this), this one-and-only morphology of the self-abating will and the self-racking flesh, which

59 Shamlu, *Born Upon the Dark Spear*, 76.

demands that we retailor all ideas of how impressions are registered and retained. For it is the ecdemomaniacal footstep that casts the harshest imprint, yet in doing so forges a different concept of legacy: (1) the wanderer's impression is registered by space itself rather than by any human narrative or textual record ('recognized by every grove and bridge'); (2) this impression is invested not in a lame-footed attachment to identity, but rather in the manic stride itself ('the memory of your strides'); (3) unlike historical consciousness, which puts the event to sleep, this impression keeps memory in a state of continual vigilance ('roads remain wakeful'); (4) the wanderer's impression is not one foretold by sacred prophecy or national myth; it fulfils no origin story, but rather comes out of nowhere as a daredevil irregularity ('an unanticipated journeyer'); (5) it is not etched into truth-telling structures (monument, memorial, state-commissioned sculpture, calendric seal), but bleached into ungoverned aesthetic tapestries such as 'song' (story, hymn, painting, nursery rhyme, graffiti sketch); (6) the wanderer's impression flips the longstanding hierarchical scales of judgment, allowing the physical ('grinding teeth') to test the metaphysical ('age-old faiths'); (7) the wanderer's impression is a force of belligerent de-ossification, erecting no legal-moral template, but rather unbolting all former blockades ('the locks of ancient barriers').

Together, these martyrological-ecdemomaniacal glitches set the backdrop for a theory of *n*th-degree severity, and with it a figure who remains impeccable (withstands putrefaction) by becoming-rumour, marching into shadowed and self-eclipsing forms. He will be the told-of, the spoken-about, this velvet colophon (from the Greek *kolophon*, meaning 'finishing touch'), this unelevated alter-*shahid* (from the Arabic 'witness'), for this wanderer went totally unwitnessed in life (and even at death's zenith) only to be colourfully recounted in remission, his fatality earning them honour, a prelude to ceaseless afterthought or aftersight.

Note: This resolves the age-old philosophical problematic of the one-player chess-game: more specifically, that the one competing against themselves will fall into an inevitable state of paralysis, an anxious stalemate caused by their anticipatory knowledge of the opponent's next move. Thus hyper-consciousness of the other self's turn causes one to second-guess each movement, to the point of arresting futility, with all these hyper-deductive layers supposedly making it impossible to ever complete the match authentically: the first move is already a 'checkmate' (mistranslated from the Arabic *al-shah mata* meaning 'the king has died', itself a mistranslation of the original Persian *shah-mat* meaning 'the king is left perplexed/escapeless'). But in the passage above we were introduced to an alternate typology of thought, one that prefers losing contests to the anticipatory self who always knows the next move, serving victory on silver plates for every approaching successor, the first figuration always ceding ground smoothly to the second—and thereby advances bravely against itself, designing its pieces for pure appropriation, in a kind of prismatic killer-solipsism. Ecdemomania thus fashions the slyest strategic route to being routed, favoring martyrdom before the one standing across the board, the becoming over the being, the emergent eternal over the mouldered past, and thereby flinging the chessboard toward imminent loss (so that the descendants might triumph).

Wandering and the test; teeth; the barrier; the unanticipated; song; recognition; wakefulness; the stride

8

> *It was as if the strange bed where I'd been spending my nights of late had become a kind of medium, dispatching warning signals to me across unseen wires from the realm of exile and homeless wandering.*
>
> GHADA SAMMAN[60]

We encounter our eighth ecdemomaniac laying back in a channelling zone, confined to someone else's bed (which is in fact more of a message-board), supposedly receiving transmissions from 'across unseen wires'. At the very outset, then, we are confronted with a one-to-many theory of nomadic sensitivity: the uprooted individual (our narrator sleeping in strangers' homes) is highly receptive to the utterances, bulletins, and communiques of her fellow displaced (the entire genus of the driven-out). Moreover, we are struck by two further paradoxical suggestions: firstly, that there is an actual specified 'realm of exile and homeless wandering'. Given that these categories are most often defined by the very absence of a binding locus, what would an exilic city or outpost even resemble (is it a shanty-town of cardboard and makeshift materials, or is it entirely structure-less, the people there sleeping outdoors beneath the stars)? And what would be the guidelines

60 Samman, *Beirut Nightmares*, 155.

of free circulation/interaction therein? Secondly, that this wandering capital 'dispatch[es] warning signals' to those still back in the regulated world—which makes one wonder about the urgent purpose of such announcements, for is our on-the-run narrator not already mortally endangered, her civil war theatre of operation compelling her to flee for her life at a moment's notice? What further squadrons or polychromatic threats necessitate her taking to this transistor portal-bed and becoming, in her turn, the listener who rummages, sifts, and gropes through half-inaudible reports (the undercover envoy, the emissary, the eavesdropper)?

In any case, this scene allows us to connect the wanderer directly to a whole anthology of counter-intelligence, surveillance, and *espionage*. Manic philosophy would therefore appropriate their coded terms in unique ways: the double agent; the bridge agent; the agent-in-place; agent-of-influence; the scout, plant, or sleeper; the asset; the babysitter; the bagman; the birdwatcher; the black bag job; the brush pass; bang and burn; covert actions; the dangle; the dead drop; the discard; the dry clean; exfiltration operation; naked operation; sanitizing; eyes only; flaps and seals; the floater, the friend, or the ghoul; the handler; the honey trap; the innocent postcard; the L-pill; the legend; the mole; the nursemaid; one-time pads, paroles, or plaintext; playback; pocket litter; the provocateur; the raven; the swallow; the spymaster; the station; the company; the take; the throwaway; the timed drop; tradecraft; traffic analysis; window-dressing; and the walk-in. Most importantly, however, this broadcasting of corrugated memoranda leads us to ask whether there is a war escalating, some campaign against the realm of bounded reality by the realm of militant exilic spies.

Wandering and the bed; medium; warning signals; wires; the realm

9

There is yet another road in the road, another chance for migration.
To cross over we will throw many roses in the river.
No widow wants to return to us, there we have to go, north of the neighing horses.

MAHMOUD DARWISH[61]

We encounter our ninth ecdemomaniac leaving blood-red flowers in rivers and crossing beyond stables full of wheezing mounts in order to concentrate the poetic gaze on a solitary figure of great importance for the question of wandering: the widow. More precisely, we find ourselves contemplating two distinct spatial imaginaries of the widow (here in its extreme version, that 'wants [no] return to us'), spatial imaginaries that almost magnetically compel her daily excursions from the empty house, but which also allow for a remarkable transversal of both the East-West and ancient-postmodern divide: namely, those of the catacomb and the architectural feature known as the 'widow's walk'.

And what is the connection between the ancient Roman catacomb and the contemporary Palestinian burial zone? A simple, reprehensible truth: that while the Romans confined their corpses to subterranean galleries, believing

61 Darwish, *Unfortunately, It Was Paradise*, 4.

it evil to bury the dead within the city limits, so too do Palestinian widows now bury their fighter-husbands underground in vast tunnel complexes, interring them below to avoid confiscation by the enemy, those who distastefully throw such bodies into unmarked graves known as 'the cemetery of numbers' (fascistic reduction to statistical non-value). And so, after two thousand years, the catacomb makes its reappearance on the scene of world history, in an era of rising scourge, with no larger sacred-cultural influence whatsoever: for this singularly Palestinian sector bears no resemblance to the conventional Arabic *maqbara* ('graveyard') or Persian *aramgah* ('resting-place'), but is rather an improvised necropolis architectonically called forward by the circumstances of chronic occupation and violent death alone, a nether-mortuary invented solely to prevent mishandling of the decedent lover.

And what is the connection between the nineteenth-century North American widow's walk and the contemporary Palestinian burial zone? Another motive at work: while the Western widow's walk was typically a railed rooftop platform from which mariners' wives would stare overlooking the harbour, anticipating their sailor-husbands' return (with ever-tautening expectation), though frequently in vain as the waves had already claimed them, so too does the Palestinian widow whose spouse is killed on the other side (in enemy territory) now trek atop the tall hills overlooking the bare wall constructed to turn their homeland into an open-air prison camp, staring helplessly across the great barricade at that cursed place which claimed the husband's body and where she can never enter. The body is denied its proper rites: eyelids and jaws closed gently, limbs bathed with untainted water at elevated height, covered in clean white sheet, while reciting prayers of forgiveness before lowered into freshly-dug earth. No, we can add to this spatial matrix of loss a third example, one that takes us back to a millennia-old Persian tradition, that of the Zoroastrians, whose widows also had no remains to visit, no ribbons to entwine in the dead's hair: the tradition of mourning along the cliffs. For these ancient widows would also ascend above the houses and cities of the living, moving slowly (a rhythm of irrelevance, of futility, of waiting to join the beloved), for whatever mandatory worlds have already since passed, speed falling beneath obliqueness, beneath the quiet groan, foraging for nothing anymore, but rather sitting observantly as a backhanded sky seems to stencil the cut-out imprint of their dead in the clouds and shades of each dusk. *Catacomb, tunnel, widow's walk, sea, hilltop, wall, cliff*: such is the spatial litany of the ultra-widow's pendant universe, both now and then, here and there, a hanging, unresolved expanse (wandering below, on high, and beyond).

Wandering and the other road; the other chance;
the crossing-over; roses; river; the widow

10

> *No, no, my father wasn't with us. Months before the uprising, he had become the madman of the city, wandering the streets singing against God and carrying his lute, which no longer had a single string. A fire broke out in our house and my mother collapsed unconscious as the rest of us leant against the outer wall of the house.*
>
> HASSAN BLASIM[62]

In our tenth ecdemomaniac we encounter a new stratum of the distraught mind. A former composer whose vast talents have won him a position making propagandistic music for the dictator, regime-glorifying anthems played in syndicated recurrence on the state radio channels, he eventually suffers an unexpected breakdown, and is thereafter found wandering the local streets and cafes each night inventing obscene songs to mock God, prophets, and the whole sacred order. The population at first quietly tolerates his sacrilegious ballads, either for fear of his prior government connections, out of respect for his once-esteemed artistic reputation, or because those spurned by God are often the most beautiful; but they grow increasingly hostile toward such conduct, his own family turning on him ashamed, casting him from the

62 Blasim, *The Madman of Freedom Square*, 24.

house to roam the alleys whistling, until the day the elder son finds his father's headless body tied with thick rope to a tractor, his corpse having been dragged for days in symbolic display.

We can propose a twofold link between this traipsing heathen composer and two other conceptual figures of undeniable importance for the topic of wandering—the fool and the heretic—though for each we are here compelled to develop a special theoretical outlook.

There are undoubtedly entire compendia dedicated to close analysis of the fool and its many derivations—the village idiot, the imbecile, the trickster, the prankster, the jester, the drunk, the famous Persian *rend* (slick-talking rascal), and the remarkably diverse Arabic etymological branches (*'ablah, balid, safih, 'abit, ghabi, majnun, makhbul, mastul, mahbul, 'ahmagh, ma'tuh, mughaffal, muharrij, jahil, sakhif*) connoting all kinds of different flavors of silliness, triviality, childishness, vulgarity, or ignorance—all of whom have their own philosophical insignia and patented deeds in literary-artistic history. There is also the well-documented history of the madman across different epistemes: in ancient societies, a relatively harmless figure regarded as a semi-ancillary part of the community; in mediaeval times, a figure tragically 'touched' by God (a symptom of having come too close to divinity), and thus embodying the human fall from grace; in the classical era, a figure holding some keener insight, able to penetrate the many deceptive layers of self-proclaimed reality's house of cards; in mystical circles, a figure of highest esoteric wisdom, reaching illuminated states that only appear to others as confusion; and in the modern age, a figure diagnosed into quarantine by pseudo-scientific doctrines that must contain, supervise, examine, judge, and punish madness at once physically, psychologically, existentially, and even spiritually (forgotten by social worlds, institutionalized into invisibility). Noting this wide-ranging dramaturgy of the fool/madman, we return to our murdered musician as the pioneer of an alternative course: not someone housed by the discourses of knowledge, psyche, or even gnosis (all of which categorize stupidity/insanity as either defect or fulfillment), but rather someone who represents sheer supra-psychotic fulmination (simplicity's gust or fusillade). The dumbfounded is actually the unfounded here, with no underlying morality or consciousness-unconsciousness relation; its manic volubility is but the marker of a now-bursting incident (the moment subjectivity becomes phenomenal upsurge).

In a separate vein, we may isolate the dueling categories of the heretic (the enemy outside; the non-believer), the blasphemer (the enemy within; the flawed believer), and the apostate (the enemy within-turned-outside; the former believer), only so as to recognize how our character above somehow becomes the combined aggregate of all three stances. This triadic synthesis is particularly evident in his various post-breakdown songs, some of which rail against the originary validity of faith itself (heresy), while others intimately tease and scorn from within the doctrinal pillars (blasphemy), while still others reflect the anger/sorrow of a turncoat (apostasy). But how could a lone strain of ecdemomaniacal experience erupt into a multilevel musical accusation of the universe? While the absolute limit of neurotic psychology, in its sadistic imperial form (i.e., that most clearly manifested in genocidal political leaders or systems) is the attempt to play God and thus to control totality, the absolute limit of the manic imagination, on the other hand, in its most visionary hour of fatal play, is the attempt to destroy all god-formations and thus to crack open totality. It therefore supersedes all of the various dialectics of knowing and non-knowing that accompany fool/madman taxonomies, and also eliminates the hyper-aware temperaments of anti-metaphysical dissidents who must distinguish their transgressive rationales (the rebel's formalized negativity), in order to invoke a bedlam aesthetic with but one manic-anarchistic goal: to overthrow power (all that rules) through creative exclamations.

Note: Things grow even more complex when we endeavour to reconcile two stunning lines from the ninth-century Sufi mystic Hallaj, a wanderer crucified, beheaded, and burned alive in the same city of Baghdad in which our composer meets his fate. Hallaj combines the spoken statement 'I am God' with another spoken statement (directed to God/Vizier), 'I trust you to kill me'. And here we discover an apparent dissonance that nevertheless joins becoming and annihilation in a single connective melody—'I am God' (becoming the ultimate), 'I trust you to kill me' (dying-killing as the ultimate)—thereby revealing the manic imagination as that which can ravage only through full possession, neither graceful ascendancy nor resentful denial but always combustive infiltration—just as the wanderer dissolves boundary ideologies not by evoking a counter-ideological pathlessness, but rather by immanent path-making (never void, only excessive action), extending itself into the productive membrane of an opponent it will fight to the death, shouldering its burden, wearing its robes, taking its first name, before collapsing it finally into a homicidal-deicidal-suicidal embrace.

Wandering and the uprising; the madman; the singer; fire; the outer wall

Cartogramania (Maps)

1

> *Opening off my room is a dark closet. The room itself has two windows facing out onto the world of the rabble. One of them looks onto our own courtyard, the other onto the street, forming thereby a link between me and the city of Rey* [...] *with its thousand-fold web of winding streets, its host of squat houses, its schools and its caravan serais.*
>
> SADEQ HEDAYAT[63]

We encounter our first cartogramaniac incorporating the figure of the mapmaker into that of *the net-maker*, for whom borders are but supple matters of woven twine, meshing, overhanded slipknots, and the symmetrical geometry of loops and rows. He brings the city's houses themselves into his 'thousand-fold web', a restrictive, twisted fabric that prompts us to interrogate the various intentions of different net-makers: on the one hand, there is the net as entrapment device (the hunter; the fisherman), its fibres designed to constrict and corner unsuspecting creatures, whether suspending victims mid-air in the forest or trawling long lattices across ocean floors

63 Hedayat, *The Blind Owl*, 51.

to dredge them up from below; on the other hand, there is the net as corralling chamber (the butterfly collector), its soft lacelike material delicate enough to hold rare beings gently, to temporarily enclose the exceptional sample, with a view to bringing new discoveries into the accumulator's compendium, before they are pinned forevermore behind glass panels; and then there is the net as offensive and defensive implement of war, whether employed in night-raids against vulnerable caravans (the hostage-taker; the renegade) or to secure encampments against such bloodthirsty types (the tribeswoman; the outdoorsman); lastly, there is the net's inversion into a calming arena, a secure enclosure for the restful (the lounger; the sleeper), the swinging hammock that provides tranquilizing rhythm or the single draped cloth that keeps at bay the limitless swarms of mosquitos and other insects. Flexible, sinuous, binding, deadly—in almost all of its diverse usages, this contrivance of filaments and holes carries the same implication: a perception of external forces as either objectified enemies or collectible properties (entities designated for capture).

Is our cartogramaniacal figure therefore capable of transferring an entire cityscape and its human citizens into the category of wanted animal or collectible thing, viewing them as mere items waiting to be snarled up in the logic of the grid? Undoubtedly so, but with this one key additional complication: our narrator has himself undergone the same conversion (from 'I' to 'it'), already renamed the Blind Owl; but here we find him in the role of another primordial net-maker of the highest calibre—the spider—as evidenced by his placing these two windows in some 'dark closet' where he presumably watches and crouches patiently. This is a common practice of predatory design: to build advantageous blind spots into the fabricated layout; to exploit the presumed transparency of the map in order to conceive sites of non-detection (arachnid lingering). A double-machination whereby the mapping of space becomes identical to the knitting of a reticulated net, permeable yet virtually untearable, balancing the physics of elasticity and tension (flexible prisons) to produce corded structures that claim both self and other, spider and caught prey, as identityless contenders of strategic incarceration, beholding, or ingestion.

Map and the dark; the closet; the window; the link; the thousand-fold web

2

I construct a mobile cognitive map of my spiritual wares, I force myself to destabilize my mind...

RÉDA BENSMAIA[64]

We encounter our second cartogramaniac incorporating the figure of the mapmaker into that of *the deranger*, for whom borders are nothing more than passageways to the 'destabilized mind'—a kind of drug dealer coordinating highs, taking delight in delivering garish sensory trips across cognitive space (atlases of pharmaceutical manipulation). Thus we enter the vistas of the heroin dream and beyond—dull euphoria of the muscle spindles, slurred speech caused by deliriants, stimulants, and psychedelics—in order to strike new conceptual ground: the hallucinatory map. Hallucination (from Latin *allucinari*, 'to wander in the mind') marks our first connection between the cartographic universe and the experience of manic visionary motion (a 'mobile cognitive map'), while the line above also confirms the link between pusher and deranger with its mention of 'spiritual wares', for this strange expression reconstructs spirit as made object or sellable merchandise, the map of which becomes silo and depository (the dealer's lab; the dealer's stash). Moreover, note that hallucinatory experience runs across

64 Bensmaia, *The Year of Passages*, 40.1.

almost all sensory modalities: visual (sight), auditory (sound), olfactory (smell), gustatory (taste), tactile (touch), proprioceptive (movement), equilibrioperceptive (balance), nociceptive (pain), thermoceptive (temperature), and chronoceptive (time). Does the deranger's map therefore unleash all such super-perceptual trajectories, including even hypnagogic hallucination (interval transitioning from wakefulness to sleep) and hypnopompic hallucination (interval transitioning from sleep to wakefulness), paranoiac suspicion (persecutory voices, talking behind one's back), or even phantom limb syndrome (feeling what is not there)? The map-maker here must gorge themselves on the world of white powders, pills, pipes, smoke, and needles, confident that no lithium salt can quell manic ascertainment, seeing plotted tributaries and rock crevices as untapped veins, surveying mountain ranges as morphine drips, and the earth itself as central nervous system (made for injection, inhalation, absorption).

Map and mobile cognition; spirit; force; destabilization; mind

3

In a map that extends, etc.
In which the word is transformed into a web whose mesh is riddled with holes
like carded cotton

ADONIS[65]

We encounter our third cartogramaniac incorporating the figure of the mapmaker into that of *the carder*, by definition a cutter who cleans, unravels, combs, and brings into parallel disorganized fibres of cotton or wool, rendering them into a sliver ready for spinning. In ancient times, the carders (derived from the Latin *carduus*, meaning 'thistle'; or from the Arabic *hall*, meaning 'disentangle') were said to possess the roughest hands, their fingers perpetually swollen and blistered to the point of becoming leathery, their skin reddened from working the vibrating bow and string instrument, teasing the disorganized raw tufts and removing undesirable yarns for later processing. Most often they were to be found travelling from village to village, employed to fill the beds, pillows, and blankets of families. So what exactly does it mean to fathom 'a map that extends' to find itself 'riddled with holes like carded cotton'? The question seats us at the sharp-toothed

65 Adonis, *A Time Between Ashes and Roses*, 49.

panels of the carder himself, one who masters conflicting sensitivities of the billowy, the greasy, the thorny, the prickly, and the granular. He wafts between bristling and lustrous flax, up to the waist in clusters both abrasive and cloudlike, bleeding into the glossy piles and tassels below like those fairy-tale seamstresses who prick their fingers at the spinning wheel. A profession that follows cruel minimalist laws of separation and subtraction (tearing apart, peeling away, paring down).

Note: If we take the carder's technique into a more refined aesthetic realm (cutting into abstract messages), then there is likely no more subversive threat to literal Truth than the figure of *the calligrapher* (once called 'Hell's locksmith'). For the calligrapher makes the textual border an occasion of pure visual enchantment; meaning is rendered obsolete beneath the sweeping extension of shapes and lines; language gets lost within the curvatures and spirals of a brush moving beyond reason (enmeshed word; mired verse). The reed-pen is thus the optimum instrument of the embroiled, the tumultuous, and the quandary—the script muddles; the stroke conveys tactful uproar. No, the calligrapher does not come to make anything known, but rather to wrest the straightedge of knowing itself into coiling furore, into the delirium of broken/flowing letters.

Map and riddling; holes; the carder

4

A thick finger rests on a couch
He traces with charcoal the outline of a woman's face
Your God will be my God
And your belly button
My perch

JOYCE MANSOUR[66]

We encounter our fourth cartogramaniac incorporating the figure of the mapmaker into that of *the miniaturist*, for whom borders are a matter of tracing manifest epics back into razor-thin outlines and brightest pigments (dyed skeletal contours). Reading of the 'thick finger' that 'traces with charcoal', one imagines the highly disciplined schools of the East, their disciples' squinting eyes into the midnight hours (many miniaturists went blind), their tightly-guarded workshops experimenting with coloured bands, gold leaf flecks, illuminated manuscripts that would decorate the halls of royal libraries. And yet the second passage reveals the conspiratorial conceit behind miniaturism: 'your belly button [is] my perch'. For here we can record a cunning prevarication in scale and measure: to flick the wrist against maturation, to infantilize creation itself and thereby to strip mythic Being down

66 Mansour, *Essential Poems and Writings*, 301, 253.

to an almost-disposable hide or rind; the once-sacred human navel becomes another creature's pedestal, roost, or branch. This implies a chipping-away at the epicentre, one that reminds us of the miniaturists' devious staging of flattened forms: illustrated warriors concentrated at the focal midpoint, while magnificent elongated trees, skies, and beasts formlessly spill into the no man's land of the book's fringes. This also resolves Western philosophy's continual anxiety over the frame or *parergon* (always related to truth, context, origin, metaphysics, and the inside-outside relation). For the Eastern miniaturists never miss the chance to rethink this visual border as *precipice*, for which two alternative concepts then take supreme hold: fatality and irreversibility. No doubt the frame is the fatal-irreversible ridge that combines the 'too far gone', the 'point of no return', and the 'lost cause' along a single tempting escarpment (the pull of anti-gravity). The bluff, the crag's face—the border here is no experience of impossibility, closure, or finitude, no fearful theology of marginality or liminality, but rather a beckoning ledge that sends once-represented forms rambling and straggling into outer space (ocular spacewalk). Thus the miniaturist's tactic of curtailment is one that allows firmly-sealed atmospheres to leak across the factorless rim, to flirt with breathtaking overhangs beyond which all things become untethered particles and enter the cerulean tract (states of abyssal gyration).

Note: If we recall the first test of wonderland, the little girl eating from mushrooms, bottles, and cakes to turn smaller, now able to slip through keyholes, then we might fathom how the figure of *the miniaturist* poses the greatest conceivable threat to the self-monumentalizing Real. For, rather than build upward, seeking vain eminence in height and stature, she instead carves downward/inward, making the conspicuous parameters of representation wilt and tighten, drawing perception into ever-lessening shapes, into dwindling and shrunkenness (becoming-negligible). This is the unique talent of the miniaturist, this mischief of the petite silhouette, one that caresses the infinitesimal: the touch of attenuation, of compacted worlds, the ability to make leaner, slighter, yet more trifling. She finds the richest subtlety in the arts of scantiness, condensation, constriction, narrowing, shrivelling, wrinkling; she finds purpose in a sculpted consort of pinched and emaciated beings. Thus the miniaturist inhabits an almost aerial vantage on the cowering realm of forms, viewing them through a poorly scaled prism of absurdity, these tiny creatures so close to the brink of complete disintegration.

Map and the finger; tracing; outline; the perch

5

I shall give up lines
and give up counting syllables too.
And I will seek refuge from the mob
of finite measured forms
in the sensitive planes of expanse.

FORUGH FARROKHZAD[67]

We encounter our fifth cartogramaniac incorporating the figure of the mapmaker into that of *the hermitess* (Persian *gusheh-neshin*, 'one who sits in corners'), for whom borders are but lineal crests of 'the mob' and its anxious predilection for accounting. The reader meets her still hesitating on the threshold of a decision to 'give up lines' and 'seek refuge', but the added references to 'counting syllables' and 'finite measured forms' divulge her former professional niche: that of *the diagrammatician*. Her former tabulomaniacal existence (obsession with tables and diagrams) has come eventually to demand a cartogramaniacal remedy ('the sensitive planes of expanse'), in which mathematical-architectural consciousness, in exasperation ransoms itself to more permissive geoscapes and anatomies...passing into the realm of jackals, ascetics, loners, and anchoresses. Thus we meet the hermetic imagination

67 Farrokhzad, *A Lonely Woman*, 126.

beyond even the captivating fold between figuration and abstraction, in a plain grey shack where abstraction has raced ahead into its next manic compartment: oblivion (Persian *dast-o-pa nashenasi*, 'non-recognition of one's own hands and feet'). For manic oblivion is the more amphibious extreme of forgetting, a contortionist manoeuvre in which reclusive hypersensitivity blots out both explicit and latent memory. And what happens to carnal, semiotic, and even forensic experience when it becomes a perfectly traceless/untraceable crime, i.e., a map of the self-disappeared (where events may or may not take place and end, but are never drafted, documented, archived, or remembered)?

Note: In thinking through the connection between mapping, hermeticism, and oblivion, we can also turn to fables of *the changeling*: that is, stories from innumerable cultures where fairies, trolls, or nymphs are presumed to swap children at birth, leaving an impostor of their own making behind in the crib while raising the human infant in their own hidden lands. According to varying superstitious accounts, the motive arises either from attraction to the child's physical beauty, general misanthropy or malice against human beings, or the desire to enslave the human child as a servant in faerie homes. Although there is also a grotesque history to these narratives of supernatural abduction and youth exchange, which may have justified parents' abusive denial of those born with neurological disorders, mental disabilities, or deformities, what intrigues us here is the radical obliteration of memory that is required for the changeling to manage their stolen existence: either forgetting their human origin to fall headlong into the spritely world, or growing up among humans (as other stories have it) and one day deciding to return to their faerie family, a self-erasing and world-erasing journey for which the changeling's search must always begin by constructing a sophisticated map of the nothing (to find the place that is not there).

Map and counting; refuge; sensitivity; planes; expanse

6

> *He'd scoured the surrounding mountains with him, rock by rock, setting up stones near some of the caves and sprinkling a white liquid on them to mark them out from the rest* [...] *It was because he'd sensed how this old, white-haired man loved the desert. He'd seen it in his eyes, and in the way he treated the painted rocks. He saw how the man's fingers trembled when they touched the caves marked with the lines the ancient people had made. As he did it, a mysterious glint would appear in his eyes.*
>
> IBRAHIM AL-KONI[68]

We encounter our sixth cartogramaniac incorporating the figure of the mapmaker into that of *the mirage-maker*, for whom borders are but cave paintings left behind by deceptive older races, godlike inscribers so powerful that even in ruined form their schemas maintain a disarming quality. This devoted old custodian's entrusted duties consist in 'scouring' and 'sprinkling', and who pours 'white liquid' on the rock surfaces surrounding the caves where 'the ancient people' first conceived their universal graphs. Nevertheless, this story's complex tribal formulations of *the leader* (where gods/chiefs can dissemble, torture, or cheat) lack the sanitizing one-dimensionality

68 Al-Koni, *The Bleeding of the Stone*, 76.

of monotheistic doctrine and modern political ideology (where gods/officials must only aid, bless, judge, or enforce), such that the white-haired elder develops affection for the wicked jokes played by the ancestors, their ingenious manipulations of gullibility, his reverence based solely in an appreciation of the great subterfuge. The desert cave drawings therefore function more as a series of cooked herbs, seeds, and salves; a pseudo-oracular brew, a cuisine of the presumptuous, meant to braise truth within lie, lie within truth, twisting tongue and sight amidst well-feigned answers—thus the curious secret behind the aged man's 'trembling fingers' and 'mysterious glint' (hints of playful treachery)—as if merely looking into such threadbare maps were in itself a process of immediate hypnosis.

Note: We are here reminded of a certain extreme kind of mirage (Arabic *saraab*; or from the Latin *mirare*, 'to look upon' and French *se mire*, 'reflected'): not the typical inferior or superior versions that result from mere temperature and sightline inversions, but the *fata morgana* appearance of luring shapes, that optical gamesmanship through which feasts, sheets of water, ships, or castles materialize out of heated thin air. This extreme mirage combines all of the many experiences of unreality, manipulating imaginary states as if they were the different steps of a ladder: the dream, the nightmare, the reverie, the hallucination, the illusion, the fantasy, the vision, and the simulation. We can uncover three further unorthodox principles of this mirage-type:

(1) The mirage occurs at the moment of pure desperation, at the outer threshold of frailty, the breaking point of survival and critical need, its clock set to the exact second of surrender; it is a vision that rules in the state of emergency.

(2) The mirage arises from the void of deepest thirst, the incarnation of a certain terrible longing, hearkening to the pleas of the unsatiated ones, its ethereal jaws set in an almost vampiric spirit of deprivation to answer the call of another's unfulfilled desire.

(3) The mirage is not a force of euphoria but rather of dysphoria, never dispensing actual pleasure but only release from pain, bringing temporary numbness to the other's agony, promising no ecstatic departure but only an anaesthetic to soothe open wounds, a calming of the unbearable.

Such is the affective logic of the mirage-unto-mania: to begin drinking the sands, to experience dry grains as refreshment (no longer knowing the difference), an ancient device of the desert's trickery, an event that takes place somewhere beyond shadow, ghost, and conjuration, perhaps closer to the concepts of *inveigling* (from 'to blind') and *tantalizing* (from the demi-god Tantalus, condemned to an underworld punishment of sitting forever in a pool only to watch the waters recede every time he bowed to take a drink). For the mirage manifests itself during our lowest hour, a falsifying spectacle of salvation, providing the mere appearance of banquets that quench no one, offerings that serve for nothing except to draw us further into the dunes, luring and inspiring the will at the instant of its absolute defeat.

Map and scouring; sprinkling; painted stones;
the marker; the caves; the ancients; the glint

7

The first new leaves of the sun
have grown across the ivy of the ancient garden's door
the playful lanterns of the stars
have been hanged upon the terrace of the sun's
passageway...
I returned from the road
my whole spirit in anticipation.
Two walls
and the corridor of silence
And then a shadow that speaks continually of the downfall
of the sun.

AHMAD SHAMLU[69]

We encounter our seventh cartogramaniac incorporating the figure of the mapmaker into that of *the lantern-maker*, for whom borders are but hiding places for proscribed intimations (conspiratorial clue-giving). This is the spatial perception of the cadre, those underground players whose secret missions depend on their ability to place half-lit clandestine markings, conspicuously inconspicuous details left hanging by the alliance, often entangled within natural formations for camouflage (leaves, ivy), lost in the jumble and kinks of an otherwise safe pattern,

69 Shamlu, *Born Upon the Dark Spear*, 33, 24.

noticeable only to the most suspecting (those of forbidden convictions). Thus we are a far cry from the traditional lantern-makers of past millennia, craftsmen who worked sometimes with paper but more frequently with cracked glass and metal frames, their pyramidal containers let upwards into the sky during festivals, set afloat in water with dead bodies during certain burial traditions (guiding the way toward the afterlife), or kept by lighthouse keepers in their upper rooms; at first a technological modification of the torch, a protective device to shield the candle's flame from outside forces (wind and rain), reducing the risk of setting fire to houses or ships (lanterns were even mandated in the earliest pirate code when walking below deck, where gunpowder might be stored). And yet the lines here speak of a perilous counter-history, one of asymmetrical warfare and revolutionary mapping, in which lanterns are 'hanged upon the terrace of the sun's passageway' by someone with 'whole spirit in anticipation', someone who studies blueprints of the enemy camp, lists coordinates of '[t]wo walls and the corridor of silence', encodes warnings of speaking shadows and imminent 'downfall', their allusive traces engineered with remarkable capacities to reveal themselves or to efface themselves at the right time. Hence this precursor figure embeds fatalistic messages for the coming abettor, as the first rock climber leaves footholds for subsequent daring souls (one must go before), counting on a theory of mutual complicity based in the strictest hermeneutic exactitude: namely, that the right one will find this subterranean map embedded within the dominant map (showing enemy positions, meeting points, attacking hours), instructions for the persecuted yet retaliatory minority (on the run), germinations of the irregular strike pattern, for whom cartogramaniacal experience is never about settling or maintaining existent worlds, but rather about radical transformation and passage to the next banned infinity.

Map and lantern; terrace; passageway; return; anticipation; corridor; shadow; downfall

8

> *Meanwhile, I continued sailing along in my stone boat at 'zero' latitude and 'zero' longitude, while my compass, rather than pointing north, south, east or west, was pointing in the 'fifth direction'—namely, straight down into the depths.*
>
> GHADA SAMMAN[70]

We encounter our eighth cartogramaniac incorporating the figure of the mapmaker into that of *the boatwoman*, for whom borders are but burning streams pouring in the 'fifth direction' (inferno). Thus we revisit a strange literary-theological tradition of underworld maps, nether cartographies that always start from the absolute nexus ('zero latitude and zero longitude'), aboard vessels built to sink ('stone boat'), and which transpose outward horizons into vertical downward layers ('straight down into the depths'). However, what remains compelling about the boatwoman is that she carries herself alone: rather than being passively employed by some hell-structure to escort others, she deliberately seeks out her own unstoppable descent, all the while steadily penning a journal of waking nightmares, much like those ancient authors who somehow composed books of the dead, except that in the

70 Samman, *Beirut Nightmares*, 376.

boatwoman's case it is her own catastrophic imagination that sets the spatial contours of the underworld: this is no universal architecture arranged according to general hierarchies of sin or punishment, but a private delineation shaped from the recesses of her individual mania, and which thus draws an essential connection between the dying-envisioning self, text, nightmare, and underworld.

Note: Historical chronicles of the boatman are many and varied: Firstly, the ancient Egyptian mythology that stations *Aken* (the papyrus boatman always in a deep sleep) and *Mahaf* (the ferryman who must always wake the patron) on the underworld's waterways, at times helming solar or lunar barques, ushering pharaohs along, while both also serving an ambiguous ram-headed cult divinity named *Kherty* or *Cherti* (symbolized by the hieroglyphic sign for 'shamble', and whose name connotes 'slaughter'). All three figures combine in the Egyptian Book of the Dead to form the one known only as 'He Who Sees Behind Him'. Secondly, the ancient Greek myth of *Charon* (a name etymologically disputed, stemming either from 'keen gaze', 'fierce brightness', 'bluish-grey eyes', or 'silence', or derived from the earlier Egyptian *Kherty*). Charon ferries souls across the river Styx or Acheron to Hades, and is depicted on stone vases either as an impatient brutish driver, winged monster, skeletal reaper, or in kinder fashion as a solemn old man, holding either oar (to row), pole (to guide), or mallet (to beat).

Brother to *Thanatos* (death) and *Hypnos* (sleep), he collects the coins left on the mouths of the recently buried as his toll. Thirdly, the Vedan, Tibetan, Buddhist, and Zoroastrian figure named *Yama* or *Yima* (which, it is speculated, means 'twin'), Lord of Death presiding over purgatorial zones and cyclical processes of reincarnation, in some readings considered the first mortal to die and thus made ruler over the southern hemisphere (*naraka* abodes, or the six *bardos* of the Tibetan Book of the Dead), most often shown riding a buffalo accompanied by two four-legged guard dogs and carrying a massive leash to harness those about to die, in his most grisly representations shown with flaky green skin and blood-red gown, taking delight in boiling souls in large oil vats and soups. And, finally, a boatwoman: the Inuit sea goddess *Sedna*, cannibal-bestial mistress, most adulated of the Arctic pantheon, her fingers mutilated after eating her parents' limbs, who takes a giant scorpion fish for a husband, and whose subaquatic home is crafted from long whalebones, its walls decorated by the clothes and belongings of those drowned at sea. Together, Sedna and her father *Anguta* (meaning 'man with something to cut'), boatman-purifier of souls in Adlivun (watery realm of the dead), a frozen lower tundra of circling ice formations and sparkling platters of seal fat, prepare once-tainted spirits for their final elevation to the Moon.

Lastly, it is by positing the above quote against the enumerated descriptions that we can actually seek a new iteration of *the psychopomp*: those 'soul-guiding' beings (gods, spirits, angels, dead relatives, anthropomorphic creatures, or animals like horses, ravens, sparrows, deer, cats, and owls) that ensure safe travel for those emitting their last breath. No longer beings of metempsychosis, only metemania (switching species for madness); no longer palingenesis, only palinmania (switching birth for madness). Thus we return to *the boatwoman* of the initial passage, whose self-steering toward the fifth direction must be seen as its own chthonic narrative effervescence—i.e., the frightful potential that writing may lead the dead, and that only authors, and more specifically those who map nightmares, are granted passage to an underworld (to be awarded aftermath).

Map and stone; zero; fifth direction; straight down; depth

9

Here we will die. Here in the final passage.
Here and there a clear line marks our route of wandering.
For how many years should we sacrifice our dead
to the oblivion mirrored in melodious ambiguity?

MAHMOUD DARWISH[71]

We encounter our ninth cartogramaniac incorporating the figure of the mapmaker into that of *the mirror-maker* and *the escape artist*, both of whom conspire to turn borders into airless rooms, tubes, vaults, and elevator shafts.

The escape artist seeks their death-defying challenge in 'the final passage' (evermore inescapable), a unique trade for which certain specialized lexicons are required. Extensive research into the historical accounts of escape artists reveals the following recurring terms (across myriad texts) from which manic philosophy might also derive new linguistic-conceptual partnerships: crowd-pleaser; breath-holder; dissatisfaction; hurriedness; unventilated circuit; second skin; antechamber; squatter's haven; inorganic; perseverance; all-cupped; vibration; aluminium; straitjacket; floorboards; columns; short ceilings; exertion; groping; fast-clung; boxed-in; plaster; vacuum; incompatible; element of surprise; gambler's debt; rapier-like;

71 Darwish, *Unfortunately, It Was Paradise*, 9, 31.

competition; twinge; cramp; worry; outreach; the square; the booth; faint scratching; lock of hair; the surmising one.

The mirror-maker answers the escape artist's request, mapping potential obfuscation into reflective surfaces of 'melodious ambiguity', a unique trade for which certain specialized lexicons are also required. Extensive research into the historical accounts of mirror-makers reveals the following recurring terms (across myriad texts) from which manic philosophy might derive further linguistic-conceptual partnerships: silk chrysalis; underbrush; anathema; canopy; trench; canister; sponge; streetlamp; intermittence; reasonlessness; grating metrics; the sombre; the lookout; reaping; sordid; shoved; here-slung; the undercover; the middle-ground; pistons; bleariness; lustre; filth; sourness; unbreathable; parcel; overlay; astigmatism; wax; hues; the close-up; the repellent; the overnight.

And what happens when the escape artist finally enters the mirror, becoming forever *ensconced* (simultaneously 'nestled', 'installed', and 'concealed')? Do they release their own *eidolon* (apparitional lookalike, spirit-image of a person dead or living), allowing an idealized spectral version to exit and walk within mapped realities, while themselves remaining trapped in glassy worlds?

Map and death; final passage; the clear line; sacrifice; oblivion; mirror; ambiguity

10

> *How could I work out where my foot was, or how could I find my hair to touch it?* [...] *You remember how to look, for example, but you no longer have the tools that make it possible to look. At the same time, I felt that I still existed as a small point of consciousness somewhere in the world. I don't know how long this lasted. The small point expanded.*
>
> HASSAN BLASIM[72]

We encounter our tenth cartogramaniac incorporating the figure of the mapmaker into that of *the amateur*, for whom borders turn one into a being wound back toward the beginnings (the novice, the street kid, the newcomer, the apprentice, the recruit, the tyro, the neophyte). He has deliberately lost familiarity with the working order of his own body, a procedure through which the highest intellect seeks pure inelegance once more: childlike demolition; unlearning; facelessness; molecularity; the non-alpha; undersupplied mind; badge-stripped; tinged; whimpering; disinclined; disqualified; thawing; self-rejected; poorly-bred; unverified; larval; the never-overgrown. This willed amateur therefore recedes back into the substandard with something like a typist's focus: they demand neatly-fitted awkwardness, messiness, gracelessness,

72 H. Blasim, *Iraqi Christ*, tr. J. Wright (Manchester: Comma Press, 2013), 53.

their credentials growing less appealing (though never mundane), their boots forming intently crammed and bundled patterns, steadily condensing themselves into a 'small point of consciousness' and thereby condensing Being's map into a smeared pamphlet, leaflet, or uncitable handout world. Much like a recreational surgeon who cannot differentiate between the intravenous (within veins), intramuscular (within muscle), subcutaneous (beneath the skin), and intervertebral (between vertebrae), here incisions are made indiscriminately. Thus the amateur's map is made not of lines but of scars; it is a compilation of synesthetic errors. The pouch; the unkempt; trimmed-down universe (soon to expand again).

Map and tool; the small point; the somewhere; expansion

Kinetomania (Continual Movement)

1

> *The fineness of her limbs and the ethereal unconstraint of her movements marked her as one who was not fated to live long in this world. No one but a Hindu temple dancer could have possessed her harmonious grace of movement.*
>
> SADEQ HEDAYAT[73]

We encounter our first kinetomaniac through the following triangulation of subject, object, and space: the dancer; the limbs; the temple. We can imagine the dark purple curtains, the slightly-raised stage, and the worn-through couches of the encircling believers—everything arranged to provide intimate access to the temple dance, in one of those rare religious atmospheres that commingle the sacred with the seductive, purity with decadence, transcendence with seediness, marvel with sick curiosity. Indeed, the royal banners of palaces and the velvet drapery of illicit lounges both partake of the same amethyst, wine-coloured, or plum-coloured portion of the spectrum. But what interests us here are the two careful insinuations embedded in the above description: firstly, that of the

73 Hedayat, *The Blind Owl*, 9.

'ethereal unconstraint' through which different body parts begin to slash independently of one another, foregoing attachment to any unifying principle of the body-as-totality, playing fast and loose with spatial-physical experience to the extent that each limb takes on an autonomous life of its own (the ever-vacillating), as when the belly dancer feigns amazement at the coming-separate of her appendages, nothing more than a series of detachable prostheses and a movement of bio-expendability wherein the hips, waist, and wrists all take their leave of the centralized will of the dancer 'herself'; secondly, that the absolute freedom of this dance exacts a fatalistic salary, as if a certain measure of grace incurs perishability (dying young), and hence as if kinetomaniacal ability itself must pay this price of being short-lived.

Note: A public codification of kinetomania might take the form of a daily existential lottery in which one could easily become king/god (exalted, worshipped) or slave/prisoner (oppressed, mutilated), alongside an infinity of middle-positions such as peasant, teacher, scientist, or technocrat (safely neglected). There are scattered literary and anthropological reports of communities organized around such cacophonous contests of luck, wherein both individual identity and social relationality are dictated by a continual drawing of respective lots. Cards are selected randomly every evening or dawn, each imprinted with a symbolic word or pictograph to assign the roles of the players for the following turn. In such a systematic invocation of chance, one could conceivably indulge every fantasy (all desires become attainable), though only in certain rounds, just as one could conceivably suffer every terror (all fears become realizable) in certain other rounds. But what kind of consciousness would be attracted to such a wildly fluctuating deal, who would voluntarily endure the lowest position for the sake of possibly reaching the highest, who would sacrifice a hand, leg, or eye to someone else's tyrannical whim in exchange for those *other* nights on which one might rule unconditionally? Moreover, what would become of subjective experience in such a state of continual flux, forever leaping from power to wretchedness to everything in-between? While the most obvious answer would perhaps be the nothing-to-lose figure, what if the kinetomaniac par excellence were actually the historical winner who had exhausted almost every possible gratification except a select few? Look into the eyes of the bored aristocrat, one who has conquered all available magnitudes within the existing social order, and now impatient to explore/conduct some breakaway postures. The hall of mirrors; conic arcs of experimentation.

If the lottery showcases the impossible impartiality of the chaotic, the twirling of proximal and distal stakes and the sorting of provisional shares, then we are seeking a theory of perpetual movement here based not on computational hierarchies but only on promiscuous becomings. Its wheel is an effective bottleneck through which, for each individual life, endless potential lives must pass, the infinity of chance overriding the finitude of time; for with this we achieve an immeasurable victory: removal of the limit of the tragic, removal of the limit of the ecstatic. A rather obvious socio-psychological critique might object that such existential lotteries would eventually lead to generalized paranoia, with any good or bad streaks interpreted as cheating; or even worse that, ironically, some totalitarian committee would prove necessary in order to regulate corruption within the game. But this again simply confirms how the manic imagination supersedes both social and psychoanalytic identity. For such fears strike only the instrumentalising mind that always plays to win; they are of no concern whatsoever to the kinetomaniac who plays only to play, and adores the free movement of chance itself. This is why the surroundings of the temple dancer combine luxurious softness with the grime of rubbish heaps, and all intermediate levels; this is why she is equally suited to the Sultan's marble domes as to the dirt floors of the tavern, the caravanserai, and the drug den, just as her own extremities forever bend and slant elsewhere, between beauty and death—for everything here honours the sliding scales of fortune.

Continual movement and fineness; the limbs; ethereality; unconstraint; the short-lived; the dancer

2

> *The only thing I have to decide is when to stop it, where to stop it, how to stop it. The sentences line up on their own power, they're crazy about living: there's a problem of stopping, don't turn it on since it all goes by itself...*
>
> RÉDA BENSMAIA[74]

We encounter our second kinetomaniac through the following triangulation of subject, object, and space: the author; the sentence; the page. We can imagine the writing figure hunched over the table, hands cramped in arthritic poses, searching for the right constructions or subversions of meaning, and yet faced here with an insane ramification: namely, that the sentences themselves contain a desperate craving to live, lining up their matchstick shapes in search of some perpetual motion that would take them beyond the forced closure of the book's binding. Now language takes on a draconian air of survivalism; it becomes a syringe grappling for the vein, as textual inscriptions scour and probe for whatever poetic algorithm might attain an undying 'ever after', resisting the formaldehyde solutions of the immutable last chapter and thereby turning the page into the locus of fatal backlash against fatal rest. Hence the description

74 Bensmaia, *The Year of Passages*, 111.

above warns of a certain kinetomaniacal threshold of expression, beyond which 'there's a problem of stopping' as the unstrung literary machinery 'all goes by itself', its words resorting to whatever pernicious antics or feral nature might avoid the embalming fluids of dramatic climax, resolution, and catharsis (a quest for the never-ending epilogue).

Note: There is a long-standing mythic archetype according to which a certain individual (heroic or villainous) is able to transmit their personal power into an external weapon or accoutrement. This often occurs before the hour of their death, but more importantly results in the birth of a kinetomaniacal implement, a legendary blade, jewel, or robe that carries forth the intensity of its prior owner (moving with inherited volition). In the particular instance above, however, it is the more abstract phenomenon of writing that is invested with this mythic principle—not even the tangible instrument, the pen, but the semi-physical construction of sentences. Thus we witness the freehand continuity of an authorless text, appearing almost like the music of the player piano as it actuates keys in a pre-designated sequence before an empty bench, though here the content is conceivably less programmatic, the page not destined for the mere repetition of past sayings but capable of productively articulating new ideational twists. It must perhaps maintain the general temperament or worldview of its former human master, but over time will ultimately find new crevices and fissures of sense or nonsense.

Continual movement and stopping; power; craze; the living

3

I travel outside my body, and inside me there are conti-
nents
that I do not know. My body
is in eternal motion outside itself.

ADONIS[75]

We encounter our third kinetomaniac through the following triangulation of subject, object, and space: the traveller; the astral body; the outside. We can imagine a prostrated or resting form, breathing slowly, in bed or on the ground, which then gradually projects itself into a subtle material that goes in search of higher ontological realms (a shadow, perispirit, or density-less double). This is an ancient philosophical-mystical precept of apparitionality and spiritual journeying (often related to 'the intelligent soul'), one that even finds a resumed version in the unconscious planes of psychoanalysis (dreaming, hypnosis); but what intrigues us here are not the former terminologies of 'celestial spheres', 'astrological energy', 'whirling vortices', or 'luminiferous ether', but rather a separate theory of the eternal (as opposed to the chronic) that would consummate itself through definitive pain alone. The harsh unquoted lines surrounding the above

75 Adonis, *Selected Poems*, tr. K. Mattawa (New Haven: Yale University Press, 2010), 379.

verse demand this relation: Pain as the ratifying gangway of becoming-subtle.

Note: Consider those ancient tribes and cultures that worshipped albinos as otherworldly messengers of some kind, first noting the incredible fact that their standard of idolized beauty was based on radical non-resemblance (as opposed to the modern framework of beauty as narcissistic resemblance), but also that the albino's sheer whiteness was conceived as a gift from the beyond. We must reconsider the astral body depicted in the above selection as a similar merchant-type, something heteromorphic that brokers the divide between material consciousness and material abstraction in order to access eternity. Nevertheless, this method would have to remain entirely divorced from soteriology (doctrines of salvation), for the astral body here is one that pursues not the highest but rather the farthest, not what is most perfected but what is most 'outside itself', not a known heavenly site of final liberation but a temporary excursion into 'continents that I do not know'—and, once more, a transit derived from some acutely pain-ridden experience of lightening, attenuation, or rarefication (the sleeper's out-of-body levitation; the albino's non-existent pigment). The eternal is not calm, serene, or releasing; instead, its cost of entrance is something closer to the insanity-inducing sensation of Chinese water torture, whereby an ever-boring groove is made by dripping water upon the victim's forehead (becoming-hollow). Hence what psychoanalysis reductively deems acenesthesia (loss of physical awareness of one's own body), anosognosia (lack of awareness of a physical defect or disability), or even, in some instances, asomatognosia (denial of the ownership of personal limbs), can be rethought if we perceive the supposed emotional excess of hysteria or the affective excess of mania not in terms of loss, lack, and deficiency of the stable self but rather as rhythmic expenditures of a fluid self-image that moves through painful exteriority, eternity, and the unknown.

Continual movement and the continent; the unknown; the eternal; the outside

4

You don't live with the dead
They slide on the rolling rug
Of forgetfulness
Admire the movements of fatal augurs
Worked up on the ceiling in their golden slippers.

JOYCE MANSOUR[76]

We encounter our fourth kinetomaniac through the following triangulations of subject, object, and space: (1) the dead; the barefoot; the rug; (2) the augur; the slippers; the ceiling. We can imagine, in the first instance, the paradoxical movement of the motionless as the deceased slip across silk fabrics into the lost depths of forgetting; and then in the second instance the spectacular movement of the seers, as their prophetic gazes allow them to tread across slate awnings and balconies (from the Persian *bala-khaneh*, meaning 'upper house'). In either instance, we are compelled to revel alongside beings who motion either too high or too low: on the one side, we are accompanied by figures like the well-digger or the grave-robber, those who plunge shovels into fresh earth and enter darkness, working in solitude, silence, and dropped registers so as to excavate some gulf of resources (associated sensations:

76 Mansour, *Essential Poems and Writings*, 317, 329.

entrenchment; declension; the unlit); and on the other side, we are accompanied by figures like the sky-walker or the roof-jumper, those who take to shaking elevations, who flirt with the alpine quarters in order to escape detection (associated sensations: openness; steepening; the moonlit). Figures of the caldera and figures of the mistral. We are told that the ceiling-going augurs are somehow 'fatal' in their future memorizations, while the dead have themselves endured fatality along the 'rolling rug of forgetfulness', but in either case kinetomaniacal experience serves to turn axes of time and space upside-down, shifting across both deranged ends of the vertical spectrum: that of the entombed and that of the uplifted.

Note: The kinetomaniacal imaginary of the dead—simulated closely by the aforementioned well-diggers or grave-robbers—bears some resemblance to the ancient nomadic Cimmerian peoples (of ninth-century Thracian origins) said to dwell in lands of permanent fog, mist, or blackness. Later mythologies further developed this ahistorical reputation of the Cimmerian shade: a clan associated with ominous capacities gained from living beneath leaden skies; wearing panther-skins, scaling implausible cliffs, speaking in mellow tenebrous tongues that mimicked the night itself, and building camps at the cave-mouth entrance to the province of the dead. Why then did the earliest civilizations fear the rumoured existence of those who moved in everlasting darkness?

The kinetomaniacal imaginary of the augur—simulated closely by the aforementioned sky-walkers or roof-jumpers—bears some relation to the scientific phenomenon of 'diamond rain' on Saturn, Uranus, and Jupiter. Unlike our conventional terrestrial model of the diamond, mined from below after having been compressed over great tracts of time, in other planetary settings they form in areas of the upper atmosphere known as thunderstorm alleys (arising suddenly from inclement weather patterns), a product of lightning, methane, and graphite placed under extreme aerial pressure. Ultimately, these uncut hailstones end up littering the planetary surface, giving off endless crystal reflections, or they melt into a liquid carbon sea, thereby forcing our unclimbing eyes to accept the order of things annulled (once the extracted-upward, now the precipitating-downward). What theories might future civilizations espouse about the cataractal movement of such gem showers?

Continual movement and the dead; sliding; the rug; forgetfulness; the augur; the ceiling; the slippers

5

My whole being is a dark chant
that perpetuating you
will carry you to the dawn
of eternal growths and blossomings.

FORUGH FARROKHZAD[77]

We encounter our fifth kinetomaniac through the following triangulation of subject, object, and space: the aspirant; the dark chant; the dawn. We imagine the invigorating figure of *the life-extender*, fleeting perpetuator of the all-too-fast and the unlasting, whose powers grant only a few extra seconds, minutes, or hours to the killing wheel. The aspirant approaches, eager for a temporal equivocation, eyes moistened by the downriver flow of the almost-ending, and petitions for the life-extender's meagre gift (not the wholesale defeat of time, but the theft of just a couple more irrelevant instants). Let us picture the desperate act: he perhaps gags upon his own pleading, offering everything (flattery, promises, servitude) to purchase even a syllable of the life-extender's 'dark chant', itself just a barely-overdrive potential that will grant three lone footsteps beyond the awful limit. The experience is one of running out of time, but grasping for at least

77 Farrokhzad, *A Lonely Woman*, 111.

something, with the life-extender's convenient trickery providing a last partial stay against unsaving, transcendent collectors. She will get you through the night; she will bring you to another dawn...but no more than this (a split-second eternity). The clock still strikes; one cannot outrace it, only nestle a while in some absconded bout of rumination. The aspirant does not aspire to immortality; instead, he kneels before the one who can make things happen just a little later (the subsidiary deadline).

From where did she derive this ability to will the minor bypass, cheating a sliver of immunized pause from the most ungiving? And what does stolen breath taste like? This much we know: that she is a figure of insistence; moreover, she is the temporal pickpocket whose gesture creates a protective kinetomaniacal annex, and in whose strange dawn-seeking presence one must become *the guest*, bathing in the horizon's firefall scraps (enemy of finality's snowfall), drinking from its fire chalices (goblets like no other). This burrowing capacity of the life-extender is also what makes her a special version of *the icon*, for the iconic here is that which turns a single image into an entire counter-movement (intercepting death's movement by mastering its likeness). No, she does not rule over time or fate; she simply holds the password to the additional (what might be called a shadow-moment or shadow-destiny); her straining chant is no discontinuation or even contestation but rather an accompaniment (thus she speaks of 'blossoming' and 'growth') that drives temporal-spatial momentum a few short measures past its intended diameter.

Note: The kinetomaniacal imaginary of the life-extender applies well to the Zoroastrian cult of fire (*atar*, meaning 'holy fire' at once burning and unburning, visible and invisible). For within the confines of the fire cult's quest for eternality (the never-extinguishing flame), we find the sacred structure of the *atroshan* (fire temple) or later *atashkadeh* (house of fire), and within their arched hallways the necessary players of the *athravan* (fire priests) and *atash sorushan* (fire angels). Picture the inexorable lighting of the fire over centuries and perhaps millennia, those who hold night-watch to certify a single flaring column of timelessness proving that the holy fire's imperishability is never a given quality, but rather must be earned through sleepless expenditures, ritual focus, and defensive heeding of invisible elemental threats. We join them in the solemn air of this monastic practice; we take our place in the semicircle of the inner sanctum; we mouth the benedictions in proper turn. We follow them even to the excarnation mounds, and into the Tower of Silence where dead bodies are left exposed to vultures and other carrion birds, the Magi (from the Old Persian *magu*) reading the rites of sky burial. They stand around the central illumination (what thoughts emerge during this silent task of refuelling?), gripping their lit torches, sceptres, and oil lamps whose function is to relay the regenerative blaze whenever the original pillar falls low, their mouths wrapped or masked in order to avoid the fire's contamination with breath or saliva. From this we deduce a brilliant principle: namely, that *atar* does indeed possess the capacity for undying life, but only if the death-bound guardians give their own lives to protect the otherwise vulnerable eternal from blowing out, monitoring its relative strength against prevailing winds, cold, and darkness. Moreover, they themselves risk directly threatening its permanence (whether through dereliction of duty, accidental contact, or malice)—accordingly, they must master distance and timing, forging a perfect technique of rekindling over many years, becoming both ideal lookout and ideal firestarter, though this formal extension-procedure is not born of pure reverence for fire in and of itself; rather, the sacrosanct ignition is prized mainly for its unique effects, and for the three specific functions it administers: 'ordeal by heat', 'light of revelation', and 'detector of guilt'. More precisely, it tests believers in various literal trials by fire; it furnishes wisdom regarding the universe's veiled movements; and it reveals fault, blame, and duplicity among those who enter its immediate precinct. Hence it is the tangible kinetomaniacal force of the hearth and its white ash that draws an acute line between the respective rewards and punishments of the faithful and the faithless. (Simple manic fact: the longer one stares intently into an object or phenomenon, building up a compulsively delicate perception of it, the more one feels one has gained admittance to the world's inner motion [the answers released]).

Continual movement and the dark chant; perpetuation; the carrier; the dawn; eternity; growth

6

Or—oh God!—had he gripped the beast by the horns, done what he himself had so often warned his son never to do? Nothing, his father had said, drove the waddan to frenzy like gripping him by the horns. It didn't matter how strong you were, how stirred by the hope of victory. If you once tried that, then the battle was lost. The waddan's madness lay in his horns. All his hidden savagery would wake, would boil over, and he'd launch his ferocious attack. The waddan was trying to escape now—he'd veered off toward the mountain. The wadi was getting deeper, the mountains higher. The waddan was drawing him on, toward that ugly, mysterious summit!

IBRAHIM AL-KONI[78]

We encounter our sixth kinetomaniac through the following triangulation of subject, object, and space: the beast; the horns; the summit. The scene before us is perhaps the most astounding example of manic certainty: a hunter-father leads his son through winding mountains in search of the legendary creature he has sworn never to harm again, and yet upon sighting the dreamed-of animal takes it by the head and wrestles it furiously toward the precipice from which they will ultimately somersault together below. Perhaps this display is meant as a final irrefutable

78 Al-Koni, *The Bleeding of the Stone*, 26.

warning to the son, issued in such lethal manner as to definitively foreclose any future attempt to capture the wild being; or perhaps the hunter-father's passion compelled him into a desire for shared death-by-entanglement, his own once-steady legs tripping into the other's cloven hooves to produce a panoramic kinetomaniacal collapse across the sill and into the mid-air nothingness.

Nevertheless, what really catches our attention here is that the author's terminology of 'frenzy', 'madness', 'ferocity', and 'hidden savagery' should not be perceived as a generalized indication of the creature's essence (for it is otherwise totally serene). Rather, the kinetomaniacal impetus is concentrated entirely in the horns; in fact, the horns harbour the one extreme sensitivity that overrides nature (becoming the runaway). What is the implication, then? That a single protrusion could stockpile the stuff of which madness is made? If wisdom is supposedly stored in the owl's eyes, vulnerability in the hero's heel, thirst in the vampire's teeth, terror in the rattlesnake's rattle, and cruelty in the scorpion's tail...then why could not mania equally lodge itself in the horns, awaiting activation? As such, let us attempt to take this observation away from so-called natural experience and into more futuristic plateaus wherein we could conceive the aforementioned 'ugly, mysterious summit' not as a psycho-emotional return to delirium, but rather as a deliberately designed technological propulsion toward delirium activated by a single manic button, switch, or device placed strategically in a single physical-sensory area. Following the horned model, could we envision the construction of an artificial manic flux, its trigger secreted in a precise spot on the body, a contrivance invented to induce technological beastliness? Neither id nor superego, neither pleasure principle nor reality principle, but an alternative scale of fury stirred by a preset movement-principle (killer-drive disguised in a single sharpened pin); the digital signal or voltage that would scramble mental transmissions. Since the postmodern era already compartmentalizes the body into a thousand consumable pieces (the hyper-segmentation of medicine, fashion, cosmetics, leisure, and athletic training), can we not equally imagine a version of technical madness whose provocation-point is grafted into its own careful scion (exploding upon touch)?

Note: We could presumably link this search for a kinetomaniacal code, lever, or synthetic prompt to the figure of the Sphinx (side-note: the founding father of psychoanalysis himself was a collector of Sphinx sculptures from antiquity). For she shares the postmodern physicality of the hybrid (half-woman, half-lion), tricking us into perceiving a visual-natural contrast rather than the sly intersectional relation between wisdom and beastliness that connects her feminine head to her feline shoulders, stomach, and claws. While the two hemispheres might at first glance seem to amass different and mutually exclusive sensibilities (the upper speaks while the lower punishes), they in fact conspire to form a flawless kinetomaniacal proclivity. More exactly, the head does indeed concoct the famous riddle, but only as a perfect excuse to strangle and feed upon the mistaken guesser at will, thus demonstrating the cooperative bond between mind and belly, reason and appetite, discourse and bite, in light of which civilized introversion proves nothing more than a portal to savage extroversion. And fascinatingly, it also moves in the other direction: for, upon Oedipus's solving of her riddle, the Sphinx kills herself, hurling herself down from the mighty rock perch or, according to other legends, devouring herself. In yet others, she willingly tells Oedipus the correct response (either out of a desire to die or to make him love her), whispering the gift-curse of the answer into his innocent ears. Thus the suicidal-sacrificial design of the human head is immediately supported and fatally fulfilled by the rest of the animal body.

This notwithstanding, we might also consider the reverse physiognomy of the minotaur (man-body, bull-head) alongside the dual-species physiognomy of the criosphinx (lion-body, ram-head) and hieracosphinx (lion-body, hawk-head), if only to wonder what other riddles would emerge if we allowed inhuman upper dimensions (the beast's question), and what manic whims would be unleashed by the layering of animality upon animality.

Continual movement and the runaway;
frenzy; savagery; madness; veering; the summit

7

And of the two of us
the one who passed across the turbulent waters of the ocean
was not he
but I.

And at this point I resembled a boat with disconnected anchor
conscious of its own eternal wandering,
once again of such horrifying truth that
consciousness
as a term
means the same thing as neck-offering submission
and consent.

AHMAD SHAMLU[79]

We encounter our seventh kinetomaniac through the following triangulation of subject, object, and space: the lifeboat; the waters; the ocean. We can imagine the charting of a rare relation between conceptual figures usually kept at odds—*the martyr* (the neck, the blindfold) and *the traitor* (the back, the dagger)—as they conjoin in the deathly metaphorical resemblance to an unanchored

79 Shamlu, *Born Upon the Dark Spear*, 57.

ark, later described as being 'carried like a coffin on a thousand hands'. To start with philosophical simplicity, then: In what lurking way is the martyr a kind of traitor (what must they betray), and in what lurking way is the traitor a kind of martyr (what must they sacrifice)? Ideological hierarchies would make any suggestion of similitude between the two appear futile, for while the martyr occupies the sanctified centre of history, the traitor remains the vintage malefactor of anti-history—the most delinquent, the uncollared one, he fiddles with lighters, playing arsonist to tribal orders and kingly domes; he is the embezzler of social conventions and legitimated power structures, borne by wiles and gambits and vinegar blood. Traitor against the state (treason), traitor against the self (suicide), traitor against the other (murder), traitor against God (heresy). But these are no longer sufficient categories; we seek more 'turbulent waters'. Hence we return to the original question of the sheer affective comparison between the one who keeps their word (to the extent of tragic martyrdom) and the one who breaks their word (for the sake of traitorous gain), the one who speaks beautifully and the one who lies beautifully, the one who dies for an idea (often at the hands of others) and the one who destroys through disloyalty to an idea (often against their own. To approach this question, one must refashion thought with the circularity of a ringmaker, not simply because these characters are often mutually indispensable to the same stories (the traitor's act facilitates the martyr, and the martyr's fall reveals the traitor), but because the 'horrifying truth' and 'neck-offering submission' of which the poetic passage above makes mention bind martyr and traitor together around the hauntingly suspended words 'conscious', 'consciousness', and 'consent' on either side. Indeed, both are practitioners of terrifyingly elevated concern, such that there remains no existential difference whatsoever between the disappeared/evicted and the self-disappeared/self-evicted (knowing in itself is a signed contract with the waves).

To couple apparent moral opposites, those of hard-won honour and hard-sold dishonour, through manic consciousness requires a palpable imagistic setting: so let us picture in intricate phenomenological detail the courtyard execution of the martyr alongside the back-stabbing operation of the traitor. We watch the martyr brought out into the open night air, while the traitor steals into the confined room; we watch the martyr led in quickstep to the wall, while the traitor creeps and then stops mid-stride in staggered motions; we watch the martyr's limp hands strapped to the post, while the traitor's tensed hands raise up slowly above their head; we watch the martyr forced to wait to receive the final piercing, while the traitor advances to commit the final piercing. And yet both are absolute paragons of alertness and non-idealized truth (this is going to happen), both alive with the ultra-arousal of one damned to complete the assignment, for consciousness accelerated to the point of 'consent' means a kinetomaniacal tremor that results in the cold stare of the accepting. They are locked into the action, their mouths sewn together in the tapestry of violence. One is the disconnected-at-windpipe; the other is the neck-snapper. The moral orientation or disparity between martyr and traitor are matters for the indoctrinating parchments and heraldry of the political; they mean nothing to the one who simply looks at them, for in either case there remains this one striking detail in common which supersedes all else: the eyes are the same.

Continual movement and turbulence; anchorlessness; horror; consciousness; submission; consent

8

> *I saw severed legs running away without their bodies and disconnected forearms waving along the roads, bearing white flags or stretching out their hands in search of someone to come to their rescue. I saw fingers floating through the empty streets and pointing accusingly at their executioners. I saw men whose blood had been drawn from their veins so that it could be given to others, running along as bluish corpses.*
>
> GHADA SAMMAN[80]

We encounter our eighth kinetomaniac through the following triangulation of subject, object, and space: the corpse; the legs, fingers, veins; the road. We can imagine the once-cohesive human body brought beneath the scalpel as *the dismembered*, and yet here the dismembered becomes the agitated, thereby finding common ground with the toy, the insect, the salamander, and certain decapitated birds, all of which possess a special biological or machinic ability to shed crucial parts of the anatomy while continuing to transport themselves regardless, strategically treating this immediate loss either through regeneration (growing another equivalent), supplement (fashioning something else), or void (leaving vacant).

---

80 Samman, *Beirut Nightmares*, 64.

On the anthropocentric side, we could conceivably picture the twitching cadaver, though more specifically only the human ghost walks headless and only the human pirate makes an aesthetic-performative enterprise out of mutilation (the glass eye or eye patch, the gold tooth, the hook, the wooden leg). And yet in the passage above, distinctively, it is no longer the central being that miraculously moves despite its missing features, but rather the vestigial organs or butchered particles themselves that take on a kinetomaniacal afterlife (the Cheshire cat's smile that remains hanging there when all else has disappeared). Hence our author presents a catalogue of hands, forearms, arteries, nerve endings, and scalped foreheads unstrung from their original house of Being and left cruising down sectarian streets. This poses the more difficult question of what happens when what was previously assumed to be essential is revealed to be inessential (to the original form), but then becomes essential once more (to the emergent formless). Beyond this, at play here is an apparent kinetomaniacal generosity ('given to others') and malevolence ('pointing accusingly'), brilliantly allowing these separated boughs to take on the symptomatic abilities of both parastasis (the masking or compensation of defects) and metastasis (the transference of malignant properties). A cutler's fantasy.

Note: If the very criterion of an object's enchantment rests in its irreplaceability (e.g., in Christian lore, the holy grail or spear of destiny, which have touched the messianic lips and ribs respectively), being indisputably unique and therefore greatly mourned if lost, then what does it mean to turn aspects of self once considered irreplaceable over to the marketplace of infinite interchangeability? Would they necessarily become intimately disenchanted? More importantly, though, consider that the enchanted sacred objects of the past rarely followed a logic of moral possession (the deserving, the chosen) but simply one of physical possession (the scavenger, the opportunist): whoever holds the artefact can win whatever singular powers it boasts, regardless of their ethical character. A number of alleged prophets stole blessings through deception or by wrestling angels into coerced utterances, and there are many theo-fabulous accounts of demons going in search of sacred objects, quite capable of thieving heavenly resources, not to mention historical accounts of fascist and aristocratic-occultist associations trying similarly to locate some reputed item or other that might offer them increased wealth, invincibility, or magical powers. The only possible conclusion being that enchantment is subject to larceny by the unintended. And so, let us ask this same question of the severed legs, forearms, and fingers spoken of above (for we are already in the age of organ harvesting): Could they be confiscated by the random bystander, like the vanquisher figure who holds out the amputated Medusan head as a shield, the very murderer becoming apotropaic heir of its evil properties, such that someone else picks up and uses the discarded remains as their own? 'Come to their rescue', she writes. What model of ingenuity might this disembodied embodiment bring forth into our midst? The body as burglar's fairground or shop.

Continual movement and disconnection;
stretching; pointing; accusation; rescue; the corpse

9

So, let this void be crowned,
for our human nature to complete its migration.
What are these flutes seeking in the forests?
We are the strangers and we, the people of the deserted temple,
have been abandoned on our white horses searching for the last station,
reeds sprouting from our bodies and comets crisscrossing over our heads.
There is no place on earth where we haven't pitched our tent of exile.

MAHMOUD DARWISH[81]

We encounter our ninth kinetomaniac through the following triangulation of subject, object, and space: the stranger; the flute; the tent. In many respects, this poetic composition strives to portray exilic kinetomania by following an almost perfect parabolic structure: the first line refers to a vacated 'crown', setting up a fragile once-upon-a-time kingdom in need of righteous leadership (the rising hero); the second line suggests that the correct heroic figure would ascend this voided throne through a 'migration' (the journey, the quest); the fourth line

81 Darwish, *Unfortunately, It Was Paradise*, 38.

rehearses the long-standing epic tradition according to which only 'the stranger' can save worlds (the arrival of the outsider champion), and some personal catastrophic experience of the 'deserted temple' will prove necessary in order to fulfil the task (the ruined sacred, the razed homeland); the fifth line speaks of turmoil and declined greatness, the fall from 'white horses', and the continued mission for lost glory to be found in the 'last station' (the final kingdom); the sixth line adds both the naturalistic and cosmological elements that the allegorical figure must somehow coalesce, interpret, or channel (the physical otherworldly); and the seventh line confirms that the heroic self is the most travelled-in-adversity, covering immeasurable distances while wandering through travesty (the trial).

With this arc established, it is the third line that holds the hidden kinetomaniacal pulse of exile. For while mythic archetypes always require movement as an instrumental means to attain idealized stasis (the happily-ever-after), it is the sudden lyrical intervention of the 'flutes seeking in the forests' that diverts us into more liberating fairy-tale straits (a where-am-I-going?). For if the mythic hero-stranger mirrors a human need for the continual creation and destruction of gods (the Crucifixion, after all, is a spiritual-kinetomaniacal story in itself, though one of ultimate homecoming), the fairy tale's flaunts a superior vision of the stranger: that of the piper whose odd whistle leads away rats, children, or spirits (into woodlands, outskirts, perpetual exile). It is therefore a matter of anarchical trajectivity ('the reeds sprouting from our bodies' and 'comets crisscrossing over our heads'); this flute-playing is itself the sound of an anti-minaret, an acoustic slinging-elsewhere, a music box designed to project listeners far from all sovereigns, homelands, and temples, into epileptic fugue-states whose origins are not psychogenic. It is tiresome to speak of retrograde amnesia; it is more interesting to speak of kinetomaniacal forgetting. The exilic piper is thus the founder of higher dissociative disorders—i.e., depersonalized memory loss brought about not by the long-term effects of traumatic incidents but by unexpected enticement toward a single aerial sensation (the siren's song).

Note: We might tie this conceptual figure of the piper to the evolution of sonic weaponry in unconventional warfare. Although often used covertly by dominant governments, these sound-attacks in fact emulate the informal tactics of the outnumbered who seek advantage in non-conforming methods; they produce ambient distress, whether in the form of high-frequency blasts or low-frequency pitches that move through walls and sealed glass. The terminology itself (that of sonic bombs, sonic bullets, sonic grenades, sonic cannons, and sonic mines) illustrates both the extremity and intricate subtlety of the violence therein, one that dances upon the myriad levels of disorientation, dread, and even paralysis. From the eardrum to the mind: nonlinear and underwater applications, nervous decibels, infrasound and ultrasound patterns. The three most common sounds used repetitively in sonic torture: insects scampering; metal screeching; children singing. The six most common symptoms of sonic torture: nausea, headache, fatigue, hearing loss, sleeplessness, and brain damage.

Hence we are actually walking along diametrically-opposed tightropes when we speak of the timeless flute-player and the modern state: the musical figure does not exploit physical debilitation but rather cheerful skipping (even unto the badlands); does not seek psychological incapacitation but rather madcap defamiliarization of interiority (to flee oneself; to flee the dark city). The piper is a one-person peripatetic concert mixing entertainment, glamour, and pageantry; an echo-seller mixing pantomime, bewitchment, and stagecraft. The piper proves that becoming-numinous is nothing more than a sleight of hand, and that all thaumaturgy rests upon the micro-exertion of nimble fingers. A tripartite method—improvisation, conveyance, conversion—that sends all transcendent hierarchies into riddance. The piper versus the political real: the movement of outer stimulation versus the movement of inner surrender. It is true that both parties enlist sonic armaments that range from clandestine to excessive bandwidths, but whereas one seeks corrective, overbearing systems, the other seeks only destinies of soft extrication. The politicization of sonic war relies upon droning audio samples and inaudible devices of totalitarian uniformity; the kinetomaniacal accentuation of sonic war lends itself to euphoric lightness, laughter, hysterical susceptibility, contagious influence, and vanguardism. Such is the crucial difference between ideology and mystique.

Continual movement and void; crown; human nature; the flute; the forest; the stranger; desertion; the temple; the tent; exile

10

> *I remembered the words the director of the Emergency Department in the hospital often used to say: 'When you're carrying an injured person or a patient close to death, the speed of the ambulance shows how humane and responsible you are.' But when you are carrying severed heads in an ambulance, you needn't go faster than a hearse drawn by mules in a dark mediaeval forest.*
>
> HASSAN BLASIM[82]

We encounter our tenth kinetomaniac through the following triangulation of subject, object, and space: the driver; the ambulance; the highway (between the accidental and the unpreventable). The Director is an enigmatic man, known among emergency room professionals as 'the Professor' for his tendency to speak in insoluble maxims, of which the above passage provides an example: For why would the ambulance driver slow down at the precise moment when the life-ebbing passenger becomes definitively unsalvageable? This goes beyond any simple nihilistic sentiment of futility, for here one must begin to acquaint oneself with two specific practitioners of deceleration: *the procrastinator* and *the perfectionist*. Both are figures who take excessive time, and both share a

82 Blasim, *The Madman of Freedom Square*, 2.

neurotic and a manic iteration worth noting: in the first instance (neurotic obsession), the procrastinator constantly delays gestures in order to avoid the event, while the perfectionist negates and repeats gestures in order to idealize the event; but in the second instance (manic obsession), both figures appropriate slowness in order to savour their doomed world. It is no longer about doubt; it is about the bliss of the indubitable. The conveyor of dead bodies might therefore consider endlessly prolonging the ride as a way to defeat inevitability, but in reality what takes place upon the highway is the perfection of this failure, a certain basking or marination in demise (a cherished undoing). Decree of the cold season; a cushioning against the sickle.

Can one speak of meteoric indecision? Yes, it is not only that the driver jettisons conviction further with every absurd mile travelled; it is that perception itself begins to gouge along separate pipelines. Thereafter, all thoughts become *memento mori* ('death reminders'), just as the road becomes a two-lane highway combining the strobes of facticity and hypotheticals. Double-dealing consciousness; a freight of deflection. His hearse-like pace is thus a kind of traction between the 'dark mediaeval forest' of incurable victimhood (the cargo of 'what happened') and the hospital bed of a clean-slate existence (the onramp to 'what might have happened').

Stated otherwise, kinetomaniacal slowness is a luxuriating in this inoperable 'if only...'.

The dangling wrist; the heavy casualty. The ride takes on the sensation of a dripping faucet, or someone dipping bread in blood, while the coach takes on the aspect of a sinking raft or crumbling multi-storey building. The driver can only stare ahead at the factual-hypothetical wrinkle before him: there are no bowls of camphor or lotus leaves in the back carriage of the ambulance; there are no valiant clinical efforts or verses recited; only the modesty of bare death amid the sense of life's quiet disapproval. This is why the driver begins to suspect the Professor of leading a cabal (from the old Hebrew *kabbalah*, suggesting a mystical tradition of esoteric interpretation, but literally meaning 'something received'), for the secret faction of a cabal has but one primary function: to set traps within permutations, to corner someone in the supposed tension between the actual occurrence and the virtual almost, the it-is-done versus the it-did-not-come-to-pass, where all subsequent run-ins with mortality occur in the form of waking a sleeping lion.

Continual movement and the Director;
emergency; injury; the patient; responsibility; the forest

Dinomania (Dizziness, Whirlpools)

1

> *My head began to swim, in a kind of intoxication. A sensation of nausea came over me and my legs felt weak. I experienced a sense of infinite weariness.*
>
> SADEQ HEDAYAT[83]

We encounter our first dinomaniac placing several important terms at our disposal, each rich with their own interpretive prospects, and all of which could serve as initial points of departure for a discussion of the coming topic: intoxication, nausea, weakness, infinity, languor. And yet it is the inconspicuous word 'swim' that demands our most acute attention, for the experiential realms of dizziness and the whirlpool require a proper guide—*the swimmer*—and in particular the figure caught struggling against some circular undertow, facing the panicked compartmentalization of the body as a single leg or hand or head momentarily rises above the liquid surface and then slips beneath again...until the point of total surrender is reached. A phenomenological equation of Being with treading water, as if individual existence itself were

83 Hedayat, *The Blind Owl*, 35.

a constant endeavour for mere survival against a riptide universe, the inexorable fight not to lose buoyancy (to the undertow of creation itself), in full knowledge that, ultimately, the game belongs to the larger vortex. Life as a thrashing and a flailing; life as borrowed time.

Strangely enough, just before this passage our narrator has spoken of how such drowning sensations occur only after a feeling of relinquishing all former kinship with humankind, claiming affinity for the palpitations of inanimate things alone, including Nature and Night—and although both of these deign to eradicate him, to drag him under and wrap him inward, his tired hands clapping against their recurring waves, he understands their desiring-matrix and acquiesces to its terrifying cause. To let oneself be taken, thereby becoming the oarless uncreated; surely this post-terror transformation elevates him to the level of another figure—*the night swimmer*—whose unmediated confrontation with the ravening intentionality of the whirlpool puts him at lasting ease, as he attains a special calm that comes only with fatal comprehension. The night swimmer voluntarily enters the blackest waters, no longer splashing his limbs in futile spasms, no longer craving any delay or exemption, no longer consumed by the supposed right to breathe, no longer lurching at the profound clamminess of skin or the seaweed entwining legs below, but rather nodding yes to the aqueous, paddling gently into the dark's bath.

Note: In fact, this metamorphosis does not result in the expected mortal downfall. Instead, in the story's aftermath, our night-swimming narrator achieves a particularly rare form of invincibility, endowed with the 'infinite weariness' traditionally attributed to the undead or living dead, but here something more like the dying alive, gliding from sphere to sphere, from bloodletting to bloodletting, with the same irresistible fluidity as the whirlpool itself.

Dizziness/whirlpool and swimming;
intoxication; nausea; weakness; infinite weariness

2

> *She caressed his face, you're beautiful, melancholic, and pale; when you recover from this horrible fever we'll go off together, we'll leave this awful city* [...] *but for now let your burning head rest in my hands and try to sleep a little. Every one of his daydreams that followed was as lousy as the one before, for as long as he never left Algiers, he would always be sick* [...] *He knew that this city had turned him into this hybrid creature, half-dog and half-goat, this creature so hard of thinking that it thirsted for death and dark tobacco! Cut!*
>
> RÉDA BENSMAIA[84]

We encounter our second dinomaniac in great need of convalescence, of the restorative gift granted by a selected confidante: she who can cool the otherwise 'horrible fever' (practitioner of the caress). Here we arrive upon a curious example whereby dizziness and the whirlpool stand as opposing forces, the former being a direct symptom of everydayness itself, of the growing stress induced by a homeland within whose irritative confines 'he would always be sick', the latter representing the rehabilitative embrace of the one distinguished as being separate and like no other. In effect, she is *the healer*—a figure of

84 Bensmaia, *The Year of Passages*, 106.6.

exceptional alleviation, selected to quiet troubles caused by both self and others by feinting medicinal efficacy, outfitted with a thousand hypodermic words and gestures of endearment, and before whose solitary waiting knees our run-down narrator folds his limp frame. The victim of 'lousy daydreams' that toss him from side to side, against the cement walls of consciousness, he now crumples into the helper's counter-swirling lap (itself imparting the peaceful sensation of lapping water). We can picture the many technical movements of her ritual: first brushing the cheek, then fondling the hair, cradling the disturbed forehead, offering sanctuary to the tensed brow, rubbing the throbbing temples, and now pressing forefingers to lips in a movement between susurration (a whispering or rustling sound) and sibilation (a hissing or whistling sound). She must act as tranquilizing agent, pacifying the infective noise of world (lulling, hushing, soothing) and thereby chasing away malcontentment; she must become absorbent, a castle or shrine into which the grumbling and protesting being sags, staying observantly awake as he falls into ultimate lethargy, her whirlpool presence encouraging a critical break from thought, from all rotted mental energies, dressing psychic wounds through dreamless rest. She permits de-stimulation by rehearsing a productive array of affectations, mannerisms, and embellishments (those of infinite assurance); she promises recovery, a future away from this, a future alone and 'together', in which the poor ready-to-die crossbreed beneath her feet—'half-dog and half-goat, this creature so hard of thinking'—can recuperate its former beauty, before the face's melancholic paleness, with a voice combining lament, trust, and promise. The healer is therefore also the patience stone (from Persian mythology, *sang-e sabour*), a receptacle forged to collect the accumulated suffering of another, drawing all worldly misery into herself, and dependably answering the petitioner (this most harrowed one) to offer him a few hours of dinomaniacal respite.

Dizziness/whirlpool and caressing; melancholy; paleness; recovery; fever; burning; sleep; the daydream; the hybrid; thirst

3

Al-Jabiya Gate—
a whirlpool inside language's head—
...Damascus,
your shadow wears my body, and your doors surround me.
Your secrets fall into me.
Happiness only resides in cuffs and folds.

This is the dizziness of someone who sees the corpse of the ages on his face and stumbles motionless

ADONIS[85]

We encounter our third dinomaniac sketching out a perceptual connection between city gate and mind's whirlpool, as if entering the ancient capital were itself an act of fatal narcosis. We recall the ceremonial magnificence of the first civilizations' gates, those of the seven wonders—their glazed bricks, tall cedar doors, blue stone reliefs, and facades decorated with painted bulls, winged lions, and flowers—recalling that their original design function was steeped in historical violence, their heavy turnstile doors and onerous iron latches meant less to welcome than to keep out (as if all settlements harboured a causal invitation to violate), recollecting images of scalding thick

85 Adonis, *Selected Poems*, 289, 99.

oil poured over ramparts to ward off charging invaders. Nevertheless, we are here met with an uncharacteristic phenomenological suggestion: it is not that you may fall into the city's whirlpool; rather, the whirlpool falls into you ('your shadow wears my body'). An event closer to possession, or to water's pervasion of a vessel, a filling and mimicry of the other's shape, a reception of its mould, with human identity (the Damascene citizen) becoming nothing less than vase, urn, or bottle. But the theoretical pattern grows yet more involved with the next detail: the city flows into its gate-crossers in order to pour out its many riddles ('your secrets fall into me'). Thus the normal coaxing pressure of the whirlpool finds itself reversed, as does the typical method of possession whereby an animated subject inhabits a resting inanimate object; for here the cityscape inscribes its byzantine world of deceit, plotting, and scheming into the opened cerebrum of the civilian, inscribing its shameful remnants not across the public squares but within the private interiorities of the residents. Exactly what kind of secrecy is at stake here, though? What is the ponderous unspoken of this stone-encrusted gate, its acrid unsayable tongue, itself a 'whirlpool inside language's head'?

To answer this question we turn to another poetic text with dinomaniacal overtones: the second passage above relates the 'dizziness of someone who sees the corpse of the ages', from which we can immediately infer a gaze exposed to certain atrocity, to the light-headed shock of the killing fields and the death squads, having paid its epochal share. Perhaps this is the profane record that the city decants into its native children, or protects them from; but then what to make of the ominous last line of the first stanza, which tells us that '[h]appiness only resides in cuffs and folds'? Is this some shred of mordant truth, advising us to hold tight to our chains and fetters, best to remain lifelong prisoner of the city walls, for beyond the gate is precisely where humankind discovers its real face: that of the wild murderer? The non-contrite; the all-acerbic. It seems to suggest a forced choice of lesser evils: either the dweller must allow the ancient partition to seize, pervade, and encrypt their mind-body, living half-content within its inescapable enclosures (the voluntarily committed), or they must take their chances, 'stumbling motionless' through the unmerciful out-there and adorning oneself with its vertiginous death-spree for years to come (*the mad staggerer*).

Dizziness/whirlpool and the gate; language; the shadow; the secret; happiness; the corpse; the age; stumbling; motionlessness

4

The little round head with its thin pale orbits
Turning like a dream
In a bilious whirlwind
Of hunger
It was cold in my mother's uterus

JOYCE MANSOUR[86]

We encounter our fourth dinomaniac in states of natal dreaming, natal hunger, natal coldness—the discomforted unborn. Things have clearly gone wrong within the belly, the infant's still-forming cranium suspended in pure fragility and rotating amid some 'bilious whirlwind' that can only suggest states of ailing, queasiness, or malnutrition. Unwell-before-life, the fine strands of her hair disintegrate into thinnest unreality ('turning like a dream'), trajectories of safe arrival now receding amid the failed duties of an unreceptive womb. But why this degenerative, frosted birth—one of famine, dearth, shortage, winter chill, punctured gestational sac, and premature rupture? What is the reason for this umbilical noose, this sprinkling of poison across the maternal innards? Does it stem from the mother's own intended self-deprivation (a cutting of the bloodline)? Are we in the presence of a damnable

86 Mansour, *Essential Poems and Writings*, 325.

matron, one who detests this most intimately vulnerable being, working against conventional desires for posterity, longevity, companionship, and reproducibility, against the neglected offspring within, and thus systematically turns her biological processes against themselves, willing revolting destinies over health, turning amniotic fluid into swampland moats, electrolytes into agents of deregulated heartbeat, membranous exteriors into wide infectious slits, so that the pathways of fetal growth now lead only to the underfed, the gangrenous, and the chanceless future? We are left reading the poetic rendition of a toxicology report, or even worse, the incriminating sonogram of she who brings all progeny into the most unsanitary crib.

Dizziness/whirlpool and thinness; paleness;
the orbit; the dream; biliousness; hunger; cold; the mother

5

the first day of my adolescence
when my whole body
began to open in innocent amazement
to mingle with that vagueness,
that muteness, that
uncertainty

FORUGH FARROKHZAD[87]

Our fifth dinomaniac provides us with an acute redefinition of *the innocent*, for whom the whirlpool-effect is contained in a rare ability to return always to the 'first day', an existential reset that brings giddiness, delight, and recurring surprise before the same affair. The stacking of axial stones, the aromas of the spice-makers: thus the time-and-again instance is recoated in a sense of the-never-before. But this is no accidental feat, for the forever-innocent devises a direct method to supersede the otherwise vitiating relation between time and event, a method based on three strategic gestures: (1) she entrusts experience to the 'whole body' rather than the analytical mind, siding with the potential durability/renewability of sensation over idea; (2) she 'mingles with that vagueness', thus circulating and interspersing experience across the

87 Farrokhzad, *A Lonely Woman*, 10.

prohibitive subject-world border by means of which the 'I' formerly differentiated itself from its surroundings; (3) she bathes perception in 'uncertainty', thereby abandoning all quest for clarity, meaning, control, or memory for the sake of the eternally diluted. What results is the grand dizziness of the impressionist, an aesthetic pact with blurring, with color free-brushed or stippled over the dominant line: to the extent that perpetual innocence would require perpetual 'amazement', she must increasingly draw the world of appearances into apparitionality, into the sheer enveloping 'muteness' whereby things become at once diaphanous (translucently full of light) and nebulous (full of clouded indeterminacy). This particular mode of innocent return conceals nothing less than a vertigo that militates against Genesis itself, for it rolls back the inaugural Edenic gesture of identification, that divine instruction to Adam to pronounce the proper names of things, and instead holds us continually in the moment before the power-complex of calling-forward was established (unrecognizability, astonishment). Softest erosion of the boundary, this reprisal of the declassified and of inarticulate watching. We walk a narrow suspension bridge between the unseen and the unforeseen, taking upon ourselves the willed myopia and cataracts of the near-sighted or the near-blinded painter, the burned or detached retinae of the sun-starer, or perhaps, even more devastatingly, entering the fog of war, that state of situational ambiguity in which friend and foe become hopelessly indistinguishable (shooting into the mist).

That this is what she intends may be confirmed in another dinomaniacal passage, which reads as follows: 'until that whirling smoke, the last gasp of fiery thirst, settled down upon the field of sleep'.[88] Here the fog of war is clearly envisioned, not as tactical breakdown but as successfully-planned tactic, deployed in order to cover battlefields of the fatigued-unto-death, a horizontal blanketing-act of 'whirling smoke' summoned by the one of 'fiery thirst'. For the forever-innocent is also the forever-thirsty: not the child with wide-eyed virtues of ignorant purity, nor the delusional-traumatic psychic subject who represses and disavows the past, but rather the adulterator whose teeming desire to escape both the event's finitude and finality compels her to throw the plane of vision into maniacal disarray.

Dizziness and body; innocence; amazement; mingling; vagueness; muteness; uncertainty; thirst

88 Farrokhzad, *A Lonely Woman*, 127.

6

He was growing weary, his strength quite ebbing away. He drew strength from the heart, and licked the wounds on his arms, the dried threads of blood. Patience, patience! He felt dizzy, his consciousness about to fail. A kind of cloud was passing before his eyes. He shook his head to rid himself of it, with the help of further screams.

He felt very thirsty but had reached a tipping point where drinking or feeling thirsty seem equivalent. He did not try to move his hand to unfasten the water skin because he felt nauseous. He was nauseated by his own body, which stank with the foulest odor in the whole desert: the smell of a body decomposing, the smell of a body festering, the smell of purulence.

IBRAHIM AL-KONI[89]

We encounter our sixth dinomaniac introducing us to two distinct yet interrelated figures of confusion: *the wounded* (or more precisely, *the mortally wounded*) and *the self-loathing*. We are given a rough picture of the first association above, finding our young tribesman again, but this time in absolutely battered condition, having fallen from a mountain cliff chasing the sacred gazelles and now bleeding out upon the shallow rocks of the

89 Al-Koni, *The Bleeding of the Stone*, 57, 177.

valley below—his bones broken, dislocated, or fractured, his flesh gashed in countless places, with sweat pouring from his brow across his eyelashes, and needing somehow to drag his mangled body into the shade (for to remain beneath the sun all day would spell certain death). Dizziness here is a furtive enemy, for it provides a staircase into ultimate submission before the nothing; its comforting sinkhole does other than what it seems; it is a counterfeit, tacitly expediting destruction while ostensibly easing pain, so that 'growing weary' and 'ebbing away' combine to offer a placid bottom-reach of fatal sleep. And yet our mortally wounded figure finds recourse to stave off this fade-to-black: first he sucks upon open lacerations, sipping his own running blood; then he starts to scream, using self-generated sound to jolt himself awake. In such maniacal appeals to taste and audition, the sensory comes to the rescue, to forestall the progress of a dizziness that would mark the end of sensation itself.

Our second conceptual figure is also linked to 'purulence', for the self-loathing perceives himself as a mildewed corpse-in-waiting. He previews and samples the unsavouriness all around him; he does not declaim his chafed form, neither dispelling nor eliding this deplorable festering state, but rather makes right with abjection, debasement, and retching. He is pure detriment, this mortified one, the man of soiled apron, of denigrated bones, living contemptuously with the fetid body ('had reached a tipping point').

He is all-over putrescence, varnished with unimaginable things, heirlooms of pestilence, firsthand earnings of the uncivil, the beleaguered, and the disrespected. He brings the underside of interspecies being; he is sometimes lax and passively accepting of his squalidness, sometimes frustrated by his physiology's misrule ('nauseated by his own body'); he outranks the rankest regiments of stench ('the foulest odor in the whole desert'); he both inculcates and propagates himself as a reeking whirlpool, his ragged and uncombed approach enough to raise alarms, to make others bribe him into farthest distance, and for them to crave his nearing obituary.

Dizziness/whirlpool and weariness; ebbing; wound; cloud; scream; odour; decomposition; purulence

7

At five years of age
I was still troubled by the striking disbelief over my own birth
and would swagger with the grunting of a drunken camel
and with the ghostly presence of poisonous reptiles

A man of the whirling of water
A man of minimal words
who was the summation of himself.

AHMAD SHAMLU[90]

We encounter our seventh dinomaniac at the unrealized and the realized levels of a self-willed world: that of *the disbeliever* and that of *the diver*. In the first instance we are guided by a 'striking disbelief' over birth itself, a dark suspicion of origin that then generates an apparent regression back to the most primal dreams of the cave-person: the child-becoming-animal, animal-becoming-ghost, ghost-becoming-reptile. But this would lead to an erroneous reading: for the swagger of the 'drunken camel' and the 'ghostly presence of poisonous reptiles' is not some Paleolithic relapse, harking back to the first spiritual-environmental fears of the hunter-gatherers or

90 Shamlu, *Born Upon the Dark Spear*, 115, 76.

to those prehistoric organisms trapped in amber, but rather the chronicle of a manic futurism. Here we are so violently thrust forward, beyond prophetic wisdom or senility, that we can devise an alternative theory, of manic sovereignty, which stands in diametrical opposition to psychoanalytic frameworks of the uncanny. For if the uncanny remains one of the most ingrained definitions of experiencing strange familiarity, the dinomaniacal puzzlement of our disbeliever, this figure of awkward motion and self-mystification, offers another way of explaining the disorienting gap between consciousness and limbs. In the psychoanalytic tradition, the uncanny often arises from an anxious confrontation with some everyday object gone wrong, a household article once well-acquainted but now turned threateningly peculiar; the object has become the embodied harbinger of some repressed impulse of the unconscious, a symbolic reminder of taboo drives or terrors that then return in a kind of archaeologically-unearthed haunting, leading the psychic subject into a valley of alienation and eerie rejection symptomatic of the castration complex, doubling, guilt, and freakish synchronicity (retracing one's lost steps, repeating the same numbers).

What we meet with in the 'troubled' five-year-old of the above passage is something altogether different: not the scared child quivering before the half-dead eyes of figurines or toy puppets in their room at bedtime, but the willed dementia of a master-poet-becoming-ex-nihilo-child whose half-alive eyes will re-instantiate the *omnipotence of thought* believed irrecoverable by psychoanalysis. No longer the distressed victim of buried psychological secrets but rather the wellspring of distressing teratological force; no longer fearfully rapt but the enraptured fearsome, at once tingling and vaporous (the funeral bell, the smoke ring). This weak-legged self therefore exudes strange familiarity as well, spreading idiosyncratically sideways and askance, though tripping and faltering and listing with the bulging muscularity of the Japanese *Butoh* anti-dancer whose mercurial post-atomic-bomb choreography admits of no traumatic memory but only zero-hurricane twitching, not the sickly aura of the this-could-not-have-happened (unadmitted authenticity) but the nuclear light of the disbeliever's this-never-happened (admitted inauthenticity). They stare at their dangling fingers, ankles, and elbows with painstaking misrecognition—half-naked, covered in white-powder makeup, with facial expressions of the almost-fainting, learning to scurry again like dry-scaled alligators, laying soft-shelled eggs in a life-turned-ooze, searching amidst the mushroom-cloud brutality that makes all unscrupulous. The outright disbeliever is a figure of the world's aftermath, of the timeless second after being's fall, and their rickety posture again signals the birth of a manic flavour of solipsism: for they themselves have become the disturbing mannequin or scarecrow, gazing in paranormal unease at their own appendages; they are themselves the unsettling object that sends the mind hurtling into omnipotent thought; their own emotionless eyes and exiguous steps are the touchstones of all things supernatural or unearthly.

Thus the 'man of the whirling of water' arrives to bring this dinomaniacal problem to resolution, for on the other side of the disbeliever's anaemic aesthetic lies the terrifying balance of *the diver*. The pearl diver, deep sea diver, highdiver, skydiver—manic silence, inhuman poise and self-possession, the wordless composure through which one becomes 'the summation' of oneself (the expanding circles of struck water). Picture the copper helmet, the oxygen tank, the ambient pressure; conceive how this lone figure helps dream a conceptual channel between ultimate dizziness (dipping through air or ocean) and radically novel understandings of autonomy, equanimity, depth, and inevitability.

Dizziness/whirlpool and trouble; disbelief; birth; swagger; drunkenness; the ghost; the reptile; wordlessness; the summation

8

> *I saw the city being transformed into a witch's cauldron. The cauldron and all it contained boiled and boiled and spun around and around in a whirlpool of bloody shrieks. Meanwhile, bullets pierced through every mouth that wished to utter anything contrary to the logic of the bullets themselves.*
>
> GHADA SAMMAN[91]

We encounter our eighth dinomaniac exploring the cauldron, an object whose basic details are quite familiar: the black cast-iron pot over the open fire, sometimes equipped with lid or handle, the scaldingly hot temperatures, the riot of bubbles, the diced herbs (mostly sage, camphor, clove, or skullcap), or body parts of various creatures (mostly small, amphibious, unsavoury), or burnt petitions (paper scraps with wishes inscribed upon them). Nevertheless, what most intrigues us here are two facts: first, that the whirling cauldron requires its practitioner to become *the hoverer*, figure of super-aerial viewpoint, peering semi-omnisciently over prognostic waters in order to somehow turn the opaque mixture into a revelatory mirror, its fumes producing a dream sequence out of soot, grit, and charred bases; and second, that the

91 Samman, *Beirut Nightmares*, 64.

boiling waters apparently draw further power from the resistance of beings (the pierced mouths of those who 'uttered anything contrary'), so that the potion's liquid churns and foretells in proportion to its victims' inward struggle, making us wonder whether the cauldron's whirlpool is best defined as parasitic or vampiric in its consumptive-energetic transference. In either instance, the cauldron is a form of evil cooking, a vessel tied to the principles of culinary malice and spiritual-material dominion, for it discloses that narrow connective path through which physical concoctions can lead to metaphysical transformations, and metaphysical concoctions to physical transformations in turn—a conundrum that belongs somewhere between magic and science, between ancient fire and modern gunfire ('logic of the bullets'), a futuristic pan motivated by the simmering of vinegar, grime, tobacco stains, and twigs. This is how one opens a skylight or porthole into visual space itself, building any unrinsed tonic whatsoever into a window for both rumination and malady; indeed, in the passage above, an entire city falls prey to the witch's ferment, its citizens slumping one after another into her many emulsions and broths. To become doused in the amalgam, this is the cauldron's law: surveillance; ribcage; dead harvest.

Note: For thousands of years, the cauldron has been tied to the realm of miracle, as a vital spyglass through which saints, prophets, monks, healers, medicine women, and mystics have sought out their exceptional results. Still, the miracle itself is a notion of very complicated origins and genres, the majority intricately tied to variations of mania. For our purposes we can break these down into five overarching categories: the first type concerns miracles that revolve around *Time*, including the abilities of Time-Travel (backward, forward, circular, or parallel temporal movement), Premonition (seeing the future), Necromancy (raising the dead), and Resurrection (bringing oneself back from death); the second type concerns miracles that revolve around *Manipulation*, including the abilities of Mind-Reading (perceiving unarticulated thoughts), Telepathy (sharing information or whispering subliminally), Dreamwalking (entering dreams), Absorption (draining special powers from souls or objects), Affliction (bringing good fortune or harm), and Possession (seizing hold of another's being); the third type concerns miracles that revolve around *The Body*, including the abilities of Shape-Shifting (taking on other appearance), Incarnation (taking on other soul), Expansion (magnifying one's proportion to immense sizes), Diminution (dwindling to miniature sizes), Emanation (changing the size of one's shadow or mirror image), Manifestation (producing crystals or electricity from one's flesh), Purification (healing scars or diseases), Endurance (withstanding extreme deprivation, including deprivation of breath), and Transubstantiation (becoming air, liquid, or solid);

the fourth type concerns miracles that revolve around *Movement*, including the abilities of Flight, Teleportation (jumping in space), Surface-Climbing (walking on water or up walls), and Invisibility or Disappearance; and the final fifth type concerns miracles that revolve around *Nature*, including the abilities of Elemental Summoning (calling forth wind, rain, fire, thunder, or earthquakes), Elemental Intuition (hearing approaching storms, or sensing weather and tidal fluctuations), Occult Communication (speaking in hidden tongues with animals, artefacts, angels, ghosts, or demons), and Luminescence (emitting light or darkness).

Dizziness/whirlpool and the cauldron; boiling; shrieking; the mouth; the bullet

9

More tense than a bow. Our steps, be arrows. Where were we a moment ago?
Shall we join, in a while, the first arrow? The spinning wind whirled us.

So, if you would, take us to You, guide us to the ungraspable land.
Take us before we whirl into deep nothingness.

MAHMOUD DARWISH[92]

We encounter our ninth dinomaniac at the transitional moment of downfall from one conceptual figure (*the archer*) to another (*the supplicant*), thus establishing a narrative meridian passing across which a once-revered sharpshooter (practitioner of the 'first arrow') somehow accepts the urgent need to seek alms ('[t]ake us before we whirl'). We are left watching an act of true genuflection, as he kneels at the bottom of the hierarchical ladder, chest bowing in formalized humility, strong-playing-weak, an arche-subject who once lived by the fixedness of his grasp now confessing helplessness before 'the ungraspable land'. Thus the first passage reads as if spoken in a commander's tone, while the second is structured like

92 Darwish, *Unfortunately, It Was Paradise*, 3, 36.

a prayer or benediction (seeking absolution before the absolute), proving sadly that mastery means nothing in the face of blind circumstance. Observing his heedless posture, we consider the great antipathy with which such longing words must now come; once a figure of the high turrets, the barracks, the patrol, the adversary, and the altercation, he finds himself reduced to the starved rationality of naked psychopathic self-interest. Desperation does not need the skillset of the bowman; rather, it requires the machete; so he speaks these softer words, adopting tenderness before the remorseless event, soliciting whatever contingent principle staves off nothingness ('if you would, take us to You'), as if the superordinant functioned as pawnbroker, matchmaker, or profiteer. He aims himself toward the lowest rung of experience (self-offering), stooping along this dinomaniacal slope from archer's perch to supplicant's baseline or substrate, the being of this former leader turning to rashness, pathogen, and deadwood along the way.

Note: This heroic collapse actually follows a trajectory that, fascinatingly, corresponds to the categories of games themselves. For if human play can be divided into four main rulesets—those of *Agon* (games of competitive skill), *Alea* (games of chance), *Mimesis* (games of mimicry), and *Ilynx* (notably from the Greek 'whirlpool', referring here to games of altered perception)[93]—then we can track the same gradual shift across our two poetic selections above. We are first introduced to the archer whose marksmanship is tied exclusively to agonic spheres of pure ability ('[o]ur steps, be arrows'), but the subsequent 'spinning wind' blows us into an aleatory sphere of pure coincidence or gamble, after which the ex-archer is compelled to become a mimetic understudy or role-playing acolyte who merely follows that which might 'guide us', finally arriving at the ilyngomaniacal prospect of an amusement-park cosmology whose only stakes are 'whirling into deep nothingness'. (Note the prospect of a fifth unexplored category, that of subversive play—games of breaking structures, a modality favored by hackers, bandits, forgers, confidence-men, and temptresses). Almost all of the prime activities of anthropological gaming are represented here, in the metamorphic shift from deadshot to death-facing supplicant, and with them the criterial spiral from learned acumen to random likelihood to frantic imitation to mortal spinning.

Dizziness/whirlpool and the arrow; the wind; guidance; the ungraspable; nothingness

93 This breakdown of game types was first articulated in Roger Caillois's brilliant work *Man, Play, and Games* (Champaign, IL: University of Illinois Press, 1961).

10

> *I saw empty bags of every colour and shape. They were hovering around me at crazy speeds, as though they were making me a special offer of leftover bones, times and places. They did not seem happy with me, nor did the force blowing them. A torn grey bag flew past and I realised it was my mother's shawl. A burnt brain flew by on giant wings. A shoal of fish swam past carrying scraps of a young girl's flesh. The flying vipers of economic sanctions flew by, wrapped around their food of humans and dreams* [...] *My whole life passed page by page, all the jams and scrapes I had been through, page after page. Even when I closed my eyes it didn't stop. Pain and vertigo had me in their power. The pages went past in the darkness, white page after page.*
>
> HASSAN BLASIM[94]

We encounter our tenth dinomaniac at the final stroke of existence's midnight, taking a last glimpse at a life flashing before the eyes, although here the procession of supposed memories goes astray in various ways: (1) the images are not subjectively comforting ('they did not seem happy with me'); (2) the images are sent by malevolent design ('nor did the force blowing them'); (3) the images become increasingly macabre ('carrying scraps of a young girl's flesh'); (4) the images become increasingly surreal

94 Blasim, *The Madman of Freedom Square*, 93.

('a burnt brain flew by on giant wings'); (5) the images become predatory forms of literary terror and oppressive messaging ('white page after page'). There is no redundancy here; these are not his own previously-lived moments but either hypothetical occasions or episodes from someone else's dealings; they are altogether incorrect, fragments of a stranger's album or a non-existent world; they form an impossible ovation, an anti-festival. His eyes participate in this unabashed proliferation, a misgiven orgiasticism so perceptually braided that the barraged mind begins feasting on itself (becoming-petrified). The life-flashing phase is therefore not that of falling fast asleep but rather that of perpetual awakening, one that shuffles our dying watcher into an entirely new specimen.

Paroxysm taken to its manic limit appears as paralysis, like that of *the gargoyle*, a figure that persists across only the most perturbed eras of fanaticism, with its locked inconceivable look, compelled to endure whatever visual bombardments and montages arise, regardless of its own wishes ('Even when I closed my eyes, it didn't stop'). Whereas the first gargoyles of ancient Eastern capitals were functional rainspouts (French *gargouille*, meaning 'throat' or 'gullet', resembling the sound of gurgling water) made in the shapes of protruding lions, dragons, or legendary intergenerics, the later gargoyles of Western gothic churches become increasingly ornamental and monstrous sculptures (also called grotesques, chimeras, or bosses). These are often long-taloned birds or skeletal batlike creatures placed to ward off evil spirits from entering the sacred space, staring out from masonry walls, aqueducts, and parapets with frozen garbled expressions, although sometimes among them one also finds the Green Man, a carved vegetal deity hidden in the rib vaults of cathedral ceilings, though also common among a range of pre-mediaeval world cultures (the earliest found in second-century Iraq), most often resembling an elder male face with foliage mask and branches sprouting from mouth, ears, tear ducts, or nostrils. This disgorging head, with leaves and vines shooting from its orifices, is almost always considered a protective mediator, like its gargoyle counterpart—one that supervises the frail boundary between heaven and hell, inside and outside, friend and enemy, and even reality and the imaginary. But what is crucial for our purposes here is not this dialectical-transgressive ideal-type but rather the specific stylistic technique through which such elevated status and power is supposedly granted: the manic elongation of the gargoyle's neck, limbs, and bones; and the Green Man's manic profusion of naturalistic flora, plants, and undergrowth. Both must enter a decoratively disfigured state, the simulacrum of mania, and must wear it as a violent guise throughout the ages.

Dizziness/whirlpool and shape; hovering; speed; offering; scraps; eyes; pages; whiteness; darkness

Labyrintomania (Labyrinths)

1

> *It was two months ago when they threw a lunatic into that prison at the end of the courtyard. With a broken piece of marble he cut out his own stomach, pulled out his intestines and played with them. They said he was a butcher—he was used to cutting stomachs. But that other one had pulled out his own eyes with his own nails. They tied his hands behind his back. He was screaming and the blood had dried on his eyes. I know that all of this is the supervisor's fault.*
>
> SADEQ HEDAYAT[95]

We encounter our first labyrintomaniac in a sparse madhouse surrounded by figures driven to exenteration (the surgical removal of organs). We are in the Persian *hezar-tu* (i.e., labyrinth, but literally 'a thousand withins'): one here cuts out his stomach (first labyrinth); another cuts out his eyeball (second labyrinth). The asylum itself must be understood as a labyrinthine zone in the following senses: (1) both promise illusory release (whether

95 S. Hedayat, *Three Drops of Blood*, tr. D. Miller Mostaghel (London: Alma Books, 2013), 10.

it is called escape or rehabilitation); (2) both sequester individuals from the outside world (whether it is called abduction or quarantine); (3) both require a diabolical, voyeuristic overlord (whether they are called king or warden). Nothing but the soft fear of the supervisor's footsteps echoing through white corridors, and with them a universal discrimination.

Labyrinth 1.
Location: Bombay
Material: White Stone
Design: Vertical; Octagonal
Inscription: 'No summer queens here, no light shadows or life elixirs, and even the lunatic never comes.'
Experience: The labyrinth appears as tenement hotel or boardinghouse with eight apartments; one enters as a paying guest, always renting a room on the ground floor in the corner of the east wing. A centuries-old elevator in the centre lobby and view of a polluted green sea from the room's single window; right outside the aperture, the incessant coughing of poor street-goers. The combined sound of people gasping and the visual image of tepid ocean bring forth only tempting thoughts of drowning oneself.

Labyrinth and prison; brokenness; the stomach; the eye; the nails; tied hands; the supervisor

2

Short pieces of writing with networks of lines cut by knives illness native lands mousetraps ravines labyrinths corridors lairs knots...

RÉDA BENSMAIA[96]

Our second labyrintomaniac describes language itself as filatory (a machine for spinning threads), thus shifting us away from the ancient literary solidity of clay tablets and into the morass of word-tendrils, splinters, and thimbles. The writing of anagrams (words formed from other words); the writing of polysemy (signs that have multiple meanings); the writing of the *polytropoi* (the wiliness of the 'much-travelled' or the 'one of many turns'). Pronunciation becomes labyrinth; comprehension becomes labyrinth; elocution and signification become labyrinth upon labyrinth; there is no mercy shown for the correctness of the oral, the aural, the visual, the proverbial, or the literal; all is made susceptible to the fine hairs of a brush.

The above passage's own descriptive lattice weaves 'knives' into 'native lands' into 'illness', 'mousetraps', and 'ravines', thereby reminding us of the Arabic-Persian scriptorial process of *I'jaam* whereby words change precipitously based on diacritical dots placed above or below

96 Bensmaia, *The Year of Passages*, 97.

an alphabetical letter in order to give it a clarified meaning or phonetic intelligibility. It is always performed as an afterthought of the handwriting process—this addition of one, two, or three precise marks suspended over or beneath the original character—and yet the entire shaking edifice of meaning hangs in the balance of these tiny circles or diamond indicators. Otherwise, a single syntactic insertion or omission can transmit sublime into wicked properties, blurring the fine-spun depreciative line between *khoda* (God) and *joda* (separate), *khahar* (sister) and *javaher* (jewelry), *ria* (a pious display) and *zina* (adultery). There is much to lose and gain, then, in this high-stakes game of fibrils, seams, and black speckling.

Labyrinth 2.
Location: Algiers
Material: Netting
Design: Skein (cat's cradle)
Inscription: 'No reflective texts are here, only memories sewn slowly into malady.'
Experience: The labyrinth appears as ribbon, cotton, floss, and gossamer (embroidered world). It leads one into the silken movement of a *casbah* (Arabic, meaning 'citadel'), though no protective feeling is granted by its curving passageways. Rather, one senses exposure before elements and gazes from dark vulturine balconies. All thoughts become needlework; all utterances are recognized as the

hemming of the seamstress (though one never meets her). There is only the constant desire for the epicenter alongside the gradual cognizance that the more one walks, the further away one gets from any essential inner point. To limp continually through well-stitched peripheries alone.

Labyrinth and writing; network; line; knife; mousetrap; lair; knot

3

Our bloods spin their dialogue
and our labyrinths are words

ADONIS[97]

We encounter our third labyrintomaniac in a blood-maze of dialogues, reminding us not only that thought's expression itself proves schizophrenic (with whom is one talking in there?) but also that this internal breaching-into-echoes is built upon a sanguinary rubric. We can imagine the labyrinth here as aneurism (a balloon-like sac causing embolic blockages, thrombotic blood clots, or fatal ruptures), for the aneurism teaches us that often the greatest risk is the removal of the very occlusion. The implication is a hypertensive cadence without recourse to any of the traditional rhetorical pillars—no *logos* (appeal to reason), *pathos* (emotion), *ethos* (value), or *kairos* (urgency); instead we speak in a blood-soaked meter devoid of all care for persuasive logic, feeling, authority, or timeliness, but for which every conceivable dialogic turn results only in diastolic murmurs and universal anhedonia (the impossibility of satisfaction).

97 Adonis, *Selected Poems*, 188.

Labyrinth 3.
Location: Aleppo
Material: Vein
Design: Capillary Branching (blood-vessel formations)
Inscription: 'No leprosy survives here, nor a prayer for death by pestilence.'
Experience: The labyrinth appears as weak arterial walls lined with abnormal protrusions; severe tissue damage makes it impossible to discern whether it is the aorta, the brain, or the spleen. Facing these oddly-sized obstructions, the heart-rate and blood pressure rise above good mercury limits (experience of the intolerant within). One persists here in a state of perpetual *Laagh al-jurh* (Arabic, 'licking of wounds'), calling out occasionally in hopes of finding the Apothecary.

Labyrinth and blood; spinning; dialogue

4

Legendary monsters with piano mouths
Lounge in the shadow pits
I sleep naked

JOYCE MANSOUR[98]

We encounter our fourth labyrintomaniac in the hollow troughs of 'the they', here meaning not the pathetic mass-gatherings of human consumption but instead the supra-pathological practice of inhuman mastication (crushing of food between teeth). There is perhaps a special beauty in predators who merely lounge, waiting quietly for long periods only to suddenly trampoline against caught prey. There are three things that we can deduce quickly then, before they come: firstly, that their 'piano mouths' grant them capacities for gaping, chasmal widening of their devouring apparatus (perhaps able to swallow things whole); secondly, that they employ camouflage (from French *camoufler*, thieves' slang for 'to disguise', or *camouflet*, meaning 'whiff of smoke in the face'), most likely through those devices of sensory concealment called crypsis (nocturnality, mimicry, coloration); thirdly, that she (the labyrinth-goer) readies herself as an attractive force to the feeding ones by both falling asleep and

98 Mansour, *Essential Poems and Writings*, 207.

taking on the hyper-observability of nakedness in their 'shadow pits'. What is meant by this offering of oneself to the monstrous diner, and what does it mean to be most desired by the labyrinth itself?

Labyrinth 4.
Location: Cairo
Material: Teeth; Jawbone
Design: Fanged (sharp-edged corners; serration)
Inscription: 'No great embalmed gods left here, no celestial horns growing behind ears, just the twice-hidden ones and the ones of many mouths.'
Experience: One enters the labyrinth brushing one's hand against walls of calcified enamel, dentin, and cementum, realizing fast enough that one is walking into the junction of another's maxilla (upper jaw) and mandible (lower jaw). Movement is therefore aligned with a forthcoming process of salivation, food-crushing, and digestion; an intuitive sense that this world itself wants you. The labyrinth once belonged to others, either temple or pyramid; it is everywhere arrayed with the red pigments of vermillion and the disproportionate statues of scarab beetles and Nile-river crocodiles; the decor of death-cult royalty. Now though, the hieroglyphs of old androgynous gods have given way to a vermin-cult, clearly chewed upon by other still-living, non-sacred dwellers. Thus one is restored here to the roots of old mammalian survival habits, and

in particular thegosis (the grinding of teeth in order to sharpen them). This is all that matters any longer.

Labyrinth and the mouth; lounging; shadow; the pit; naked sleep

5

The earth in elevation reaches repetition
and air wells
change into tunnels of connection.
And day is a vastness

FORUGH FARROKHZAD[99]

We encounter our fifth labyrintomaniac in a sequence of aerated wind tunnels (at once gusting and tapering); the walls themselves stray between materiality and immateriality, leading ultimately into soundproof rooms of the salacious. Here the elevated is brought down into venal paths, into the thousand words for the immoral being: rakish, wanton, debauched, reprobate, licentious, unscrupulous. The language of obscenity is therefore its own labyrinth, and not just the repositories of curse-words and expletives themselves but also the complex accusatory terminology invented to describe the demeaned soul. The result is the birth of a class somewhere between the French *demi-mondaine* (literally 'half-worlder', one given to extravagant or decadent pleasure-seeking) and the Persian *havasbaz* (literally 'taste-player', one given to corrupt indulgences of desire or appetite). The courtesan, the fiend. Labyrinth of the miscreant.

99 Farrokhzad, *A Lonely Woman*, 161.

Labyrinth 5.
Location: Darband
Material: Wind; Breath
Design: Cylindrical-Aerial
Inscription: 'There will not be another birth, just the cold season without beginning (always remains).'
Experience: One enters the labyrinth through a series of over-oxygenated corridors; this hyper-respiratory logic of its architecture results either in allergenic or asthmatic reactions. Squalls; tempests; tornados. However, quickly one develops an ability to hear the drafts for what they truly are: guttural sounds, rumor, gossip, insinuation, backhanded claims, innuendo, conspiratorial whispers. The muffled, low-pitched voices of judgment are everywhere; they fill the days and nights of this talkative place.

Labyrinth and elevation; repetition; the well; the tunnel; connection; vastness

6

> *I am your secret. I am your amulet. I am your lost name. I am your lost coordinate. I am the one who searched in your embrace to find himself there. I am the one in whom you searched for your unrecognized man so you could discover in his embrace your lost truth. I am the seventh coordinate... I sowed in your wombs six of the names. I cannot, however, divulge the secret of the seventh name.*
>
> IBRAHIM AL-KONI[100]

We encounter our sixth labyrintomaniac speaking to a Creator that defines itself as semblances of the most lost (lost name, lost coordinate, lost truth), introducing us to the unrecognizable within and gifting us unsafe amulets that drive souls to their worst potentialities (becoming-culprit). Theological secrecy therefore turns out to be nothing less than the secretion of worldwide trouble (joke of the laughing godhead). Here the tautological unity of 'I Am That I Am' is replaced by 'I Am None and Many'—a chandelier-cosmos that means many things and signifies many aliases, and in whose vague reflective presence we appear responsible to many selves (each carrying several wombs).

---

100 Al-Koni, *The Seven Veils of Seth*, 210.

What does it mean to be guided by someone who will not tell you the way? What is to be done when contacted by powerful beings with spotted records of instruction? Let us ask the namesake of the book's own title—*The Seven Veils of Seth*—for he is none other than a derided god of the red desert, war, anarchy, and foreignness. He is a mutilated and mutilating god; he is a usurper god; he is a fratricidal god; he is a god of coercive, unselective sexuality, while also himself being deceitfully impregnated; he is an ill-matched lord of storms, one of unfit kingship (the miscellaneous one). His physiology is that of a mixed-breed species, his face combining various uncategorized animalities (jackal, fox, giraffe); he goes by countless metamorphic titles and diverging signatures, remaking identity into a congestion of epithets.

We are told elsewhere by this same author that 'For those in thirst, homeland is a labyrinth'.[101] No doubt this is a nomadic fact of life (the desultory search for water), but does it also mean that every human desire for worldliness just invites further disinformation; does 'worlding' itself only encourage the unfortunate penchant of otherworldly beings to parlay this thirst into a labyrinthine ruse?

Thus we are compelled to estimate the implications of thinking metaphysics itself as a labyrinth of veils,

---

101 I. al-Koni, *A Sleepless Eye: Aphorisms from the Sahara*, tr. R. Allen (Syracuse, NY: Syracuse University Press, 2014), 47.

equivocations, and chaotic deities. To divorce the metaphysical realm from truth and relinquish it to the will of multiple revolving visages (all unresolved) is effectively to grant open warfare between the mystical and the One. Not the traditional humbled mystic who falls passively into universal bewilderment, but rather the divine confounder whose sole arrogance rests in an ability for sacred deception, bad advice, unkept promises, negligent deals, and hollow revelations. This is where belief comes to rest across the stained mattress of discrepancy, or becomes a gamepiece on a cheater's board (twisted in the gods' mixed metaphors). We are no longer debating the lie of metaphysics, but rather the metaphysics of the lie.

Labyrinth 6.
Location: Ombos
Material: Fool's Gold
Design: Disks (hammered thin sheets of false gold leaf across immense round circlets)
Inscription: 'There is no gold dust left, just the nomads turned cosmic puppeteers.'
Experience: One enters the labyrinth as an apparent burned library (not an erased archive; an archive of erasure). It is full of scrolls, pendants, holy ointments, and small bottles filled with the collected tears of virgins, saints, and martyrs. One tries everywhere to find the labyrinth's god, but to say the Name is to instantaneously

transform it into another; to speak the Word is to repel the Overseer (serious disciples of an unserious master).

Labyrinth and the secret; the amulet; the lost;
the unrecognized; coordinate; womb; name

7

In the city with no street, they thrive
In the decomposed web of alleys and dead-ends
Coated in furnace smoke and kidnapping and jaundice
A colored frame in the pocket and a bow and arrow
in the hand
The children of the depths
The children of the depths

AHMAD SHAMLU[102]

We encounter our seventh labyrintomaniac where extreme youth meets slum, shanty-town, emigrant camp, or war zone. Here alone can one witness the premature aging of the orphan, the runaway, the child criminal or child soldier; here alone can one theorize the unique styles and techniques of the children's street gang. Forcibly brought into criminality or war; the juvenile turned missile-maker or pickpocket.

Their accumulative physiology is its own labyrinth: the unclipped nails; the untrimmed hair; the frayed, unwashed clothes; the dirt caked on pockmarked faces. They make an advantage of their smallness (swarming in great numbers); they make an advantage of their vulnerability (hugging around the waist or clasping hands).

---

102 Shamlu, *Born Upon the Dark Spear*, 98.

They manipulate assumed innocence, flashing eyes of false helplessness and turning tricks beyond their years; and when this fails, they resort to their becoming-hurtful.

The unprepared; the unvaccinated; recipients of unfair determinism. Certain ethnographic works tell us of the things they say to one another at night, by the street corners, bridges, or cardboard boxes that supplant proper homes and bedrooms. They are fascinating philosophers of the backstreets.

We can glimpse another dimension of labyrintomania in the clever movements through which these child gangs manipulate verticality (climbing walls, trees, apartment building ladders), sneak into restricted places (the dumpster, the junkyard, the arcade, the train compartment, the theatre back-door), or scurry away into hiding-places (corners, closets, crevices, stairwells, under beds). They master backsliding; they shoplift negligible items (never more than a handful); they temporarily inhabit the guise of the stowaway and the beggar. Petty infractions of those who never had a chance.

If the child's imaginative parameters already encompass dueling bouts of automatonophilia and automatonophobia (the love and fear of human-resembling objects), then we could conceive of a situation wherein the labyrintomania of these tough thoroughfares could provoke an explosive convergence of love and fear into automatonomania—a passion severe enough to make one adopt the modality of the human-resembling object: a child wearing a doll's face.

Labyrinth 7.
Location: Zahedan
Material: Concrete
Design: Intersectional (indigent boroughs)
Inscription: 'There are no more fairies crying beneath crumbled domes, and even the man with no lips has left us.'
Experience: The labyrinth appears as a massive conglomeration of ugly boulevards, side-streets, dead-ends, and back-alleys; there are unused toys littered everywhere, amid discarded trash and syringes (pure untidiness). One plays pretend here in order to survive; one grows older far too fast; one is compelled to kidnap the child within oneself, and ransom it to daily circumstance.

Labyrinth and the street; decomposition; web; dead-end; kidnapping; the pocket; the hand; the child

8

> *I rush to the metro. I have become accustomed to the suffocating daily crowds* [...] *the little daily battle to occupy a metro seat that would spare me from standing at a door or in the aisles of the train, exposed to shoulder shoves—becoming part of a human block whose waves go to and fro, carry me, and hurl me against the metal walls, a human block throbbing with exhaustion, vitality, and stench* [...] *the river of humanity that almost sweeps me off as it gushes down through automatic metal doors that open with a slight circular pressure on the handle, which appears like the last thing distinguishing the relation between what is mechanical and what is human, and perhaps is the last communication between them.*
>
> GHADA SAMMAN[103]

We encounter our eighth labyrintomaniac grappling with crowd formations, which she rightly diagnoses as a condition of acclimatized suffocation. The crowd is itself a labyrinth for many reasons: it paralyzes through movement (the rush of everydayness takes one nowhere); it masks universal entrapment in a false appearance of individuation (delusions of being the one who could actually

103 G. Samman, 'The Swan Genie', in *The Square Moon: Supernatural Tales*, tr. I. Boullata (Fayetteville, AR: University of Arkansas Press, 1999), 98.

get out); it is constructed by an unknown, perhaps long-gone ruler (the social contract that no one has actually signed). Furthermore, like the labyrinth, the crowd is a decentralized power-structure behind which there lurks a certain genius, though now diffused, transferred out of the hands of an original nefarious author into the walls themselves (space as malevolent will).

She confronts us with a 'human block throbbing with exhaustion, vitality', from which we must gather that the crowd is always somehow approaching both the exhaustion of its vitality (becoming too perfect) and the exhaustion of its exhaustedness (becoming too unbearable). For this reason, the crowd-labyrinth induces both ecstatic and horrific feelings. The ecstasy derives, strangely enough, from the sensation of absorption, anonymity, and disappearance (drowning in the mass); this is not simply a timid wish for belonging, identification, or acceptance but in fact a suicidal wish for the suspension of difference altogether. The horror, on the other hand, derives from the growing self-consciousness of being stared at, named, and appraised, as if at any moment all crowd members might turn around and form a catastrophic focused circle around the individual (fleeing from extreme recognition). Thus the ecstatic dimension is the death of the one in the many (the liberation of being ignored), while the horrific dimension is precisely the death of the one by the many (the oppression of being called-out).

Note: We could stop here to irrevocably dismiss the term 'egomania' for good, since maniacal experience is precisely what allows no ego remnant, no subject torn between interior and exterior judgments. Mania, rather, is the complete victory of the outside; prologue to sheer excoriation: something flayed beyond both self and other.)

Going on, we are also met with the crowd-labyrinth's continual 'shoulder shoves' and thrusting against 'metal walls', revealing the hyper-arousal and kinetic (in)sensitivity of the collective whose members are roused to violence by mere touch (the riot). The heat, noise, and friction of the gathering make them increasingly cantankerous and irate, at once a fifth column and a third rail. Hastening; numbness; blank eyes; herd-like, livid compliance; dysfunctional machinism. No single figure, no one body seems liable, though someone, somewhere must be keeping the ledger.

We are told in a separate work by the same author that she sometimes longs for a more orphic counter-labyrinth, '[a]n inner river of obscure suffocation stretch[ing] its dark veins between me and the elements of the universe, joining me to the circulatory system of an unknown, mysterious planet.'[104] Thus we find the maniacal aspect in waiting: the crowd's thoughtless congregation generates as an offshoot this desire for some alternative suffocation

---

104 Samman, *Beirut Nightmares*, 139.

in the cosmogonic elsewhere, not a negative escape from connectivity but another experience of infinitely voluminous contact that takes place on an 'unknown, mysterious planet'. This is what comes after 'the last communication'—untenable pressure finally giving rise to a visionary outburst.

Lastly, let us consider the paranoiac leader: Is there not some mad justice in the mad empress who lashes viciously at those closest to her (abusing the inner circle above all others), for what are they doing in such close proximity to her brutality anyway? Does the crowd not always somehow deserve punishment? Does its vacuous momentum not warrant a becoming-rueful? Labyrinth of the better-off-dead.

Labyrinth 8.
Location: Beirut
Material: Limbs (cadaverous or half-alive)
Design: Mass Grave (sprawling; grotesque seamlessness)
Inscription: 'No square moon, no local nightmares or old ports shining beneath a billion eves, just a costume party for the nearly-living and the nearly-dead.'
Experience: The labyrinth appears brimming, awash, mobbed with insensate bodies and body parts. It stirs together/apart, this pure indiscriminate; too many brought into unprincipled commingling. Hands fall across backs; legs strike across faces; some bleed, trample,

or lose physical track of themselves; one cannot tell where self begins and other ends (becoming-unwary). No possible transfiguration, no ascension, no epochality. This place wears the feeling of the purgatorial middle, a useless wave or mechanical wilderness. One keeps going here, for there is nothing else, all the while wondering about the logic of its penance.

Labyrinth and rush; the accustomed; suffocation; the crowd; the block; the wave; exhaustion; vitality; being-swept; pressure; communication

9

My heart exceeding my need, hesitant between two doors:
entry a joke, and exit a labyrinth.
Where is my shadow—my guide amid the crowdedness on the road to judgment day? And I as an ancient stone of two dark colors in the city wall, chestnut and black, a protruding insensitivity toward my visitors and the interpretation of shadows. Wishing for the present tense a foothold for walking behind me or ahead of me, barefoot. Where is my second road to the staircase of expanse? Where is futility? Where is the road to the road?

MAHMOUD DARWISH[105]

We encounter our ninth labyrintomaniac disturbed by contradictory inquests: (1) the pursuit of the immediate road (that of need, the present tense, and the rightful connector between the ancient stone and the Day of Judgment); (2) the pursuit of the second road (that of excess, barefoot expanses, and futility). We notice the prolific use of the secondary here—'two doors', 'two dark colors', 'the road to the road'—alongside suggestive remarks that the second door leads both to misanthropy ('insensitivity toward my visitors') and an affinity for the shadow-world

---

105 M. Darwish, *The Butterfly's Burden*, tr. F. Joudah (Port Townsend, WA: Copper Canyon Press, 2007), 255.

('the interpretation of shadows'). Something perhaps akin to the schismatic formula of the prophet who leaves their tribe to chase a collateral voice into caves and mountains. Thus the labyrinth constitutes the domain of the unnecessary decision, the turning of a door's handle that leads one into an alternative ultra-hermeneutic beyond ruled by half-sightings and undecidable beings. Is the attending shadow something of presence or absence, here or not here, appearing or disappearing, human or inhuman, living or dead, friend or enemy? Answers are not clearly given anymore, for in each instance the likelihood is that they are at once neither, both, and not-quite.

On the other hand, the emphasis on 'afoothold for walking behind me', 'the road to the road', and the 'ancient stone' in 'the city wall' could also be statements regarding the labyrinthine futility of the search for origin. Not because the origin remains forever unknown and therefore sends us along labyrinthine paths, but rather because the origin is itself paradoxical and thus embodies a labyrinthine estate. To demonstrate this, we need only turn to the earliest surviving work of world literature, the epic journeys of Gilgamesh, to find an originary figure full of circuitous paradoxical streams: (1) he is a demi-god (two-thirds divine, one-third human) at once magnificent and despotic; (2) his very Sumerian name translates to 'The Ancestor is a Young Man'; (3) he carries the incipit titles 'Surpassing All Kings' and

'He Who Saw the Deep'; (4) through tests of strength, he binds a rampaging figure named Enkidu ('The Wild Man') into lifelong alliance; (5) he kills an immemorial death-bringing forest guardian named Humbaba ('The Terrible'), and thereby steals his seven 'radiances' or 'terrors'; (6) he meets an immortal being and survivor of the flood named Utnapashtim ('The Faraway') who nevertheless cannot teach him the secret of immortality. Limitless, sinuous paradoxes embedded in a single origin story, for according to the above details the great precursor is one who simultaneously embodies beauty and cruelty, the divine and the human, the ancestral and the young: he is one who allegedly supersedes all sovereignty (though the King represents precisely the absolute limit of earthly power) and perceives the imperceptible (though the Deep represents precisely the absolute limit of the unseen); he uses tests (the absolute limit of separation, struggle, and rivalry) to somehow create loyalty and moreover bests an untamed being in a physical challenge (though Wildness represents precisely the absolute limit of brute force). He then ambushes the Terrible one and takes its spiritual gifts (though Terror represents precisely the absolute limit of surprise, abduction, and non-spirituality) in a miraculous gesture of terrorizing terror in order to thieve radiance (though Radiance represents precisely the absolute limit of something innate and given), and he then councils with an immortal to demand knowledge of the everlasting (though Eternity itself represents precisely the absolute limit of thought).

The second road is hence that of a kind of foundational mania, a road back to the first road and a hesitant beyond, to a regal forefather of segmental inheritances, a ruler without rules, disclosing an origin of resplendent paradoxes. Labyrinth of the supra-orbital.

Labyrinth 9.
Location: Uruk
Material: Rock; Sand; Steel; Fur; Water
Design: Assemblage (incongruent parts)
Inscription: 'There are no murals, burdens, unfortunate paradises, or ordinary griefs left, only a wish of the "If I were another" that was granted from first breath.'
Experience: The labyrinth appears amid raised platforms and indigo-coloured tiers made from fired bricks; it stretches into both impossibly compact and long ziggurats, though one senses power in the shortest halls and weakness in the most immense galleries. Things appear both larger and smaller than they actually are (the sixth sense here is disproportion). Things challenge assumptions: the ziggurat-labyrinth does not bridge heaven and earth but rather confuses them interchangeably. Things simultaneously mean exactly what they say (excessively transparent), exactly the opposite of what they say (excessively reversible), while conveying a third message of

something radically other than what they say (excessively unrelatable). Meanwhile, an old poet dispenses paradoxical whispers, repeating the words 'a river dies of thirst' over and again. Depending on the turn, one becomes either the apostle or the vandal.

Labyrinth and hesitation; need; the shadow; the ancient; interpretation; shadow; wish; foothold; behind; ahead; barefootedness; the second road; expanse; futility

10

> *While my friend Dawoud was driving the family car through the streets of Baghdad, an Iraqi poet in London was writing a fiery article in praise of the resistance, with a bottle of whiskey on the table in front of him to help harden his heart. Because the world is all interconnected, through feelings, words, nightmares, and other secret channels, out of the poet's article jumped three masked men.*
>
> HASSAN BLASIM[106]

We encounter our tenth labyrintomaniac exploring an old aesthetic premise: What if the characters of an author's imagination could claw their way beyond the stage, canvas, or book to join reality's surface? Similarly, we could ask how it would alter so-called artistic experience if we were to believe in a subtle ricochet-effect whereby to read, recite, or watch a certain piece would automatically activate some occurrence (fatal or transformative) in the world at large. A lowering of the aesthetic barrier; the restoration of sorcery; a pact with the 'three masked men' behind every thought—a single poem is inscribed and elsewhere a single stranger falls into impalement or rises to nirvana.

This trap-door theory opens our conversation to treating the labyrinth as a site of immanent manifestation,

106 Blasim, *The Madman of Freedom Square*, 5.

collapsing the boundary between vision and event (palpability as supreme law). But do the arriving cohorts come in peace or do they seek revenge against their author? Do they possess the ability to multiply themselves, gifted the same rules of imaginative procreation through which they themselves emerged? Are they somehow more attuned to the objective world (things, spaces, phenomena) or to the sensorial world (images, sounds, touch) that would give them a clear advantage in becoming? What are the defining bounds of their vulnerability (How are they hurt?) and their mortality (How do they die?) What is the nature of their interrelation (Do they form loyal bonds of a race, tribe, gang, blood alliance?) when they pass another figmentary being along the way? Given that they leap from literary pages, are they imbued with a superior eloquence in language, and do they import the text's carnivalesque laws of time and space into their new sphere? Do they desire reality or do they savour their inauthentic core? Do they perceive themselves as superior or inferior forms? Can they ever return to the fictive zone, and do they fear this return? Can they bring us back with them?

Labyrinth 10.
Location: Baghdad
Material: Image
Design: Kaleidoscopic (film-reel loops; palimpsestic overlays)

Inscription: 'No freedom squares or corpse exhibitions, just reality's recording played over and again.'
Experience: The labyrinth is constructed from photographic tape and cinema negatives. The rule here is endless overexposure: radiological atmospheres; sensation of being in black-and-white scenes, backstage environments, or X-rays. Here one merely plays oneself, the first step in recognizing the original illusion of consciousness (subjective malfeasance), as if seeing oneself built through electromagnetic detectors.

Labyrinth and the friend; resistance; hardening; interconnection; the secret channel; the masked men

* * *

There is no time or space left, at least not here and now, for those further iterations of restlessness that would fill out the entire manic imagination-in-movement. The sixty interpreted above are only a prelude to thousands that remain unaccounted for, each its own archive of aisles and potencies and neo-Bedouin turns, each forming an overture to the unceasing ones.

Part 20

Monomania (Aloneness)

Isolomania (Isolation)

Megalomania (Self)

Catoptromania/Eisoptromania (Mirrors)

Colossomania (Giants)

We arrive at a critical stage where it now becomes possible to steal psychoanalysis's favourite plaything—the self—and inspire in it maniacal, post-psychological modifications. For what if mania were capable of turning subjectivity into its external object of desire and fascination? What if someone stared fixedly at the 'I' as if it were an outer portent to be enshrined, quickened, grasped, interpreted? To become obsessed with the individual character as an entirely separate edifice (idol, artefact, story, natural disaster) would constitute a release from the typical narcissistic frailty of the modern subject, for it would free thought, sensation, and vision from their endogenous prisons and release them into a long-awaited exogenous abyss. It would be nothing less than a graduation into true rarity.

One of the grossest mistakes of early psychoanalysis was to construct taxonomies in which symptoms were seen as inherent to a disorder itself, rather than as by-products of the collision between said disorder and the social reality that names, condemns, and persecutes it. For instance, it remains an unresolved question whether schizophrenia possesses an essential propensity toward violence or whether schizophrenic violence emerges precisely from the rancorous confrontation between the schizoid imagination and the surrounding majority, confident in the rigid presumption of their own general sanity (never realizing that normalized everyday culture is itself deeply psychotic at almost all levels). Similarly, the psychoanalytic (mis) understanding of mania as self-obsession (delusions of grandeur) rather than as obsession with a fully redefined concept of self (grandeur of the illusion) misses the subtle annihilative procedure that must be followed in order to enthrone this once-inner 'I' in the farthermost reaches of speculation. Not to see oneself in the stars, but to see the stars as convertible selves. And we can be sure that, in each case, this hyperextension will be established only by a fatal passage: from extreme solitude (monomania) to extreme distance (isolomania) to extreme watchfulness (megalomania) to extreme reflection (cataptromania) to extreme magnification (colossomania)...and to perish therein. For this is what must come to pass on that strange night when mania turns its special gaze upon the voice in one's own head: the maniac must touch identity in ways like no other, tapping on the glass window of its sanctum, making a forced entry so as to take it as a headstone or hunter's trophy. This is how a lone misspent persona becomes a new specimen, simultaneously immanent, transcendent, singular, multiple, universal, molecular, and disappeared.

Monomania (Aloneness)

1

> *Do not the rest of mankind who look like me, who appear to have the same needs and the same passions as I, exist only in order to cheat me? Are they not a mere handful of shadows which have come into existence only that they may mock and cheat me?*
>
> SADEQ HEDAYAT[107]

Our first monomaniac presents us with a quintessential aspect of the condition: hearing voices (voices of totality, of world, of the everyone). These voices are responsible for a blight of the lukewarm and the mediocre (Persian *velengari*, 'idle chatter'); they turn perception into an abscessed, ulcerative haven. That they come only to 'cheat' our speaker above is further indication of a residual shred of non-nihilistic consciousness that believes it is owed something (that he deserves better); that they utilize trickeries of resemblance by hiring lookalikes only makes them more worthy of complete obliteration, thereby taking us out of the domain of trauma and into the domain of sworn revenge. Manic paranoia, which would constitute

---

107 Hedayat, *The Blind Owl*, 3.

the outer limit of the paranoiac structure, would not be a fear of victimhood, but a reciprocation of hostilities: 'I' am also out to get *them*; 'I' exist only to win against their cause. This monomaniacal type therefore persistently seeks the triumph of the one against the all.

Aloneness and mankind; the lookalike; the cheated; the shadow; mockery

2

It's the plan of the entire world's egoism leveled against me.

RÉDA BENSMAIA[108]

We encounter our second monomaniac with head placed on the slab, facing his headsman in the form of what might be called an ego-syndicate. The entire world's populace are the unneeded; they glean whatever pares away from others' forlorn scalps. Nevertheless, the central link here between 'egoism' and 'the plan' betrays their inner weakness: namely, that the collective always represents itself through a kind of false hedonism, when in actuality the highly predictable nature of universalized ego renders it entirely devoid of pleasure. Rapture is the province of mania alone, attained through a precarious combination of obsessive vision and smooth adaptation. Sadism, conversely, is marred both by its ideological blindness and by its complete lack of spontaneity—and ego-becoming-world is (by definition) pure sadism. Moreover, the plot for all-encompassing identity is theoretically nothing more than an excuse for the ultra-personal (hollow individualism complementing itself with hollow universalism), whereas the richest effluxes always burst forth through impersonal experience (the

---

108 Bensmaia, *The Year of Passages*, 112.3.

casual brings casualties). What results, then, is a bitter war of hangmen: on the one side, the throng's unwieldy, joyless 'levelling'; on the other an unheeded loner with a capacity for extemporaneous sensation.

Aloneness and the plan; the entire world; egoism; the levelling

3

> *No steps, no traces [...] You truly are alone with yourself now. You fall into light, light and free. You test your silence and fragility. You have the power now to ask it, are you who you are?*
>
> ADONIS[109]

We encounter our third monomaniac having gone where none can follow, into states of semi-hibernation where solitude, contemplation, and self-awareness do not strengthen ontological unity but rather bring about a season of utmost fragility for Being. Here, the mind's brooding does not win the perfect prize of self-confirmation—'I think therefore I Am'—but instead descends into a state of silent imperfection. Far worse than the existential crisis that asks 'Who am I?', this untold aeon represents the more definitive, grave realization that 'I am someone other than who I think I am' and that therefore 'I misunderstand my own thought', or even 'My thoughts are not my own.' What kind of power can be drawn from these dangerous dissensions? If monomaniacal consciousness is itself this test of potential brokenness, under what specific circumstances is fragility a desirable quality? There must be some conditions of struggle, atrocity, or survival

---

109 Adonis, *Selected Poems*, 297.

in which weaker bases are more valuable than stronger ones, where the fractured soul fares better than the tightly bound one. Introspection, retrospection: philosophy for millennia, and psychoanalysis for centuries, have been anxiously obsessed with the presumed existential gravity of these acts (truth, trauma, subjectivity, metaphysics), whereas the counter-obsessive gaze of mania has found the sole exemption by which to turn them into pathways of the 'fallen into light, light and free' (illusion, forgetting, annihilation, chaos). In essence, manic aloneness is the place where one answers 'No' to the interior voice that wonders 'Are you who you are?' In fact, to become-monomaniacal is precisely to never again be what one is.

Once more, this is not a matter of repression, the unconscious, or the negated double, but rather the visionary effect of birthing the maniacal one: the one who goes where no others pursue, not even themselves, who calls forth great ruin, shattering identity and demanding more than can be given. Indeed, it is in the coves of manic solitude that one finally finds the one who asks too much. Hour of interrogation; hour of the Inquisitor.

Aloneness and the step; the trace; light;
freedom; the test; silence; fragility; power

4

I am myself
I am the enemy
Alone...

JOYCE MANSOUR[110]

We encounter our fourth monomaniac designating the lone 'I' as enemy, and actively seeking a method against the inability to destroy oneself (forever misfiring). Someone in her wants to kill; someone in her has to die. We might call this a confrontation with the Vehement (from Latin *vehementia*, meaning 'eagerness, strength', but stemming from the verb *vehere* meaning 'to carry'). A deadweight theory of ferocity, then: Does this mean that we carry the Vehement within for as long as possible, or does it in fact carry the self, until the knees buckle, the lower back breaks, and the self must be discarded, forever left behind? The superior; the obsolescent. Sacrifice of lesser fury.

Three lesser-heard pieces of trivia: (1) Certain parasitic plants from the Indonesian and Sumatran rainforests called *titan arum* and *rafflesia arnoldii*, also known as 'corpse flowers' for giving off the smell of rotten meat, have

110 Mansour, *Essential Poems and Writings*, 109.

the largest inflorescence in the world, though devoid of stems, leaves, or proper roots; (2) A black-magic superstition among tribal communities in Madagascar states that twin babies bring evil, so that parents are compelled to take these new-borns (representing bad luck, taboo, and familial affliction) out to the bush to die alone; (3) A widowed heiress to a firearms manufacturing fortune spent her entire later life compulsively building new floors and wings of a mansion in northern California, creating hidden closets, blind chimneys, disproportioned risers, double-back hallways, and staircases to nowhere in order to trap the ghosts of those supposedly killed by her husband's rifles. Three oddities that intersect in the monomaniacal figure of *the holoparasite*: a species obligated to undergo a parasitic phase in order to sustain its life cycle. In the first instance, the corpse flowers whose stench brings forth swarms of flies and other insects upon which it will subsist; in the second instance, the twins believed to practice witchcraft, gaining life at the expense of tribal doom; and in the third instance, the victimized phantoms whose afterlives consist in pursuing a parasitic torment of the living. Cadaverous flowers; accursed twins; gunwoman's ghosts. A new definition of the assailant, whose monomaniacal formulation began in the first paragraph's discord between two halved selves (leeching subject versus vehement supersessor): not that which destroys life, but that which drains life in order to live, and that which then enjoins madness to end the former's parasitic reign.

Aloneness and the enemy

5

I feel that the table is an unwanted barrier
between my hair and the hands
of this stranger.

FORUGH FARROKHZAD[111]

We encounter our fifth monomaniac siphoning her desire into the sole wish to be left alone with another; more precisely, an apparent desire for aloneness with a 'stranger'. Here the seemingly romantic principle of being-alone-together escapes its usual straightforward interpretation, for the other is no well-known intimate, but an unknown figure sitting across the table (Why are they there?). His intentions fall into a bottomless well of the undiscovered, the unheard, or the unidentified, and therefore his own desiring-configuration resembles something transoceanic in nature. But let it be fully understood: *she* is the enshrouder here (making others incognito); *she* is what grants him the allure of remoteness and potential touch (placing his hands upon her hair); and it is *she*, ultimately, who is the architect of the 'unwanted barrier' that prohibits consummation. Heartache is simply a poetic justification to bring consciousness into more segregated straits—for the stranger-companion is invoked

111 Farrokhzad, *A Lonely Woman*, 124.

to embody infatuation, and infatuation itself is a secret channel back to a loneliness measured in sea fathoms and nautical miles. She gauges the optimal distance at each turn, a carpentress of the dividing table and its seating arrangement: close enough for seductive attraction, far enough for seductive retraction, like the gradual ebbing of the tides. Such is the trickery by means of which one draws oneself into fatal depths.

Let us consider another elemental connection, via the rarely used term *obnubilation* (literally meaning 'to darken in cloud-like fashion'), which names an exclusive talent of the monomaniac: for it is in radical aloneness that one first learns to wilfully cloak oneself from something. The term also has an idiomatic counterpart in Arabic (*ja'alehu ghamidan*, meaning 'to becloud'), alongside countless other Arabo-Persian sub-typologies of obscurity, each with a special criteria for dimming worlds: *maghmoor* (sunken); *muzalam* (darkened); *mahjoob* (covered); *mob-hem* (hazy); *ma'atam* (dusky); *moltabas* (equivocal); *makhfi* (hidden, esoteric). To know exactly how to cloud, mystify, submerge, shadow, drape, haze, overcast, equivocate, or conceal a certain force at any given moment becomes a critical ability in the game of obsessive desire: once again, to project obscure air between oneself and the alluring object (in order to allow evacuation), a balancing-act of inclusions and preclusions that eventually brings one into the lattermost radius. For if some strands of monomania hold within them the dream of pure evaporation, then blindness is always the first key to mastering invisibility.

Aloneness and the unwanted; the barrier; the stranger

6

So you're the herdsman [...] *the one who's happier living in an empty desert than being with other people.*

But I can't live near anyone. That's what my grandfather taught me, and that's what I must teach you. All I want is peace. Do you understand?

IBRAHIM AL-KONI[112]

We encounter our sixth monomaniac drawing an equivalence between humankind and war, such that the ultimate peacemaker would live at an impervious distance from the rest. What is most striking here, however, is not this anti-humanist philosophical assertion itself but the tangible performative impact that we later discover it has on our herdsman and his few personal effects (those of guardianship). We must return to a historical dualism pertaining to the ancient shepherd, whose staff was an instrument of assistance (for walking) and unification (for herding) when alone or among innocent grazing animals, but would immediately become an instrument of violence upon the approach of a wolf or outsider human. The ancient implement bound together both care and the uncaring; it tapped lovingly across the valley stones

112 Al-Koni, *The Bleeding of the Stone*, 12, 21.

and warm flanks of goats or sheep, and just as easily bludgeoned the settler, raider, or warlord. An elegant monomaniacal principle: to be like the handheld possession or equipment, the shepherd's staff, simultaneously gracious and forbidding.

The grandfather's lesson above has a long tradition within both Eastern martial arts and Western aristocratic combat, for which decorative pieces or ceremonial garb would metamorphose into deadly armaments: the Shaolin forms that taught rural populations the potential of household items to stab, impale, and puncture (pipe, fan, flute, cup, hairpin); the European styles of aristocratic combat (cane-fighting), duels that would begin at the drop of a silk pocket handkerchief, accoutrements of sudden death appearing from within the formal attire of the gentleman.

Aloneness and the herdsman; emptiness; teaching; peace

7

I have tired from an agony not my own
I have sat upon an earth not my own
I have existed with a name not my own
I have wept from a pain not my own
I have extracted life from a pleasure not my own
I have entrusted life to a death not my own.

AHMAD SHAMLU[113]

We encounter our seventh monomaniac chanting a single cipher (from Arabic *sifr*, meaning 'zero'), itself a refrain (repetition) of one who refrains (abstention) that leads to the enigmatic zero-rung of Being. What does it mean to compulsively list every single facet of self-extrication, to make catalogues of all those things that are 'no longer' one's own? Not even the dearest, most intimate assets of individual experience are salvaged: neither pain, pleasure, death, nor first names. Monomania here takes us into a process of unsparing excision.

To whom do these indexed events belong once they have been rendered impersonal, though? Let us avoid the obvious assumption that 'not my own' indicates some oppressive commander who has appropriated the deeds to the author's ontological property, and instead consider

113 Shamlu, *Born Upon the Dark Spear*, 29.

a more throwaway possibility: What if this admission of lost custody implies that Being simply goes to waste? What if the subject's agony and earth just fall into the weeds, mislaid into a perpetual drift, henceforth belonging to no one (forever unclaimed)? If certain versions of monomaniacal thought lead to ascendancy, supremacy, and valorisation, then we can imagine others leading to the utmost worthlessness. The one who does not linger; the one who cannot be compensated.

At this point we should be less interested in the poet's own choral indifference and more captivated by the imaginative influence that this washing-of-the-hands-of-self might yield for others yet to follow (who could vouch for the neglected chests). Indeed, what happens when we etymologically and conceptually disentangle legacy (image, story) from legitimacy (truth) and legality (law)? Open rights to existential piracy; no proper heir. When there is no longer ownership, do we enter a free harbour of invention, fabrication, and unscripted narration about the one who desisted from all subjective control? Could anything now conceivably be said about this figure? Could successors emblazon whatever aspects they wish upon their forerunner's brow? Weirdly, is it not precisely those most divested of any stake in life (the prophet, the rebel, the martyr, the warrior, the monk) that have the most extraordinary stories told about them in the aftermath? For so many years after their deaths the people still dream, project, and credit everything to the one who had wanted nothing. Hence the conceptual link is established between becoming-zero and becoming-cipher.[114]

Aloneness and the unowned

114 A small dose of practical (non)reality: this poet himself, despite the clear attempt to dissociate himself above, is commonly considered a populist and societal champion within his official country of origin. His monomaniacal requital against the life that had been arbitrarily assigned as his property would only fuel the drive of others to seize upon his image, making the one 'not of my own' into 'one of their own'.

8

> *But the night would have been less dark and the roaring of the bombs less fearsome for both of us if we'd been able to hold hands. After all, in an earthquake even wild animals huddle close together. To die communally, as it were, is less terrifying than to die as a solitary individual. He who dies alone dies twice: first because he's alone and then again because...he's died!*
>
> GHADA SAMMAN[115]

We encounter our eighth monomaniac reflecting upon the aloneness to be found in death itself. If another Eastern writer herein reminds us that to die alone beneath a tree somewhere is worse than a death in the operating room, precisely because in the latter case one sees that everyone fights urgently to save them while in the former case one feels at once left-behind and singled-out by the whole world, then we must understand monomania as the most refined intuition of this simultaneous sense of betrayal and election at the moment of death—a tension between the god-sent and the godforsaken.

Still, two peculiar things happen in mania's confrontation with mortal solitude. Firstly, a hallucination of the ideal death-mate, the image of a potential consort offering

115 Samman, *Beirut Nightmares*, 41.

warmth, for mania renders the imagination excessively productive, and the imaginative prospect of holding hands is what gets her through the visceral 'roaring of bombs' and the metaphorical 'earthquake'. It is precisely because she obsessively watches over this lonely death that she does not die (only *he* dies alone; she continually lives within his death), a survival mechanism based on the strength to be located in trembling and in tremulous vision.

The second occurrence is something harsher, for here monomaniacal experience transitions into a 'loneliness that knew no bounds, a loneliness that mingled with the sounds of the bombs that threatened me with every passing moment'.[116] Let us pay close attention to the term 'mingled', for it suggests a kind of morbid telepathy: one can no longer tell oneself apart from the military arsenal; one *becomes* the very explosion that shatters one's form, the very knife that sinks inward. Yes, she has paid enough of a price to gain the rudiments of a fatality *savant*: one inclined to think death itself, to think *as* death itself, to inhabit the death that walks and to sense its metallic caches, or even, more precisely, to step into the dying.

Aloneness and the night; the fearsome; holding; huddling; communality; the dying alone

116 Ibid., 116.

9

Do not believe me if I return and I return not.
I was neither living nor dead.
Only you—you were alone, the utmost lonely one.

MAHMOUD DARWISH[117]

We encounter our ninth monomaniac in both the interim (suspension of time) and the interregnum (suspension of power), which requires that we allow mania to redefine the very experience of *the meanwhile*. If another Western philosopher reminds us that we only conceptualize time as something passing, without ever reflecting on the fact that time also always arises, then we must understand monomania as the most refined intuition of this risen temporality. Essentially, the end is generous; the end comes to us, and it comes precisely 'in time' (this is more than a mere expression).

So what does it mean to warn the loneliest one to 'not believe me if I return and I return not'? He is the clockmaker (he lives between the ticking hands); he is the rainmaker (he lives between the falling droplets). The monomaniacal meanwhile is that which disbands all dialectical-messianic categories of returning and non-returning, every living or dead god—for to be the

---

117 Darwish, *Unfortunately, It Was Paradise*, 144.

monomaniacal figure is to never quite be gone, while always remaining the only one and the most alone. When will you find us? In the meantime. When will you abandon us? In the meantime. This is how time rises, uplifted in pure division.

Aloneness and the return; the non-return;
the neither living nor dead; the utmost

10

> *I was happy in my seclusion, with the gifts of the forest, oblivious to the world of humans. I would drink wine, in moderation. But the disaster was that none of the creams with which I covered my face and body deterred the mosquito attacks. And how could I relax when a swarm of them was hovering over my head all day long like Christ's halo in those old paintings?*
>
> HASSAN BLASIM[118]

We encounter our tenth monomaniac cheated of self-fulfilment at the very last moment; he is *the ascetic*, but also an intermittent user of the flask, drinking wine and allowing other 'moderate' indulgences, and ready to reach contentment amid the 'gifts of the forest' were it not for a single invading presence. Thus we find ourselves at the instant when monomania reaches its combustible limit (it is never alone enough). He proceeds beyond misanthropic ire, accusing other species; all sound becomes intrusive; all movement is uninvited. Paranoiac-irritative sentiment expands almost orchestrally: from an initial questioning of other subjects (suspicion against the lover, the boss, the child, the simple neighbour), it then widens to include the object-world (suspicion against insects,

118 Blasim, *Iraqi Christ*, 50.

stones, flowers, wooden walls), and then widens further to include the phenomenal world (suspicion against wind, dust, flame, dripping water) and the sensorial world (suspicion against sounds, sights, tastes, aromas, and all forms of touch), and then widens further to include the absent world (suspicion against beings not there, spectres, the dead, imaginary companions) and the cosmological world (suspicion against gods, prophets, demons, guardian angels).

In another short story, the same author writes that 'they are all killers and schemers' and that he has proof of their 'connivance and vile nature'.[119] The charge is now levied against everything that is or could be. We have seen similar behaviours and attitudes before, but here radical aloneness seeks an even more concentrated atmospheric home; it demands a theatre of operations that is closer to the *anechoic chamber* or *sensory deprivation tank*. The anechoic chamber is a space designed to allow no reverberant sound or electromagnetic waves, absorbing all vibrations, interfering energies, and signals. The sensory deprivation tank is a soundproof, lightless capsule where one rests floating in salt water of skin temperature. The sable; the ebony. But what if the higher goal would be to allow monomania to spin paranoiac thought so voraciously that it would lead to a non-euphonious mode

119 Blasim, *The Madman of Freedom Square*, 11.

of perception itself: that is, without aid from tanks or chambers, to be capable of shutting off the lights of Being, dampening and deafening both self and world to the extent of achieving a living oblivion? What would it take to become the creature that, upon closing its eyes, would close the eyes of all existence?

Note: While we engage with a very specific idea of paranoia here, we continue to resist psychoanalytical compartmentalization. Firstly, psychoanalysis would almost certainly place mania and paranoia in entirely separate spheres, never wondering what alchemical combinations might emerge from their alloy, and never locating the missing link between them in solitude. Secondly, this paranoiac reaction does not proceed from the centralized psyche of a paranoid subject, but rather takes the shape of an ever-spreading inkblot of thought that begrimes both interiorities and exteriorities in like fashion. And thirdly, this paranoia, strangely enough, is not based in persecutory anxiety but rather unlocks the ecstatic dimension of both fear and hate. It discovers a relish in universal conspiracy, a conspiracy-unto-delirium that 'I' too join in my loneliest hours, such that the radically-separate 'I' becomes nothing less than a worldwide 'connivance' (and the wonderful darkness therein).

Aloneness and happiness; the gift; obliviousness; moderation; disaster; deterrence; the swarm

Isolomania (Isolation)

1

> *I withdrew from the company of man, from the company of the stupid and the successful and, in order to forget, took refuge in wine and opium. My life passed, and still passes, within the four walls of my room.*
>
> SADEQ HEDAYAT[120]

Our first isolomaniac manifests an overpowering attachment to the concept of *the shelter*—not the place where nothing happens, but the place where the Nothing happens. Notice, however, that that the Nothing must be induced by something: hence the need to be stimulated by agents such as wine and opium. The four walls form a workshop (complete with the appropriate instruments), and with it the desire to let nothingness do its work.

In a later scene, two elderly men—twin brothers, the narrator's uncle and father—step into a locked temple room where a cobra awaits them. Theirs is a trial to the death: one is bitten, screams, and expires; the other emerges from the temple quarters with white hair, a blank inattentive gaze, no personal memory, no temporal

120 Hedayat, *The Blind Owl*, 5.

recognition, and loss of all visual-spatial understanding. Note that these accurately outlined symptoms are those of *dementia* (from the Latin 'out of mind') or the Arabo-Persian *zawal-e aghl* ('declension of mind'), two terms revealing two distinct approaches to the damaged mind's orientation: outward or downward. We will return to this question of directionality below; for now let us note that this event was systematically caused by the experience of a certain shelter (the cobra-room), and thus we are speaking of an author's procession toward willed dementia through isolation—not some gradual, progressive decline accompanying old age or brain trauma, but a specified sequence of acts or situations within space concocted deliberately to generate an inescapable mindlessness.

Implicit in the two distinct etymologies of declension and outlying, then, are also distinct tactics of exhaustion: to run down or to run aground; to drown mind in deep or shallow waters, either taking reason too low (to the point where it overdoses) or too far (to the point where it starves). Whereas meditative practice seeks a clearing away of mind (a pact with emptiness), becoming-demented is a ritual of over-engagement (a pact with excess) one way or the other, whether vertically submerged or horizontally distended. The sea or the desert. In language, we could see this as the difference between using repetition and nonsense: the first technique (a subduing of mind) is a path of degeneration, deterioration, and dissolution wherein the incessant saying of the same thing over and over eventually forges a heavy, strangling chain (like the dragon devouring its own tail); the second technique (a driving out-of-mind) is a path of the rattled, the aghast, and the thunderstruck, wherein the speaking of unlike meaningless exclamations leads one to insensibility and self-muttering (like the hyena laughing to itself). The sinkhole and the loose thread. Either way we approach an essential raggedness.

But what if our narrator does both? That is, what if he repeats nonsense with the strictest compulsive circling, both abusing and overextending rational energies, and thereby making consciousness choke on itself (saturation) while also dragging it into the place it cannot go (confusion)? The shelter is the site that combines vertical and horizontal erasure, its isolomaniacal air providing the connective stage for a mental reunion between father, uncle, and mind-losing narrator. The anniversary of a falling-off and a going-away.

Isolation and withdrawal; forgetting; refuge; wine; opium; passing; the room

2

> *I've blocked a door with piles of paper, going out of the house isn't a solution, breathing the air outside isn't a solution either. I've cordoned off the front door with yellow police tape...*
>
> RÉDA BENSMAIA[121]

We encounter our second isolomaniac dabbling with isolation's relation to the concepts of *the barricade* and *the crime*. When confronting the barricade, we are struck first and foremost by the architectonics of stacking: all items become preventative forces; all solidity becomes obstructive hardness. The sentimental universe of the room, with all of its collected objects each with their separate meanings, now takes on a single unified function: to form an impenetrable obstacle. They are no longer psychologically or emotively valued, but are arranged only in terms of respective height, mass, shape, jaggedness, movability and immovability, and thus stripped down to a lone question: Can they hold back the menacing outside? A fence of desperate insularity.

But what is the crime whose commission is betrayed by the clue of the yellow police tape? Perhaps we can infer from the other tell-tale sign of the piled paper that

---

121 Bensmaia, *The Year of Passages*, 90.1.

the criminal act is associated with writing itself—which would place us within the isolomaniacal province of three clandestine literary genres associated with totalitarian societies: the *samizdat* (Russian, literally 'self-publishing house'), referring to the secret reproduction and circulation of underground publications; the *tamizdat* (literally 'published there'), referring to the international exporting and distribution of outlawed works among émigré circles abroad; and *literatura yaschika* (literally 'writing for the drawer'), referring to 'delayed literatures' wherein subversive manuscripts were stored and not brought to public light until many years or decades after their original formulation. These textual products were considered either too ideologically antagonistic, morally obscene, or aesthetically unacceptable by the state's standards, and also often corresponded to three specific political-cultural destinies: the internal revolution (*samizdat*); the external revolution (*tamizdat*); and the untimely or futural revolution (*yashchika*). An unexpected conceptual tissue between isolation (the most disjointed) and revolution (the most encompassing).

Still, what captivates us even more than the inner content of this isolomaniacal writing-act is the inception of a new visual appearance linked with the banned, smuggled, or punishable book. Several exhibitions and museum displays throughout the world now showcase the samizdat's yellowed frayed pages, its smudged ink, typographical errors, inconspicuous bindings, false covers, and cheap carbon paper, the optical cues of a cloak-and-dagger world of thought and a lingering hope that the keys to the kingdom could be stolen from within a dark room.

Moreover, the samizdat's release is almost always accompanied by a notable authoritarian twist: the regime's own censors are naturally those most well-acquainted with these subterranean monographs, for they require such intimate knowledge in order to effectively prosecute the offending authors. This exposure however often leads to an ideological rupture among the government professionals themselves (the phenomenon called 'dual consciousness'). Hence the counter-intelligentsia finds an ironic audience among the intelligence officials themselves, its contraband information moving influentially through the information ministries (torturer becoming reader). Makeshift imprints housed, in some instances by the millions, in *spetskhran* (Russian, 'restricted access collections'), command increasing loyalty among those sworn to censorship, surveillance, and even fatal suppression.

And yet there is another approach to negotiating an isolationist textuality, one that takes the shape of a literary flurry or landslide that conceals writing through writing. Imagine an author who writes seven books as a distractive screen to hide an eighth. This eighth work would be the isolated primer meant to be read either by none, by only one, or by a select audience of a few (each implying very different consequences). In a similar vein, some thinkers have speculated on those rare books that were never even written, introducing us to an elusive breed: the failed artist, the (non)author who has chosen otherwise, electing for the active passivity of saying no to writing itself, denying the potential fruition of their vision for whatever reason (distaste, circumstance, laziness). Those who interpret these unfulfilled, called-off pieces make a strong case for the idea that, rather than simply disappearing into non-existence, they form a sub-archive that steers the very course of the literary future. Another unexpected conceptual tissue between isolation (the most careless) and the forthcoming (the most cared about).

A revered Eastern mystic once said that he had spent his entire life banging on the doors of insanity only one day to realize that he was knocking from the inside. We must also ask ourselves on what side of the door we belong, in respect to the criminal work of the samizdat suggested in the above passage. Are we the intended secret audience, or are we the secret police crashing down the front doors of dissidents?

Isolation and blocking; piles; paper; solution; cordoning; the front door

3

We meet no more.
Denial and exile separate us.
Promises have died.
Space is irrelevant.
Death becomes our only point of contact.

ADONIS[122]

Our third isolomaniac offers a renovation of the concept of *the promise*, or more particularly the death of the promise, which then promptly brings about a condition of *vilification*. For what does it take to deny ever having known the other? The above verse epitomizes the final farewell, which will hold until the impending instant of finality itself (thus 'death becomes our only point of contact'). The opposite of the marriage ceremony's 'until death do us part' is the vilification ceremony's 'until death brings us back together'— invariably meaning a cruel, imposed death, itself a last promise that comes to seal or crown what went unpromisingly before. Remember, after all, that this is the same poet who once wrote 'And I love Golgotha' (literally 'place of the skull').[123]

---

122 Adonis, *The Pages of Day and Night*, 92.

123 Adonis, *Victims of a Map*, 99.

For what reason does one break vows, and at what moment does the oath no longer pertain? Often when the other party fails to uphold their side of the bargain (in cases of mutual promising) or when the pledged-to object is compromised beyond hope (in cases of failed protection). Nevertheless, a little-mentioned third factor rests upon the extent to which said promise is founded upon metaphysical, subjective, or social-psychological obligations. These are in fact the most uncertain criteria of affirmation, but let us start with this first critical recognition: society does not have actual rules; nor does religion; nor does Being itself; these discourses flaunt the ideological pretence and appearance of effective rules, but there are no true rules in the alley when the adversary slinks out from some corner; the rules are imposed only later, when supposed heavenly judges, political authorities, or nagging voices of conscience arrive in the aftermath to clean up the blood spilt. Enforcement rarely takes place in real time; it is a cover-up negation and retributive restoration of false order that always occurs too late.

Historically, the promise has been romanticized as belonging to the province of idealism; it is assumed that the most emotionally devoted figures are the best keepers of promises (the lover, the soldier, the prophet). But these are actually weak bonds based in transcendent loyalties that fracture far too easily: the lover's desire wanders and he breaks his promise to the beloved; the soldier falls into traumatic fear on the battlefield and breaks his promise to the nation; the missionary and even the prophet momentarily lose their faith and break their promise to God. No, these idealistic types are in fact the most unreliable regarding their word.

Accordingly, it is necessary to consider exactly the opposite proposition: namely, that radical coldness (ice in the veins) is the strongest guarantor of the promise. And doesn't our poetic author cited above embody a parallel iteration of *the hitman*?[124] The hitman, who needs no explanation, only directions; the hitman, who feels nothing for their target, guided only by unfeeling contractual duty; the hitman, who fears nothing because they recognize themselves as already owned by death; the hitman, who desires nothing and expects nothing, demanding only the agreed payment; the hitman, who respects no moral structure, yet follows an iron code precisely under the auspices of indifference. These are the most unwavering: the least romantic, the least idealistic, the least attached or believing (leaving no reason for hesitation). No, they do what they say (though such experts in fact speak the least); they pull the trigger; they come through; they are incapable of psychological crisis, because from the very

---

124 In past works—*Insurgent, Poet, Mystic, Sectarian: The Four Masks of an Eastern Postmodernism* (New York: SUNY Press, 2015) and *Inflictions: The Writing of Violence in the Middle East* (London: Continuum, 2012)—one finds developed philosophies of the mercenary and the assassin.

outset they are not psychological creatures (it is not about them; it is about what must be done). Ironically, their occupational isolomania grants them inhuman levels of trustworthiness. Stated otherwise, the only professions to be trusted are those of the professional.

Note: Those paying close attention will notice that a certain famous Western philosopher's theorization of the figure of Abraham is actually nothing short of a hitman's profile. Whereas almost all of the biblical monotheistic God's other devotees betray him (Satan's pride, Adam and Eve's transgressive curiosity, Cain's rage), or at least show crucial moments of weakness and doubt (Moses's frustration toward the stone, Christ's questioning of his abandonment upon the cross), Abraham abides by insane divine commands with metallic consistency. He is quite literally God's assassin (deployed to kill the son), but existentially he is also fully steeped in the assassin's non-psychological, non-transcendent, amoral mentality. He does as he is told: a stark principle, but one he upholds to the maximal limit. This perhaps allows us to contravene older archetypes with a different definition of faith, one too humble for aspirations of religious belief but rather disposed to a far barer notion of the word. The promise is made not to higher powers (the divine source is irrelevant); rather, it is made to the immediate power of an action undertaken. The price is agreed upon; the deadline is set; and the hitman's world is maintained in its spiritless harmony. We therefore stare into the face of the coldest lunacy, a mania for the command-in-isolation. There is no abstract complexity here; we must marvel at the simplicity of its lines. 'Knight of Faith' means nothing more than 'he who gets things done'. Perhaps in a similar register, Job too exemplifies this practicality of the mere practitioner: that is, the one who does what he is supposed to, keeps his mouth shut, sticks to the job at hand, serves his warrants, and ultimately recognizes the hitman's nature in God himself. Loyalty to the stated deed; risking vilification in order to keep the deathly promise (of the end of all promises). And he is rewarded above all others in the tales; he too collects his purse in the end.

Isolation and non-meeting; denial;
the promise; irrelevance; death; the contact-point

4

The walls rise up
Have pity on us, God of our fathers, we who are damned
The brown walls of despair circle our heads, our skies, our homes
Spare us the anger of envious men

Death to spirals
Death to the weak
Death to those who frequent the uterus
Death to those who stand isolated

JOYCE MANSOUR[125]

We encounter our fourth isolomaniac composing a poetic helix out of the concept of *damnation*. For damnation creates irreconcilable separation; it is the ultimatum, the final word spoken at the border between relation and the unrelated. It is therefore the genre of isolation itself, operating not by moving oneself away but by forcibly moving others away, in an onslaught that casts them out to an ungraspable distance.

Much can be said regarding the first passage's walls, pity, anger, and envy; equally, much can be said about the second passage, and why it is spirals, the weak, and

125 Mansour, *Essential Poems and Writings*, 115, 279.

womb-goers become the objects of the author's death-wishes; but our more immediate purposes draw us to the last line—'Death to those who stand isolated'—to ask what specific stylistic components constitute a damning writing-act. And what does it mean to speak of a mania for damnation? Initially, however, we must observe that the technical construction of damnation requires a continually-loudening and far-reaching language, its proclamations forming spires ('circle our heads, our skies'), for which the cancelling momentum grows ever more inclusive (to damn one thing is to damn the adjacent, and then onward). Hence, if the first passage exemplifies the voice of the damned, in the second passage the authorial voice has learned the active tongue of the damning. And the latter must be tonally the exact opposite of the former: it must be without pity, envy, or despair. This is where writing can be described as *the bedevilled*, for good only abstractly arbitrates damnation, whereas evil coordinates the very instrumental practice of provocation, facilitation, and accompaniment toward damnation. This is why evil, in most mythological-theological traditions, also takes responsibility for eternally housing the damned, for interestingly, like our poetess above, it occupies both what is itself most damned and what rains damnation upon the world.

Isolation and the walls; pity; damnation; despair; anger; envy; spirals; weakness; the uterus; standing

5

O God, who knows what I did
in that dark and quiet seclusion?

FORUGH FARROKHZAD[126]

We encounter our fifth isolomaniac in the midst of a dramatic conceptual redefinition of *angst*: a single unthinkable gesture fastens her to the moaning of the divine name (becoming conversant with the ultimate). She calls God forth to survey the profane height, and even to answer for what escapes her (some act committed in 'dark and quiet seclusion') not in a gesture of self-shaming or evasion, but in gleeful incredulity at her own hands and their unaccounted potential for the impassioned offence. She petitions the Creator to bestow a new title upon her ardent, sultry feat; she waits anxiously for a denomination of aphrodisiac quality. Without malaise, trepidation, worry; instead, here angst is the disquiet of the seventh heaven (delectation, ferment, pyrexia). Where philosophy has long been harassed by a thinking of this ponderous experience as existential neurosis, in one quick movement our poetic figure cures us, allowing us to fathom a mode of angst-as-bliss. Let us start with the subtle manner in which this is performed: namely, by reframing the acute

126 Farrokhzad, *A Lonely Woman*, 77.

view of Being not as state but as action, such that the central question becomes no longer 'Who am I?' but rather 'What am I doing?' This swift manoeuvre takes us down a slippery track between *erotomania* (mad love) and *erotetotmania* (mad questioning)—just as the classical Persian lover is always *Majnoon* (the lunatic) infinitely begging for updated reports on the beloved's activity. The delirium in unknowing; this is the correct identification of wonder as an accolade, not a depressive lever. Angst can thereby take on a manic flavour—this is why, at the height of their pondering over an unknowable existence, Persian mystics and sensualists drink and compose wine-songs. It is a celebration of perplexity; one toasts the primeval riddle, a banquet in honour of the prevaricating everything, the totality-that-knows-not-what-it-does. It is a feast best shared alone: angst thus raises its glass in isolation.

Isolation and God; unknowing; the doing; darkness; quiet; seclusion

6

His mother would be on her own now, until the day she was finally devoured by wolves [...] *She too would pay the price of solitude. The price of freedom. The price of living apart from people and their malice.*

It's a thing like thirst, like hunger, like life in the wilderness; it's the fate of isolation, the fate of the desert. God has set a price on everything.

IBRAHIM AL-KONI [127]

We encounter our sixth isolomaniac pursuing a conceptual reciprocity between isolation and *the price*. The willingness to satisfy this set price is what determines who is to become *eligible*, and who *ineligible*—which is to say that isolation establishes its own hierarchical structure of exclusivity. The mother will make her payments to the many phenomena of solitariness around her (thirst, hunger, God, desert); this is the toll of keeping company with a natural domain that continually pulls away from human presence, for elsewhere the author tells us that 'Nature is by instinct a hermit'[128] and 'The Sea only talks to strangers'.[129] The elemental world instinctually retreats

127 Al-Koni, *The Bleeding of the Stone*, 56, 35.

128 Al-Koni, *A Sleepless Eye*, 6.

129 Ibid., 59.

and at the same time communes with those who mirror its estranged patterns. If mere Being is neither free nor unconditional, becoming-isolated proves a far more expensive proposition (its cost measured in blood, flesh, and displeasure).

These statements remind us of an obscure work by a Western author who demarcates the layers of a highly isolomaniacal 'Land of Magic'.[130] The first thing we learn is that its landscape is surrounded by buoys made of dead bodies, and that they ring alarms to warn of trespassers, so that the Magi can then lead them away. From this we might first wonder whether the cadaverous bobbing signals are themselves former trespassers; but more substantially, we could deduce a certain hypothetical scenario wherein every interrupted train of thought in life, every room entered only to forget the initial objective, was not simply some kind of random lapse or distraction, but rather the result of the Magis' concerted effort to throw us off track. Which would mean, necessarily, that such instances of the slipping mind were in fact most significant proof that we were onto something close to the magical, upon which we would no longer surrender these disjunctive incidents to absent-mindedness (the dismissive 'What was I saying?')

130 H. Michaux, 'In the Land of Magic', in *Darkness Moves: An Henri Michaux Anthology, 1927–1984*, tr. D. Ball (Berkeley, CA: University of California Press, 1997). The following fragments are in reference to this work.

but instead insist compulsively upon their retrieval, fighting against the artificial confusion sent by shamans.

Secondly, we learn of spontaneous waves that sometimes occur across random highways, runaway forces that no longer possess any connection to their oceanic origin. This is apparently a kind of magical ricochet of energy discharged from some magus's spell. So how might it change the cast of consciousness to consider the entire sphere of accident as a by-product of leaked magic? Someone breaks a tibia bone; another's house burns down; another smiles for no reason. What if all seemingly accidental events were the tangential offshoots of otherwise precise, willed acts of sorcery? Would the horrific death of a loved one then impel us to discover the unrelated intent of the spell, to at least confirm whether they were lost to some vain prestidigitation or to a truly worthwhile cause?

Thirdly, we learn that the magical disciple's first trick is to split himself so as to walk across two riverbanks simultaneously; we are warned not to break his concentration and bring upon him the shame of reunification. We are told this with an ominous hint that a penalty will be payable, as later we meet the executioner magus who rips offenders' faces off their bodies (this being an intricate, difficult spell in itself).

Fourthly, we read a fragment pertaining to those magical practitioners who can see fatalistic doors open (appearing beneath the water), and who can thereby outline the entire course of an individual's day from one happening to another. This power, admittedly, derives from an isolomaniacal portion of thought and has been treated before in a thousand synopses of those figures referred to as a medium. But would one actually want to know the things that could have been during the day's affairs, once these possibilities had already expired—a kind of enhanced retrospective vision or hindsight? Wouldn't this likely produce a grievous compulsion to dwell over what might have been improved at every single crossroads of those moments, a neurotic search for the ideally lived twenty-four hours? And what happens when one learns that most attempts to replicate those lost opportunities would invariably fail, or rather that the fateful encounter on the third day of the week would not translate into the same results if staged on the following day (even at the same time and place)? Beyond this, we might imagine another intuitive-perceptual ability to see forward, but only into the extreme distance (glimpses of what will occur decades later), such that the chain of events leading to the envisioned result would be difficult to discern or influence.

Lastly, we are told that each magus possesses a limited quantity of folds over their lives, and that these folds correspond to various periods or conceptual identities into which one enters over the years (death therefore marking the culmination of the final fold). This is an isolomaniacal definition of time that explains why mystical and magical circles are almost always led by well-aged elders, for the countdown effect of being conscious of such precise finitude (i.e., the knowledge that one will die instantly upon exhausting the twenty-second fold) leads to an existential trajectory of ever-elevating complexity. More exactly, with time one would stay longer in the various stitches, savouring each crease-like juncture, demanding only the richest grooves as finale. This is what the elder's wisdom means: an increasing attunement to honing the most bountiful stages as the end approaches, aware of the vaporescence of experiential passages and hence the need to sculpt them each with the greatest of magical acuity (as if fighting for air). This is the price, to return to our original paragraph's content; this is how one wins eligibility.

Isolation and devouring; payment; the price;
freedom; malice; thirst; hunger; fate; God; everything

7

and an isolation
that with heaviness
like a cane-holding elder
passes through
the corridor of silence.

To subside upon the sharp edges of self-respect
and to plunge beneath from the pure-hearted honor of isolation
with a scream of terror before every downfall.

AHMAD SHAMLU[131]

We encounter our seventh isolomaniac in mid-oscillation between the seemingly opposing concepts of *silence* and *screaming*. The first dimension perhaps signifies what another Western philosopher already called absolute solitude—i.e., to be so alone that one is no longer even alone with oneself, thus inaugurating a period of unbreakable silence—but the second dimension (that of the scream) takes us into phases addressed only by the Eastern philosopher-poet's complicated equation of honour and terror. Is it in profound isolation alone that one realizes pure terror as the most honourable position before existence?

131 Shamlu, *Born Upon the Dark Spear*, 33, 63.

The image of the cane-holding elder and his slow-trodden steps through silence-filled corridors appears to mirror a Sisyphean stride (always in 'heaviness'), and yet the later movement over the 'sharp edges of self-respect' appears to mirror the mad trial of Prometheus (always before 'downfall'). Thus it is no coincidence that this same author, in another work, names these two mythical figures together, though casting a staunch existential division that disowns Sisyphus (as death-cheater) and instead claims Prometheus's tragic-heroic line (as fire-stealer). Both are recipients of eternal punishment, both are tormented by massive boulders, and yet our poetic voice repetitively paints only the awful scene of the latter: the Titan's naked body, wrists and loins chained to rock, and the jinxed eagle who feeds upon his exposed divine liver at each daybreak. No doubt the kindred tie between contemporary poet and condemned ancient god is flagrant, for we must remember that this particular author's literary foundry is the torture chamber; hence, both are guided by the same philosophical principle of dual isolation whereby a single creative act is equated with tearing oneself away from all else, and following this creative separation both accept the appropriate lived symbolism, the punishment of being physically ripped apart for ages thereafter.

While it is perhaps important to identify the reason for the cosmic gifting of the secret—for it matters in the story of human ambition whether fire was lawlessly trafficked out of love for the human race, or pity, or simply out of an entirely indifferent inclination to defy the other gods—it is even more pressing to detect how, amid this double isolation (the creative and the vengeful), some transitional rationale advances from silence to screaming. This speculation leads us to a potential theory of *ingratitude toward the benefactor*, for there is little historical evidence of a single thriving Promethean cult in the ancient world, and only scattered traces of a shrine, prayer dedication, or ritual practice to venerate the one who delivered survival. Nothing at all to acknowledge the manic kindness that enabled such otherworldly theft. Does he scream, then, at the thought of the infinitely unappreciative humans who continually warm themselves around his offering while remaining dumb as he dies shivering night after night, only to release successive generations of similarly thoughtless traitors to follow? Is it the thankless aftermath of the event, the disrespected risk of trading miracles beneath closed skies, that raises outcry? And does this same insult—their obliviousness, their greed, their uncredited technologies and their delusional progress before the original Promethean will—not then form a third isolation (between the decentred one and the self-centred many)? While the struggle is borne in silence, the offense is met with unbearable sound. Treachery; disbelief; howl.

Our rebel poet's isolomaniacal experience corresponds well to this same nexus of honour and terror through which creative generosity is turned into a banquet for birds of prey or prison guards: few tales tell of humans venturing to save their saviours, whether the latter are slung up on hot granite or thrown down across cold cell floors. Everyday arrogance can never perceive eternal benevolence, and almost none remember to bow their heads to those superiors who gave everything, who liberated worlds, and were disappeared for their troubles. But then, would the isolomaniacal subject be precisely that rare one who perceives human existence as mere stolen chance, a violation of the intended law by a brave scapegoated exceptional, and thus seeks to free the criminal god from their universal banishment?

Isolation and heaviness; the elder; the corridor; silence; subsidence, the edge; respect; plunging; honour; screaming; terror; downfall

8

My brother and I didn't exchange any conversation. It was as if the sound of bullets flying through the air had rendered language ineffectual, or had created some sort of insulating wall, increasing each person's awareness of his individuality and isolation, an isolation in which each of us had fallen into his own personal well...

GHADA SAMMAN[132]

We encounter our eighth isolomaniac inciting/enduring a new conceptualization of *the anti-social*. She stands on the outskirts of society's failure, witness to the collapse of its unifying dream (the mask) into its underlying horror-show of conflict (the face). The social has always been genocidal, at all institutional registers and in every facet of its coerced bonding order (house, school, temple, economy, state), all the while fooling itself that its chronic malignant experiment will work better next time. History, in this regard, is pure debacle, overestimation, and anti-climax; it is a neurotic repetition-compulsion from whose futile bias only an isolomaniacal break could undo consciousness. Thus the catastrophic setting of the above passage hatches an emergency useful for demonstrating the uselessness of the social effort, slitting once-sacred

---

132 Samman, *Beirut Nightmares*, 9.

loyalties down even to their most core myths of identification: No kinship left; even the brother turns stranger; language crumbles into perfect incommunicability; there is nothing more to be said across genetic pools and traits. The 'personal well' into which each hostage descends is therefore the very eradication of personhood as a relational, communal, or universal paradigm; it reflects what exists on the other side of society's rendered impossibility, a near-apocalyptic predicament both more powerful and powerless than even monadic awareness, for it is won only amid the conclusive perpetration of the disaster of the last human exercise (to never try again).

Isolation and exchange; language; individuality; the well

9

In vain you drive us from journey to journey.
You have tossed us away from our kin,
from our water and air, and you have ruined us.
You have emptied the sunset of sunset.
You've robbed us of our first words
and looted the peach tree of our days.
You have stripped us of our days.

MAHMOUD DARWISH[133]

We encounter our ninth isolomaniac protesting against *unrighteous time*, in a poetic invective against the enemy who has isolated them from their own destined selves. What remains is what was not supposed to exist (the very definition of monstrosity): the turned-into-something-else; the what-have-I-become? Hence the immediate cause of isolation here is a vainly consuming injustice, that of the unrighteous theft of rightful time ('our days'), for it hollows out possibility itself, stealing the interior of all possible experience ('emptied the sunset of sunset'). The violation goes even farther, however, when it rips into the essential past and scrapes out at once the lineal sense ('away from our kin'), the inceptive sense ('our first words'), and the elemental sense ('our water and air').

133 Darwish, *Unfortunately, It Was Paradise*, 41.

The result is something akin to the optical illusion of infinite reflection caused by two opposite-facing mirrors, or the bizarre undulation in the chest felt by backgammon players and other dice-throwers who instantly know their ideal number and then instantly lament its non-occurrence when other numbers surface. Breathlessness; suspense; abrupt stunting of the expected/the expectant by the likelihood/unlikeliness of a loose flick of the wrist. Thus anticipation and deflation are separated temporally-spatially by the slim duration of a single roll, the roll of isolomaniacal extraction, itself always accompanied by a gambler's hyper-consciousness of the high-low that chisels, wrings, and scores one into what 'ruined us'.

Isolation and vanity; being-driven;
kind, water, air; ruin; sunset; robbery; looting; stripping; the days

10

> *Many people burst out laughing when they heard the insults which my father's imagination came up with, but they soon began to keep away from him and ask God for forgiveness. Some of them avoided meeting him in the street. One of them told him in jest one day that he hoped a truck loaded with steel would run him over, but everyone was frightened of his connection with the government.*
>
> HASSAN BLASIM[134]

We encounter our tenth isolomaniac back in the story of the mad father-composer, he of the rough stylistics belabouring the base materiality of the prophetic, the angelic, the messianic, and the divine. He is not the wandering mystic relying on the kindness of strangers; he is not the atheist intellectual burned at the stake; he is the composer behind closed doors who wrests divinity into bodily capsulations; he is the walking eyesore of the city's everydayness, improvising scandalous scenes for the main characters of a supposedly inviolable history, entering the sacred cave of revelation to bounce too-revealing echoes off its stalactite walls. And on account of this unblessed artistry of disgrace, so we learn two things: (1) they all wish him dead; (2) they all fear him.

---

134 Blasim, *The Madman of Freedom Square*, 22.

In this respect, he resembles the Japanese supernatural fox *kitsune*, a miraculous entity that grows as many as nine tails over the course of the centuries it lives, its hair turning white or gold as it gains the ability to shape-shift into human form (often appearing alone as an enchanting woman or old man), to weave elaborate illusions, and to omnisciently see and hear all ongoing movements within the world. One is warned in folk tales to avoid this figure, to look away from its hypnotic eyes and to shun conversation with the fox on whatever ill-fated night it might cross one's path.

But here the composer's antipathy goes beyond mere reproach or disfavour; the father's songs inch toward a more brutal empyrean suggestion than even the Platonic, Manichean, or Gnostic traditions of *the demiurge* (lower divinity, builder of flawed physical reality). For the demiurge is typically an artisan-god, responsible for earthly matter, but always standing beneath the 'Supreme Being' or 'the One', often working blindly and altogether devoid of spirituality itself, a poor maker of fulguration (lightning flashes, thunderbolts). Thus our existential imperfection forever arises from the hopeless attempt to replicate and trap shreds of divinity within material forms, the only question being whether the demiurge fashions this impaired material world out of malevolence toward the higher Being or mere ignorance of its proper composition. Is the forging of defective corporeal entities (as inevitable mixtures of good and evil) a pathogenic-pathological defiance of the otherwise apathetic lord of the One (which itself creates nothing)? But this would be to presume that there still persists a perfect, introverted, and full godliness behind the scenes of the rash amateur-creator worshipped in error by humans as the ultimate form. Whereas the radical content of disgust in the father's songs implies that there is only the demiurge; that both terrestrial and infinite creation are concoctions of profane substances; that material life is no 'unconscious semblance' of the unknowable Supreme Being but rather that totality itself is ruled by a fundamental drive to build incorrectly. Isolomaniacal cosmology is therefore predicated on the creational bitterness that isolates each dimension and leaves them in pentagons of mutual hostility: the demiurge's contempt for its own makeshift animations; the creatures' contempt for their divine framer's miscalculation; the individual's contempt for all others as embodied disappointment; the individual's contempt for itself as ill-conceived thing; the demiurge's contempt for its own failing hands. From all five sides of the incongruous condition, they cannot stand the look of one another. The demiurge is hence not antagonist, deviant, fool, or evil; it is the fire and the blood of all things, in all their sickening nature. Creation as gastric, animal, somatic muscularity and rage; creation as unforgiving, carnal mistake.

Isolation and laughter; insult; keeping-away; forgiveness; avoidance; the meeting; jest; fright

Megalomania (Self)

1

> *My face had a natural talent for comical and horrible expressions. I felt that they enabled me to see with my own eyes all the weird shapes, all the comical, horrible, unbelievable images which lurked in the recesses of my mind. They were all familiar to me, I felt them within me, and yet at the same time they struck me as comical. All of these grimacing faces existed inside me and formed part of me: horrible, criminal, ludicrous masks which changed at a single movement of my finger-tip.*
>
> SADEQ HEDAYAT[135]

First principle: comicality.

We encounter our first megalomaniac cultivating the skill of facial contortion, for with these many caricaturing gestures comes the recognition of the comedic (un) truth of self. He studies the pathways of facial masking; his finger traces the brow, the forehead, the corners of the mouth; he slips seamlessly between tragicomic states with the clown's manic grace. In this way, he gradually

135 Hedayat, *The Blind Owl*, 114.

becomes adept at both exaggeration and subtlety: such is the frightening power of minimalist variation, revealing how the tiniest inconstancy of atmosphere, the slightest shift of faciality, can undermine entire worlds. The very core logic of subjectivity wanes: It is no longer *my* face (identification) but the face that has somehow been given to me (circumstantial possession) as stage property. Moreover, it is through this perceptual approach that one cultivates the talent of inducing mimicry in others: like the martial artist who exploits the opponent's own momentum, here the narrator uses the other's unconscious insecurity to manipulate their affective output. There is no intersubjectivity here; there is only a marionette theatre. The other's inferior concept of self (that which believes, needs, defends) makes them a windup doll for the megalomaniac (who plays, exuviates, inflicts). He cringes, they cringe; he grimaces, they grimace; he winces or smirks, and they follow suit blindly. The clown's bending smile causes others to feel awkwardness, discomfort, and unsurety toward their very existence. A new definition of black humour, then: no longer simply the cynical trivialization of abstractly negative phenomena (violence, death, illness, eroticism) or their particular symptomatic objectifications (the hand-held skull, the gangrenous limb, the leprous flaking skin, the flung garment), but rather the conversion of the very 'I' into the object of the darkest laughter, one that sheds its chameleon scales onto all beholders, with all former resonances of the gallows and the grotesque, but this time in order to change subjectivity itself into the categorical reference for ludicrousness and cruel hilarity.

Self and the comical; the horrible; the expression; weirdness; shape, the unbelievable image; grimacing; the ludicrous; the mask

2

What happiness, what happiness, what joy! what pleasure! what liberation, an eternity! <but we stiffened up, full of defiance, to wander again, with panting breath, lost and ravished, among the craters!>

RÉDA BENSMAIA[136]

Second principle: going-lost.

We encounter our second megalomaniac moving against all typical paradigms of pleasure, instead privileging something that finds fulfilment only in sudden excursions to the atrium, the hiatus, or the lost city. The egotist is often overcome by a need to preserve or increase pleasure as a sign of being alive; the ecstatic mystic seeks excessive pleasure so as to attain the annihilative diffusion of the living self into an eternal force; the ascetic radically denies pleasure in order to attain moral supremacy, enlightenment, or spiritual-experiential transcendence. So what constitutes the difference between these indulgence-based or deprivation-based attitudes and that of megalomaniacal 'defiance', and how exactly is the latter a delirious principle? The answer lies in the careful alignment of descriptive terms above: wander, panting, lost, ravished. Firstly, 'panting' and 'ravished' suggest

136 Bensmaia, *The Year of Passages*, 52.2.

a nearing of the exhaustive point of desire (the apex of sensation), meaning that to 'wander' and go 'lost' at this juncture is to sharply redirect one's libidinal momentum before the meridian of intensity is attained. Megalomaniacal 'defiance' therefore comprises a turning-elsewhere (not a repression, denial, conservation, or prolonging) at the eleventh hour of pleasure, precisely so as to enable a kind of horizontal escalation.

And where does it go? 'Among the craters', we are told, which necessitates knowing about these bowl-shaped cavities and circular depressions found across the surfaces of earth and moon. Specifically, we can distinguish three different geomorphologies of the crater: impact craters (caused by the collision of celestial objects or meteoric bodies), volcanic craters (caused by lower magma chamber activity in eruptive volcanoes), and subsidence craters (caused by nuclear subterranean explosions), a typology that informs our speculations on potentially unique formulations of emergent pleasure/desire. We could imagine our megalomaniac's going-lost among immense holes in the ground as corresponding to: (1) a newly-formed desire (near the climactic point of a previous pleasure) to find the one most impacted by contact; (2) a newly-formed desire (near the climactic point of a previous pleasure) to find the one most incapable of protecting their surface-appearance (perhaps the face, body, or speech) from embedded, churning intensities;

(3) a newly-formed desire (near the climactic point of a previous pleasure) to find the one most devastated by the radioactive fallout of a past test, almost swallowed up or entirely contaminated to the point of collapse. Such are the awaiting manic diagrams of interstellar, molten, and detonative satisfaction.

Note: There is a long history of fixation with craters among Islamic civilizations, and so it is no coincidence that at least twenty-four moon craters are named after mediaeval North African, Arab, and Persian astronomers, astrologers, and scholars.

Note: A form of Mediterranean war architecture resembling craters is called *embrasure* (a splayed opening in battlement walls, strategically enlarging toward the inner face, often accompanied by arrow slits made for archers, cannon, or iron darts).

Note: The Wabar Craters of Saudi Arabia were first reported to the Western world by a colonial intelligence officer and geographer-explorer who had gone in search of a lost city called 'Iram of the Pillars' (or Ubar) mentioned in the Qur'an. The craters reside in the oil-rich sands of the *Rub al-Khali* (Empty Quarter), considered one of the vastest stretches of desolate wasteland on earth, and near them were also discovered fragments of large iron meteorites. The lost city itself was said to have been destroyed when God sent a thunderstorm to forever bury it in the desert sands, a scourge against the people's corruption in defying the prophet Hud's warnings to stop practicing idolatry.

In the final stride, we return to the initial megalomaniacal question: Why would someone arriving at the pinnacle of a certain desire suddenly break pattern and angle off toward some remote basin of experience? Why would the astronomer's genius, having charted star trajectories and solar systems, suddenly start to stare blankly into the open ravines of asteroids or comets? Why would the architect's genius, having designed great structures of fortified enclosure, suddenly start to carve 'murder-holes' into the curtain walls and gates of the castle? Why would the political genius, having achieved the highest ranks of ministerial recognition, go in fanatical quest of a legendary lost city of 'empty dwellings' rumoured to have been smote by 'the wind which carries the grievous punishment'?[137]

Self and happiness; joy; pleasure; liberation; defiance; wandering; panting; the lost; the ravished; the crater

137 Qur'an, Surah 46 (Al-Ahqaf), ayah 24–25.

3

He is the wind that never retreats, water that never returns to its source. He creates a race that begins with him. He has no offspring, no roots to his steps.
He walks the abyss, tall as the wind.

ADONIS[138]

Third principle: expulsion.

We encounter our third megalomaniac realigning subjectivity with the winds, and thereby becoming the master smoker (opium brazier, water pipe). Picture the tilted-back head, the contracting chest, the mouth's slow extension of the oval shape, the white rings or serpent tails blown aloft into surrounding air. There is a careful artistry to the most sedated gestures, especially this puffing-away of self: to relax, forget, and expel; to recline during dispersal. Tongue, teeth, breath: a multipart apparatus of emanation.

Note: It is a recorded detail of victims' testimonials that some officers of the Ottoman Empire would occasionally entertain themselves by wagering bets on whether a pregnant Armenian woman's unborn child was male or female, then ripping open the stomach to confirm the sex and collect their respective winnings. This is

---

138 Adonis, *Selected Poems*, 23.

the look of internal identity (neurotic power), always desperately tied to weak metaphysical phantoms (ethnicity, nation, religion, ideology). We must acknowledge the pivotal contrast between this mundane horror-logic of identitarian origin, belonging, and domination, and the megalomaniacal freedom of our above-mentioned figure who 'never returns' to any 'source', and who 'has no offspring, no roots to his steps.'

These smoke rings bespeak an evacuation process whereby one literally watches a once-internal phenomenon (moving through lungs, throat, flared nostrils, pursed lips) dissipate into external semblances and forever disappear. This is not some lofty ontological notion but rather the acutely physical practice of exhaling a piece of individual Being beyond itself; a sensorial display whereby what was once tangibly within me is no longer within or even mine, as it drifts smoothly into intangibility. The megalomaniac smoker thereby provides us a neutralizing theory of effluvium ('tall as the wind') through which all acts of origination ('he creates a race') then immediately go the way of an ozone-bound gust ('He walks the abyss'). To join the momentarily clear vortex; the unavailing wisp.

Self and wind; non-return; creation;
the race; non-offspring; non-roots; steps; abyss

4

Call me by my last name.
Hang my clothes on planets on stars.
Let my fruitless legs walk the earth
Seeding my despair in animal hearts
Let my final answers ring like bells of death
To call men forth to their absolution.

JOYCE MANSOUR[139]

Fourth principle: formality.

We encounter our fourth megalomaniac speaking in almost royal or divine tones of commandment, and cannot miss the extreme formality of the first line's demand for last names (the honorific). Also, the hanging of clothes constitutes a decorous, stately gesture, complementing all approved laws of the well-mannered: mid-level bowing, removing shoes or hats, lowering shoulders or eyes, extending or kissing hands, maintaining a stoic expression, offering gifts. Thus we are brought before another culture of pretence, etiquette, and customized respect, but this time with megalomaniacal implications that extend to 'planets' and 'stars', echoing the ceremonial liturgy of death-bells. Furthermore, we wonder what sin warrants the last line's mention of absolution. After all, mercy and forgiveness are, in themselves, exceedingly formal gestures.

---

139 Mansour, *Screams*, 18.

Note: There are historical accounts throughout numerous cultures of specific punishments for those who fail in their tasked formality, most often involving exclusion from the palace, temple, or criminal syndicate's inner circles, but often relayed to more severe forms of mutilation (the breaking of kneecaps) or demands for rituals of formalized atonement (the severing of one's own finger). More broadly, the family name is also often black-listed, defamed, or even revoked, and the family estate confiscated or ransacked.

Inferiority. We are advised that everyone below our author has an 'animal heart' and that she continually 'despairs' in their company. Hence they must beg tolerance simply for being lower in her presence; they must seek pardon for the inevitability of their impoverished essence, since apology at least proves awareness of the hierarchy of titles and entitlement. They must wear the proper vestments, arrive at the designated hour, make the artful address, and then still plead for exoneration at the superior's throne. Whether or not the pleas are accepted quite rightly depends upon the whim of she who doles out the 'final answers', and certainly the final absolution would also mean the most formal absolution (i.e., the absolute's collection of the absolute fine), itself a warning that the next vulgarity will bring the onset of a wrathful conclusion.

Self and the last name; hanging; fruitlessness; seeding; despair; the animal heart; the final answer; death-bells; the call; absolution

5

And this is I
a woman alone...
...and the simple and sad pessimism of the sky
and the incapacity of these concrete hands.

FORUGH FARROKHZAD[140]

Fifth principle: cosmic pessimism.

We encounter our fifth megalomaniac invested in a sort of immanent commiseration, whereby an atmospheric sorrow (pessimistic sky) takes its place beside the equal helplessness of the author's will (incapable hands) in invalid unison: neither side (neither self nor world) can rescue existence; rather, it is this mutual capitulation of the particular and the universal that causes an infinite laying-down. They deplore, they share their remorse, but they make no amends.

Note: One of the crucial points of contention among Persian new wave poets was not whether or not to draft apocalyptic proposals—they all entertained such end-world visions—but whether one ought to perform a brief lamentation of some kind before unleashing floods, fires, darkness, or hailstorms. Is it the moral duty of the fatalist poet to kneel respectfully, to shed tears, to pause silently,

140 Farrokhzad, *A Lonely Woman*, 125.

or to elegize Being one last time as it falls apart? Some opted for merciless executions, while the above author proved to be one of those who preferred manifestations of regret, sorrow, and thoughtful hesitation (even in the midst of violent delirium), as evidenced by such titles as 'Sometimes I Feel Sorry for the Garden' and 'Let us Believe in the Beginning of the Cold Season'.[141]

What remains original here, though, is the megalomaniacal conversation between a lonely woman and an equally lonely earth when concretion fails—as if mania alone could bring about this united compassion between subjective and objective territories. This cohesive crying-out of inner and outer space is something she unsurprisingly describes as an instant of *simplicity*—that is, the reduction of once-complex ethical questions to a single answer: 'no more.' She hangs her head to welcome the coming typhoon (likely from the Persian-Arabic *tufan*), and recites words of poetic dreariness synchronized with the life that renounces itself.

Self and simplicity; sadness; pessimism; incapacity; the concrete

141 For further articulations of such elegiac-apocalyptic modes, see J.B. Mohaghegh, 'The Captive and the Exile: Vulnerability, Sensation, Desire' and 'Paradox, Ecstasy and the Catastrophic Mind: Apocalyptic Writing', in *The Radical Unspoken: Silence in Middle Eastern and Western Thought* (New York: Routledge, 2013).

6

> *Was it because they rent the veil of illusion, made plain that, if a man lost his links with people, he'd lose his links with himself: that if he lost others, he'd lose his own self, which would come to lack all point?...Was he weeping because his sad father's muwwals somehow captured the nature of their strange life in the eternal desert, where nothing else seemed to exist in the world?*
>
> IBRAHIM AL-KONI[142]

Sixth principle: rending.

We encounter our sixth megalomaniac approaching the limit of *the non-obsequious*, a figure who 'lacks all point' and has 'lost links' to both people and self. That 'nothing else seemed to exist' is the key to understanding this megalomaniacal dimension, for it is a feeling initially spurred on by the choice of a perfect locus where none can give chase (the desert): to exist where no one else will exist; to exist where no one else can exist.

Nevertheless, the rending of these bonds has a productive result: in fact, it furnishes the optimal conditions for one who controls Being through amorphousness (shapeless mastery). Consider *the snake charmer* (again we come back to a relation between megalomania and

142 Al-Koni, *The Bleeding of the Stone*, 36.

mimetic power) who formlessly mimics the snake in order to gradually govern the field of mimicry. At first they follow the creature's swaying body, side to side, side to side, but at some point in the dance the cross-legged snake-charmer stops imitating the creature and the creative momentum shifts in the other direction (impersonator becomes influencer). A new theory of halcyon and its sub-mythic calmers: for now the snake stands mesmerized by its clone pulling it along at subtly different rhythms, beholden to a persuasive gift of the rending-figure who answers to no other, not even to itself.

Self and the rent veil; plainness; the lost link; pointlessness; capture; nature; strangeness; the nothing-else

7

— 'Who created the universe?'
— 'The universe,
I
created!
Who other than one with miraculous fingers like mine
would have the power of creation?
The universe
I created.'

AHMAD SHAMLU[143]

Seventh principle: masochistic conceit.

We encounter our seventh megalomaniac in a state of maximal pride, fielding his own rhetorical questions that treat universal creation as an individual exploit deserving of self-congratulation. Bravado, grandiloquence: the language of gallantry and overstatement. This is a destination of aesthetic mania that select painters, sculptors, dancers, musicians, actors, architects, philosophers, and authors often reach: to believe all others incapable of such creative work; to believe that no other could have done this. But in the very same moment, this utterance opens up a chasm: such bragging rights are only earned on the outer edge of torment, where to win and to lose begin to

143 Shamlu, *Born Upon the Dark Spear*, 112.

mean the same thing, where the most victorious one is *the flagellant* whose whip picks up speed and force with every sequential lash. This is why the possessor of these same 'miraculous fingers' will eventually call himself 'Abel standing on the platform of contempt, the honour of the cosmos, having lashed myself'.[144] The haughtiness is still there, but it now begins to circle around claims of ultimate negativity as well, serving at once the most unsurpassable initiator and the most wretchedly slain brother, the two roles progressively coinciding as the vociferation pours forth line by line. Double-edged writing: with one hand it applauds, with the other it reprimands or even mauls.

Note: A certain type of anti-psychological fighter gains strength the more they are hit, becoming more dangerous as they take on damage. The sight or taste of blood, the sound of a fist's impact, and the sudden onset of intense pain to ribs or jaw become intoxicants. At this point they will either proceed to a devastating knockout or be rendered unconscious themselves (fatal propulsions). This is a manic virtue: the love of annihilation or, more precisely, discovery of this love within annihilation's sting.

As such, megalomaniacal conceit reaches a level of vaunting, ostentatious word play that also ropes in abjection, disdain, and counter-insolence. For pure greatness would by definition have to include the greatest examples of *all* things, from the most praised and approved to the

144 Ibid., 117.

most derided and berated, all valued similarly within the mad clamour of the infinite boast.

Self and universe; the miraculous; the fingers; creation

8

After eight months of life in a city whose streets remain darkened and eerie night after night, eight months of gruesome nightmares whose sounds seem to take up residence in your pillow, ringing in your ears like a tape recording that plays nonstop, you'd feel that you needed to be able to encounter yourself, if only just once, without at the same time either being in flight under a barrage of gunfire, hiding behind a barricade or kneeling at the epicenter of an earthquake.

GHADA SAMMAN[145]

Eighth principle: centralized fear.

We encounter our eighth megalomaniac with the mentality of *the pulverized*, a minesweeper who nevertheless sets off every conceivable assault 'at the epicenter of an earthquake'. It would require scrutiny of several psychoanalytic figures over centuries to explain their varying scales of supposed psychopathologies, in the process offering a cautious differentiation between hysteria (with symptoms including heightened responsiveness, playfulness, irritability, fatigue, and hyper-sensitivity to stimuli) and psychasthenia (also sometimes referred to as neurasthenia, with symptoms including irrational fear, anxiety, guilt,

145 Samman, *Beirut Nightmares*, 166.

and multiple phobias).[146] In the classic framework, the hysteric's abnormality originates from a 'narrowing' of the conscious world despite continued interrelation between dissociated aspects of the individual identity, whereas the psychasthenic's abnormality derives from a deep-seated bifurcation of the so-called 'reality function' itself. These two strands of extreme fearfulness, in turn, become the foundation for early psychoanalytic models of extroverted and introverted personalities, with the hysteric driven to overwrought 'automatisms' by subconscious ideas and 'contingent symptoms' and the psychasthenic prone to weighty complexes of mind characterized by restraint, conservativism, lack of confidence, depersonalization, tics, and pre-emptive fright before certain situations. The former erupts into involuntary states of surprise, while the latter remains perpetually harassed by their conscious thought and by the perceived probability that a malign occurrence lies in wait around every corner.

However, here our author introduces a novel prototype of fear: one that maintains all the excessive reactivity of the hysteric ('ringing in your ears') *in addition to* the evasive techniques of the psychasthenic ('hiding behind a barricade'), but for whom the 'I' also becomes the receptacle of all worldly disaster ('under a barrage of gunfire').

---

146 The formative creators of the discourses of hysteria and psychasthenia are Jean-Martin Charcot, Pierre Janet, Sigmund Freud, Carl Jung, and Karl Jaspers.

To run away is to run toward, as will (the self-inflicted) and event (the inflicted-upon) become interchangeable, resulting in a sense that 'I never die', while concurrently bringing destruction to everything around me (invincibility, accursed association), and also that 'I die worst and every time' (super-mortality, accursed responsibility). Megalomania as a distillation of maladaptive concern, the thought that all peacelessness must be digested here in myself alone. This is the work of something combining the audacious, the craven, and the scoundrel: it sucks in every existent and non-existent fear, a high-wire act coupling and thereby superseding conscious and subconscious terror, shock and paranoia, inner and outer causation, in the fatalistic-manic certainty that I am being followed by and am drawing forth all manner of catastrophic forces.

Self and the eerie; the gruesome; residence; ringing; the nonstop; flight; barrage; hiding; the barricade; the epicentre; the earthquake

9

You cannot trap the immortal.
So do with us and with yourself whatever you wish.[147]

Oh, my father, did I wrong anyone when I said that:
I saw eleven stars and the sun and the moon, I saw them kneeling before me?

MAHMOUD DARWISH[148]

Ninth principle: the immortal imperilled.

We encounter our ninth megalomaniac extending the besieged sensibility of our previous prototype, subscribing to an enemy-ridden worldview for which the abiding is always the most targeted, the termless one drawing attention from those with terminal plans. But what happens at this mysterious crux of the Persian *jang-e tan-beh-tan* ('body-to-body war') between immortal and mortal structures? What happens when the immortal continuum slices into itself, when that which stretches eternally backward (Arabic *azaliyah*, 'immemorial') truncates its own right to unroll eternally forward (Arabic *abadiyah*, 'everlasting')? 'You cannot trap the immortal', he warns us, for there is always a hidden annihilative-manic mechanism ensuring

---

147 Darwish, *Unfortunately, It Was Paradise*, 139.

148 M. Darwish, 'I Am Yusuf', tr. A. Amireh, <http://www.naseeb.com/villages/journals/1-palestinian-poetry-oh-my-father-i-am-yusuf-68387>.

that what has always been is no longer what will always be, becoming the dark side of its own moon.

Note: The particular skeletons of megalomaniacal subjectivities—i.e. the precise criterion establishing each respective 'I'—proves indispensable to understanding the ten renditions here. The fact that this same author writes elsewhere that '[a] few thousand poetic years ago, I was born in a darkness of white linen, but I could not distinguish between the dream of myself and my self' refers us back to an initial schism between vision and truth.[149] As is typical of all manic approaches, only the visionary component matters—permitting us to discover the following megalomaniacal equation: to kill the immortal, one must kill the dream of the immortal.

To conclude this line of thought, let us interpret the second passage, in which the poetic author describes himself as the prophetic figure Yusuf (Joseph), proleptic dreamer and dream-reader, betrayed by jealous brothers and metaphorical wolves, handled by slave-trading caravans and handler of the grains, wells, and silver cups. He is the person of many roles (favourite son, chief prisoner, pharaonic vizier, messianic ancestor) and many garments (multi-coloured coat, captive's rags, royal dress); he is also the recipient of all radical affirmations (paternal love, divine blessing, captain's approval, mistress's lust, familial

149 Darwish, *Unfortunately, It Was Paradise*, 147.

reconciliation) and all radical condemnations (siblings' homicidal envy, captain's punishment, mistress's scorn, apocalyptic martyrdom). What emerges as a result is a poetic formulation that borders upon these same duelling realms of blessedness, purity, innocence and malice, anger, and misfortune, through the megalomaniacal recounting of a dream that serves: (1) to establish the prophet's name as synonymous with immaculate survival; (2) to hurl accusations and cast blame upon mortals; (3) to unmask a perpetual sequence of conspiracies; (4) to emphasize the supremacy, elitism, and hierarchical distance between the perennial self and all others before whom 'eleven stars and sun and moon' are not found kneeling. But remember, this is also the figure whose redeemer offspring is supposedly selected by a monotheistic tribal god to perish in battle during Armageddon, still fighting enemies as part of the destiny of the four horns or four craftsmen/horseman, thus sending us back to the first matter of how the Untiring might someday choose self-abolition. And what will happen when the immortal rescinds itself, beating the percussive drums of euthanasia? Will this also spell the reciprocal death of all mortal beings—or something far worse hinted at in the permissive 'whatever you wish' (mortality left to itself, without recourse to the immortal, without even the ability to dream the immortal ever again)?

Self and trap; the immortal; the wish; wrong; kneeling

10

On these videotapes I murdered, raped, started fires, planted bombs and carried out crimes that no sane person would even imagine. All these tapes were broadcast on satellite channels around the world.

Perhaps I've told you too much, but let me tell you frankly that I'm worried about you, because you're either an idiot or a genius, and agents like that excite my curiosity. If you're a genius, that would be gratifying. I still believe in genius, although most members of the group talk about experience and practice.

HASSAN BLASIM[150]

Tenth principle: image radiation.

Our tenth megalomaniac combines the qualities of the main characters in two different short stories about extremist movements, figures in which vast histories of post-mortem aesthetics take an avant-garde turn. In the first account, our narrator is abducted, thrown into the trunk of a car, and forced to portray himself on videotape as the spokesperson of several militant causes. He is such a convincing envoy that he ends up being continually traded, passed from one ideological sect to another,

150 Blasim, *The Madman of Freedom Square*, 10, 48.

reading fiery scripts and declaring himself as the terrible face of crimes he barely understands. In the second account, our protagonist finds himself recruited by one of the Directors of the Creativity Department for a secret society of 'Corpse Exhibitionists'. These specialists—with codenames like The Nail, Agent Deaf, and Satan's Knife—are increasingly renowned throughout the land for presenting highly stylized displays of death (using bodies freshly-killed): from the draping of bisected legs across electric wires to the setting of lifeless breastfeeding mothers and infants beneath palm trees to the staging of children in restaurants with mouths hovering over bowls of blood soup filled with family members' eyes.

This configuration of fatal actor and fatal installation artist leads us to imagine a megalomaniacal subject able simultaneously to harness the powers of the video recording (infinite reproducibility) and the situational exhibition (once-in-a-lifetime singularity). There is no positive or negative hierarchy of effect here, whether striking an impressive or infective chord. Both are figures of laundering, fame, and inoculation; both actor and exhibitionist hand death over to the hyperbolic, the sensationalized, the conspicuous; both are practitioners of overkill and of the overdone, gaining their laurels of recognition and taxidermic memorability through frightening visions of decrepitude. To make finality ground-breaking and seminal; to make of darkening fate a luminary's showroom.

All is promulgation; all is spreading-word. To make the pen-name blare and the look/visage gain instant reputation (through revulsion). For mania here turns the most distant simulacrum of self into the most intimate presence (to touch the face of God, or rather the many death-poses of gods).

The idiot-genius that fuses terroristic role-playing and corpse exhibitionism therefore resembles those schizophrenic painters that never take their brushes off the canvas (swirling pastels, waters, night skies). His is a practice that becomes tenacious, ingrained, etched equally into the conscious and unconscious spheres of all sentience. For to broadcast or three-dimensionalize images megalomaniacally means to grow ubiquitous across all temporal orders (pasts, presents, futures [un]realized; lost time, skipped time, wasted time, forgotten time, resurrected time) and all spatial orders (virtual, subaqueous, cosmopolitan, site-specific, trans-cosmic); it is to let the image rule in both surreptitious and overt forms, as pinched nerve and dull pain; to occupy the dream, the real, and the interstitial daydream; to make exposure pandemic.

Self and crime; broadcast; the tape;
the satellite; the channel; idiocy; genius; curiosity

Catoptromania/Eisoptromania (Mirrors)

1

> *But on the wall inside my room hangs a mirror in which I look at my face, and in my circumscribed existence that mirror is a more important thing than the world of the rabble-men which has nothing to do with me.*
>
> SADEQ HEDAYAT[151]

We encounter our first cataptromaniac in a place where mirrors are partitions that no longer reflect worldly reality but rather end the once-bilateral relation between this 'circumscribed existence' and the world at large. We perhaps recall the many superstitions, customs, and belief-systems surrounding mirrors, such as the bad luck associated with its shattered glass, or the potential entrapment of spirits within mirror worlds, or the early treatises of Diocles, Ptolemy, and Ibn Sahl on Burning Mirrors; but what happens when it becomes a den of occultation for a godlike being that no longer wishes to project itself into existence? The messianic figure that withdraws but never returns finds permanent, uninterrupted refuge in the mirror's borders (its surface or depth?), a perfect hideout

151 Hedayat, *The Blind Owl*, 52.

forever removed from the spastic ‘rabble-men’. Human interiority can by no means provide such an impregnable space; all rational, sensorial, and perceptual avenues of self-reflection are useless here; for to think, to touch, or to consciously behold the ‘I’ does not go far enough in granting separation. Only the mirror gifts sovereignty; only the shards’ logic makes it possible to believe that all has ‘nothing to do with me’ (the non-partaken).

Mirror and hanging; the room; circumscription; importance; the rabble

2

Your body is now naked. You can look at yourself in the mirror. Are you the one I am seeing?

RÉDA BENSMAIA[152]

We encounter our second cataptromaniac in a place where mirrors provide an anti-Edenic reversal of the problematic of self-consciousness, the assumption being that the garden's first ancestors could not stand to view their own nakedness (original shame, guilt, repression). It is only through the mirror's prism that nakedness allows one to stare scopomaniacally, although like the little girl's looking glass it disturbs the piers of subjective recognition, allowing only fascination with one's own bodily curvatures as if viewing them for the first time. Bareness moves away from identity here; bareness disarms both knowledge and memory. Something remains in the glass, an apparitional question with no answer, something of unclad skin that embodies the very definition of a pure secret: namely, that which becomes yet more secretive the more it reveals itself.

Mirror and nakedness; looking; the one

152 Bensmaia, *The Year of Passages*, 98.9.

3

> *Light itself is glittering, a mirror in which people find their faces as they enter and leave. There are soldiers there, like angels that the eye can't see*
>
> ADONIS[153]

We encounter our third cataptromaniac in a place where mirrors become a seat of war, but of a particularly offensive kind that resembles the Persian *shabi-khun* (night-raid, literally 'blood-night'). Indeed, the night-raid has its own unmentionable place in the history of civilizational combat, whose annals are filled with images of sleeping enemies stabbed quietly in camp. The classified mission; the covert operation. This is why 'there are soldiers there... that the eye can't see', for the mirror-world apparently constitutes such a conflict zone of ambush, stealth killing, and recondite movement. But why does this moment of facial discovery approximate such fatal incursion and escape ('they enter and leave')? Why does it require tactical surprise, waylaying, and malefic trickery? Without doubt, the night-raid comprises the most obscene portion of war: it prefers the depravity of the unfair fight, its very nature arising from an excess that overspills the established rules of honourable violence; it is the demoralizing

153 Adonis, *Selected Poems*, 287.

weapon of the immoral warrior (like the disgraced, face-covering ninja), leaving us to wonder about this supposed manic relation of mirror-gazers to unseen murder and to those who prowl against the defenceless, the unarmed, and the unconscious.

Mirror and light; the face; entering; leaving; the soldier; the angel; the unseen

4

Then collapsing in the closet near your bed
Throw your omega together with a fistful of salamanders
In the mirror where shadows leap
Does your husband flee from you?

JOYCE MANSOUR[154]

We encounter our fourth cataptromaniac in a place where mirrors are flaw-disclosing artefacts, something that offers two acute oppositions to the psychoanalytic notion of the *imago* (the idealized image of the parent, lover, god): (1) the mirror that reveals all hypocritical cracks of the idealized figure (fall from grace); (2) the mirror that reveals the anti-ideal figure, in all its most loathsome possibilities (nemesis). The unripe; the misbegotten. Accordingly, the reflective image exists within a kind of degrading sepulchre ('the closet near your bed'); it humiliates the ideal's birthmarks and its unfinished plans; it invalidates every 'omega' and steals sight away, into the hateful quarters of salamanders, shadows, and unfaithful husbands.

Mirror and collapse; the closet; the bed;
the omega; salamander; shadow; husband; leaping; fleeing

---

154 Mansour, *Essential Poems and Writings*, 201.

5

In the eyes of mirrors,
movements and colors and images
seemed reflected upside down,
and over the heads of base clowns
and prostitutes' shameful visages
a holy bright halo
burned like a blazing umbrella.

Ask the mirror
the name of your savior.

FORUGH FARROKHZAD[155]

We encounter our fifth cataptromaniac in a place where mirrors extol the wicked and the shameful, a radical inversion of the moral universe in which hellhounds enjoy 'a holy bright halo' and carry 'the name of your savior'.

Three dark folkloric structures from Eastern Europe resound through different villages of the Balkan mountains to forge a particular connection between the mirror and evil: (1) The Transylvanian construct that soulless beings (like the vampire) are not reflected by mirrors; (2) The Black Sea construct that spectral or demonic beings only become visible in mirror reflections; (3) The

155 Farrokhzad, *A Lonely Woman*, 49, 123.

Serbo-Croatian custom of burying supposedly evil persons with a hand-mirror so that their spirit cannot escape the coffined earth. In all of these Slavic formulations, evil is either trapped or unlocked by the mirror's influence; but in no circumstances does it alter the original evil, as in the case of our poetic verse above in which evil, when reflected, becomes the most beloved, hallowed, consecrated. Is the mirror a simple healing device (turning evil into good) or a more preternatural reverser of values (favouring evil over good)? Or does cataptromania actually open onto that rarest of mythical archetypes whereby the villain must somehow save the world? An entire philosophical volume could be devoted to interrogating that strange instance where an evil god or brutal anti-hero must become the rescuer: perhaps, in order to ready ourselves for such a possibility, we should store up countless mirrors to free the bloodthirsty, infernal, ghostly, and wicked women at the hour of need. A time when those of 'base' and 'shameful visages' must lift their eyes to aid us all.

Mirror and eyes; the upside-down; the base; the shameful; visage; halo; blaze; the saviour

6

After fastening the veil securely around his head, he approached the water to inspect himself in its mirror. He leaned over the surface of the submissive pool, which was flooded by the golden dusk and saw another creature there: a haughty, terrifying demon, as unfathomable as a god.

You, my beauty, don't know that Mirror is one of my names, since I am a mirror for everything. I am the mirror that does not show people their faces but reflects their souls. Anyone evil sees evil in my face. Anyone good, sees good in my face.

IBRAHIM AL-KONI[156]

We encounter our sixth cataptromaniac continuing the above thread, seeing mirrors as intimately attentive to the question of evil (though here linked to a more active process of making-evil). Obviously, the first mirrors of ancient times were pools of water; less obvious is the premise outlined above, that early peoples felt they were not perceiving themselves in the lake, river, or font: instead, they were beholding an image of unstoppable terror (something without brakes, crutches, reins). Something creaks,

156 Al-Koni, *The Seven Veils of Seth*, 19, 205.

flutters—'another creature there', he mumbles, alluding to its godawful stature.

Note: We are also told in the second passage that one of the more devious god's counter-names is Mirror, thereby divulging a slippery truth of the ultimate: human beings are not made in the image of gods. Rather, duplicitous gods are continually remade in duplicated images of their human worshippers, such that divinity implies being caught in states of ongoing sulphurous transfiguration. It also raises the disturbing question of what happens to destiny in those rare trustless moments when the reflection precedes the real (i.e. when the mirror comes first).

To become inspired means almost literally to steal spirit. This is what the mirror-in-mania does: It thieves attributes; moreover, it violates the stolen feature and converts it into an instrument of evil potency. Mania therefore solves the riddle of how noble traits may give rise to ignoble acts (through mirroring): hyper-reflected devotion becomes jealousy; hyper-reflected bravery becomes arrogance; hyper-reflected kindness becomes burden; hyper-reflected contemplation becomes masochistic doubt; hyper-reflected passion becomes daredevil risk, dejection, or even murder. For certain, this is a less well-travelled rim of philosophical analysis: that of detailing the exact pathways through which an initial virtue becomes a potential vice, learning in what special circumstances an affirmative thought or desire gradually morphs into a heinous occasion. Cataptromaniacal thought, then, is lodged precisely in this perceptual venture, for it passes qualities through various phases of becoming-execrable (from Latin *exsecrari*, 'to curse'), whether by means of exacerbation, contamination, or suspicion.

Mirror and veil; approaching; inspection; submission; the pool; the creature; the unfathomable; the name; the everything; the anyone; soul

7

You have come from the suns, have come from the daybreaks
you have come from the mirrors and from the silken cloths....
I arise!
A light in my hand
a light in my heart
I polish the rust off my soul
and place a mirror across from your mirror
so as to create an eternity of you.

AHMAD SHAMLU[157]

We encounter our seventh cataptromaniac in a place where mirrors serve as a proponent's weapon (valiance refracted). He arises for the mirrored her; he rides forward for her silken image, an advocate-by-force with torches ablaze in both hand and chest. Here obsessive loyalty is met by an urgent wish for infinite replication: the manic figure will not rest until the desired one gains endless control over reality; she must become queen; she must become the all-ruling; everything must belong to this one 'come from the mirrors'. And he is the deliverer of such prizes: it is his charge alone to ensure dominance

157 Shamlu, *Born Upon the Dark Spear*, 38.

and to commit dynasties into her open palms. Strangely, though, universal power here is not attained through unification of the world into a manic object, but rather through the fractal multiplication and division of the original manic object into a swarm. Her felt presence must hang everywhere, and it is the placing of 'mirror across from mirror' that allows this mass securing of strongholds, leading to an almost imperial perspective through which the conquest of space is equated with the conquest of time: the more land and cities taken, the higher the chance of winning eternity for her across the narrating lips, memories, and rituals of the future living. For it takes a militant cataptromaniacal drive to turn a single being into an inextinguishable emblem.

Mirror and the coming-from; the arisen; polishing; rust;
the across; created eternity

8

As I gazed through the opening, I saw five bearded men staring down at me. I noted with alarm that they all had the same face and were wearing the same clothes. It was as if they were a single man surrounded by four huge mirrors.

GHADA SAMMAN[158]

We encounter our eighth cataptromaniac in a place where mirrors serve as nerve centres for cult-garrisons, thus allowing us to revisit older ideas of the sectarian, a figure of partisan shares whose partialized ferocity matches the segmental nature of glass itself. Indeed, she first sights them through the mirror-barrel of the keyhole: these men with the same uniform, long beards, and sleeved tattoos, an ultra-exhibitionism wherein all visual facets must confirm the state-of-alliance. They are those who enter closed doorways, to kill everything for their minor persuasion—for the island, the neighbourhood, the corner, the sermonic notion—beholden to a cataptromaniacal fanaticism of the follower/denizen. This is how they become identical operatives, a 'single man surrounded by four huge mirrors'; this is where the symbolic world becomes the uncontainable event, storming down halls

158 Samman, *Beirut Nightmares*, 239.

as pure self-reflecting faction, while ideas seal themselves into self-fulfilling prophecies.

Mirror and the opening; staring; alarm; sameness; singularity

9

But no one can cast the reflection of Narcissus back on the mirrors of night.

MAHMOUD DARWISH[159]

We encounter our ninth cataptromaniac in a place where mirrors participate in a manifold philosophy of Night. The Watchman's Night. The Traveller's Night. The Coward's Night. The Corpse-Washer's Night. The Drunkard's Night. Someone must say more about these inhuman nocturnes for which no narcissistic disorder can survive, and yet the mirror remains all-prevailing. The Smuggler's Night. The Runner's Night. The Lamplighter's Night. The Bag Lady's Night. The Crow's Night. There are such evenings when identity sleeps, and something else awakens to be hosted by reflective surfaces (to think darkness as mirror). The Harlot's Night. The Satyr's Night. The Insomniac's Night. The Stonecutter's Night. The Rebel Prince's Night. A table of contents, perhaps, for a book never to be written (a text that sees no light of day).

Mirror and casting-back; night; picture; dream

---

159 Darwish, *Unfortunately, It Was Paradise*, 15.

10

> *If he had not had trouble with fantasies in the past, he would have behaved like any sensible man, looked in the mirror and said: 'Impossible.' But he was used to surprises and his experiences had taught him not to waste time looking for reasons for his predicaments and to look for the emergency exit instead.*
>
> HASSAN BLASIM[160]

We encounter our tenth cataptromaniac in a place where mirrors act as exit portals, assisting those with a developed sixth sense for leaving situations at the right moment, finding the speculum's 'emergency exit' before the onset of some ecological, political, or individual massacre. But what is the provenance of this departing intuition? Is it similar to the instincts of animals whose sensations warn them of cyclones, cloudbursts, and hurricanes before arrival? How does this manic figure, given to insensible behaviour, know to enter the escapable glass ahead of the disaster? Perhaps the answer lies in his troubled relation to fantasy, which by definition rarely ever includes images of things already possessed. Instead, fantasy most often copies patterns from the unattained object and the unfulfilled wish, using wilder imagination to bridge tangible

160 Blasim, *The Madman of Freedom Square*, 86.

distance and thus remaining stuck in the dialectics of real and unreal planes. Nevertheless, our cataptromaniac stays sober; he does not suffer from fanciful tendencies that invent 'reasons' for loss or pleasure, but rather sits listening for the predicament's predicate; thus he finds himself browsing, skirting, 'used to surprises' and aware 'not to waste time' before immediately getting away from ill-evolving scenes. Stated otherwise, it is when one trains thought against tempting fantasy that existence begins to reflect its intentions more clearly, for the diabolical event always mirrors itself in advance to those who choose the slipaway sense over the wallowing mind.

Furthermore, it is altogether likely that this art of safe disappearance is linked to the omnicidal instinct itself. For those who harbour all-devouring visions of the world gain a kind of second sight for similar plots on the part of others, or, further still, are able to hear the rumblings when the world itself turns omnicidal.

Mirror and trouble; fantasy; insensibility; surprise; non-wasted time; the predicament; the emergency exit

Colossomania (Giants)

We must return to antique fables and pyramid walls filled with pictograms of enormous beasts and divinities. Their excessive frames generate a kind of wonderment exclusive to forces of the titanic, the engulfing, the unconquerable. But let us ponder the intellectual-experiential possibilities opened up when we fall beneath such monumental or disproportionate manifestations. This bids us to step into the stories of hovering gigantic beings, those who possess such otherworldliness and cosmological stature that they provoke intimidation, delirium, bewilderment, silence, ecstasy, or terror in their onlookers.

It is perhaps telling that mania alone could allow us to cast glances across such colossal imaginaries: to stare upon the indecipherable, the foreboding, the outstretched, and the overpouring; to follow the cryptic motions of those who persuade, enthral, or devour at will. By focusing on these narratives of gargantuan prototypes—scandalous creatures who can irradiate their moods or swell their limbs beyond the dominion of the law, the known, and the real—we can begin to contemplate how such strange movements toward immeasurability are in fact attempts to render a counter-current to absolutism. Against paradigms of oneness or unity, here we are faced with multiple contenders to apotheosis: giants and leviathans that are never inaccessibly far-removed from mortals, but are instead menacingly apparent in their fathomless, towering presence. We must probe the secret of their loathing for the structures of humankind, the angered swinging of their arms, and their supra-mythic madness. In other words, we must read these tales of colossi as subversive anti-totalitarian gestures (tectonic shifts toward vulnerability and chaos). For it is beneath their shadow that one might dream beyond the enclosures of a world.

1

> *It was as if the surroundings, the souls of all the dead, and the power of their thought, which was aloft over the crypt and the broken stones, had forced or inspired me, because things were no longer in my hands. I, who had no belief in anything, fell involuntarily to my knees before these ashes from which the blue smoke rose, and worshipped them.*
>
> SADEQ HEDAYAT[161]

Our first colossomaniac is an archaeologist whose explorations have led him to spend the night among ancient faraway ruins. That evening, he suspects within the stone formations a subtle animus, which then escalates into a full-blown palpitation, as former kings and gods resuscitate themselves in grand procession around the fire. Their sudden march, breaking forth from the marble in a dynastic necro-festival beneath the stars, is the source of unsurpassed awe. Though they do not belong to the archaeologist's own cultural backdrop or belief system, their radical untimeliness overwhelms his faculties, bringing him to the brink of reflexive colossomania (puppeteers of the imperative). The highest form of exoticism, whereby the outsider phenomenon turns one inside out,

161 S. Hedayat, 'The Fire Worshipper', in *Three Drops of Blood*, 43.

a gutting and effusion of subjectivity's pillars toward foreignness.

The word 'surroundings' reveals that the colossus is experienced less as a figure looming above (transcendent divinity) and more as a current circulating around (electrical immanence)—a question of atmospheric power above all else. Moreover, the statement 'the souls of all the dead' prompts two compelling and counterintuitive realisations: (1) that the colossus is in fact an entity comprised of many particularized legions; (2) that the colossus is itself a spiritual conspiracy. This multifarious collusion is further confirmed by the phrase 'the power of their thought', which links the startling resurrection of the statues to the plots of a premeditating will (*they know what they are doing*). The fact that this mysterious collective consciousness drapes itself 'aloft the crypt and the broken stones' demonstrates a sly ability to transmit its vision onto other entities and supposedly inanimate objects, a sort of magical contamination designed to enliven things with the embers of a new mandate. Thus we are in the sphere of a command, one which 'forces or inspires', in the sense of breathing spirit into one's being without consent, as the enraptured archaeologist (himself now excavated) rightly notes. For it is in fact an inspiration-by-force that now mobilizes his limbs to flail, his head to sway rhythmically, and his eyes to roll backward into drunken oblivion. The colossus takes all without mercy or permission, reducing him to one last remaining realization: that 'things were no longer in [his] hands'. And this colossomaniacal subordination of volition, we note, leads to a type of imitative worship that oversteps the domain of belief, for our traveller recounts to us curiously that he 'had no belief in anything' and yet 'fell involuntarily to [his] knees and worshipped them'. It appears, then, that the colossal monuments of this empire abide by a logic of practical sorcery rather than by some abstract tenet of theology: they compel discipleship and seductively gain devotion through various trickeries of sensation, movement, and light—the primordial function of miracle itself. Though external to his ideological-geographic origin, and in fact *because* of this very drastic externality (that they are not him and yet they are greater than him), these figments are keen to wrap him in the blue smoke of their hallucination (the glory that demands passivity). To kneel, surrender, and undergo the going-under.

Colossus and the surroundings; dead souls; power; thought; force; inspiration; non-belief; worship

2

In the attic I found an old card from North Africa, a glove that must have belonged to a giant, and an object that looks like a Neanderthal's heavy club...

RÉDA BENSMAIA[162]

Our second colossomaniac has climbed up into the attic to rummage through trunks and crates of old keepsakes, searching aimlessly for a token or relic to entertain the weary imagination. This kind of minor curiosity typically implies a minimal level of enchantment, seeking a random pseudo-magical object to grant just a momentary release from everyday being. The wistful gift from days gone by serves as a justification to retreat from the world's banality, providing a small pocket of autonomy in which thought can rest, dwell, speculate, or convalesce. But what happens when, in the process, one accidentally stumbles upon massive and disturbing items, no longer harmless recollections of incidental and known things but glaring interjections of bizarre and potentially cataclysmic forms? What particular crisis or schism occurs when, attempting a whimsical gesture, one instead locates the reservatories of inexplicable elder races, sealed for millennia, their contents appalling in nature?

---

162 Bensmaia, *The Year of Passages*, 76.6.

One can begin dissecting this act of colossomaniacal finding by considering the spatial phenomenology of 'the attic', by definition a site intended for abandonment and rediscovery. The attic is a throwaway realm comprised of waste and forgotten junk, though also capable of providing occasional bouts of nostalgia and sentimentality. Thus our narrator apparently starts out on the right track in his extraction of an 'old card from North Africa', offering just the right dose of oddity—a slight and weathered artefact, a remote locale, and some personal narrative therein (enough to satisfy the weakest criterion of reminiscence). But it is the second object that troubles the rafters and timbers of the attic's otherwise indulgent psychology, for then we come upon 'a glove that must have belonged to a giant'—a piece of deductive reasoning that leads to a ridiculous conclusion. We thus detour from casual searching into the severity of an unwelcome revelation. The oversized accessory organically lures the imagination toward a vision of the hand within it, and from the hand to the startling forearms... an inescapable bodily sequence that will cause the atticgoer to reconstruct the entire physiology of the glove's owner until he stands before the most thorough, daunting crystallization of this giant. Rather than achieve the initial goal of some narcissistically simulated self-image of past times, the mind finds itself clouded by the insane apparition of the colossus (without identity). But it is the third object that compounds this misfortunate trek up the attic stairs, taking it beyond the outer limits of its own tolerance: something resembling 'a Neanderthal's heavy club'. The implications are unmistakable: the club is an instrument of violence (survival, war), and the Neanderthal is not the far-off or deceased relative whose souvenirs typically haunt the attic but rather the estranged cousin of distant ancestors. Not the intimate relation who intrepidly travelled the world but the hostile, unnerving precursor who confronted the ghastly infinite; not a light-hearted sojourn into historically irrelevant moments (the attic as repository for the most useless memories) but a grasping of the cruel emblems of prehistory (the attic as portal into the most essential shame/fear, that of the race's inception). And what does this estranged forebear portend? How have the glove and club come to be in our possession? A violation perhaps, the unnatural theft of the colossus's weaponry in order to spite their clear supremacy. Or not envy, but the desperate preservation of a last conduit, a mimetic shroud or article that would lead man back to the vigour of the progenitors. Or, just as likely, they have been packed away in anticipation of a return, awaiting the instant when the ancestor comes back to take what is rightfully theirs (the chieftain's claim).

Nor is this ancestral influence easily dismissed, for the author who trespassed upwards into the ageless speaks elsewhere of a 'Gigantomachia of sentences at high speed in the Marseilles-Nice Express, the Phocean. I've got to do everything in my power, and while there's still time…'.[163] Language itself begins to emulate the gigantism, speed, and power of the old exemplars, and with it the creative urgency of those who give 'everything' and fight 'while there's still time'. To write with the massive cudgels of once-colossal leaders…in advance of their inevitable resurgence.

Colossus and the attic; the artefact (the glove, the club); the ancestor; the origin; return

163 Bensmaia, *The Year of Passages*, 52.3.

3

He comes unarmed like a forest, like a destined cloud.
Yesterday he carried a continent and changed the position of the sea.
He paints the back of day and creates daylight out of his feet, borrows the night's shoes and waits for what will not come.
He lives where the stone becomes a lake, the shadow a city—he lives and fools despair, wiping out the vastness of hope, dancing for the soil so it can yawn, for the trees so they can sleep.
And here he is speaking of crossroads, drawing the magic sign on the forehead of time.

ADONIS[164]

We encounter our third colossomaniac in this portrait of a whirlwind figure that boasts extraordinary features and attributes. He arrives with emancipatory abilities that blur or supersede the established boundaries of reality itself, deranging and re-arranging, forming and malforming at a breath's notice. With almost fantastical grace, this unknown figure emerges to wrench apart the borders of definition and to seamlessly cast his touch across the surface of all existing things...so as to invite the inexistent.

---

164 Adonis, 'Psalm', in *Victims of a Map*, tr. A. al-Udhari (London: Saqi Books, 2008), 107.

With this passage we stand at the heart of a centrifuge (too many dimensions in simultaneity) and therefore can only attempt to distil the elements potentially at stake here in isolated succession. We are told first that 'he comes unarmed like a forest', suggesting either a state of pure vulnerability (masochistically plunging himself into danger) or pure invincibility (incapable of being wounded), or perhaps a combination of both whereby the more damaged he becomes, the more immortal he becomes. There are indeed stories of such gods who thrive in their laceration. But we are then told that he is also 'like a destined cloud', marking the second time this apparently human form is referred to as a force of nature (forest, cloud), this time with the added twist of an inherent destiny. The notion of his being 'destined' means that there is fair warning of the turbulent entrance of this colossus onto the scene, no longer an anomaly or rupture but a long-awaited storm. But even more importantly, one wonders whether this implies a self-inflected fatalism (he sends himself forth) or whether he is just the prosthesis of a yet higher entity (sent by another). The next articulation—that 'yesterday he carried a continent and changed the position of the sea'—speaks to his aggressive capacity to carry out mammoth transpositions of unworlding and re-worlding. And the fact that he does so while 'painting the back of day' and 'creating daylight out of his feet' reveals that it is an act of cosmic aesthetics rather than a sacred requirement. This is an artisan-colossus who waves a chiasmic brush to reverse whatever colours and shapes cross his path, just as he 'borrows the night's shoes' in a gentle reciprocity and can 'dance for the soil so it can yawn'. A painter, a dancer; he is a being of artistic rejuvenation who does not anthropomorphize the earth, but rather renders former classifications obsolete with such radical freedom that anything can take on any given trait (trees that sleep, night that walks...). This is also the secret behind his dual powers of transfiguration and aggrandizement, for it is worth noting that he 'lives where the stone becomes a lake, the shadow a city', thereby storing the ingenuity with which this particular colossus makes all things colossal in kind. He widens, orbits, and magnifies extant beings beyond their former finitude, in an expenditure so concrete that it militates against the far-fetched axioms of both 'despair' and 'hope'. For in the place of petty existential conditions that always await 'what will not come', we find him stationed boldly at 'the crossroads', conscripting the oncoming, making silhouettes turn against their own accord, and 'drawing the magic sign on the forehead of time' with inventive extravagance. The colossus signals an interval of unstoppable alterations; he conveys new lineaments through a smooth manipulative grip, where nothing is allowed to remain as it once was upon meeting the pliant hands of a roaming master sculptor set to unhinge, to refashion, and to revel in the grand plasticity of foundations.

Colossus and the forest; the unarmed; the destined; change; creation; despair; hope; dancing; the crossroads; the forehead; magical sign; time

4

Anxiety holds the heart
With its tiny iron hand
Mud stirs in the belly of a giant woman

In the shower with their giant drops

Here
The naked sultan whimpers under his silken eyelids
Unhappy
By walled-in-giants in ether
Who no longer carry their whips in hand

JOYCE MANSOUR[165]

We encounter our fourth colossomaniac amid three separate juxtapositions of bodily experience, each tied to a distinct organ or appendage depending on the specific impulse in circulation. What this teaches us is that the colossus should not always be perceived as a unified creature, neither overall nor throughout, but rather often emerges as a compartmentalized assemblage whose sovereignty is tied to a single branch, extremity, or area of musculature. Indeed there are thousands of folkloric, heroic, and even prophetic examples of exceedingly

165 Mansour, *Essential Poems and Writings*, 301, 327, 331.

strong beings whose dominant functionality resides in some exclusive part of themselves (the hair, the eyes, the left hand).

If the unleashing of colossomaniacal potential here requires an acute sensory trigger, then we can look to the first stanza's reference to 'the heart' and 'the tiny iron hand' alongside the 'belly of a giant woman', wherein it appears that a certain combative animosity arises between different portions of the human composition. If anxiety should triumph in its constrictive clutching of the heart, then the colossus's manic overture must revolt against the heart by selecting the stomach as its ideal anatomical sphere. Moreover, rather than align with some sacred property such as blood, this colossus (the giant woman) is found stirring mud in the belly, a foul yet highly corporeal substance from which swampland offspring (those who slither and burrow) emanate to feed or sleep, rather than their angelic counterparts (those who perch and impose) who apprehensively institute and engrave the law in the cardiac cores of the fearful. 'Stirs' (as a method of fluidity) versus 'holds' (as a method of constraint).

In the second stanza, we again see this turn towards liquidity over solidity in the wake of a 'shower with their giant drops', reflecting a certain manic experience of torrential downpour. The above registers are no longer pristine metaphysical kingdoms or even self-contained holy provinces, but porous arenas of surge, deluge, and inundation. Colossomaniacal skies are therefore envisioned as perpetually streaming and soaking the ground below (the feeling of immeasurable rainfall, incalculable wetness).

Lastly, the third stanza arrests us in yet another negative existential state before the '[u]nhappy' visage of a 'naked sultan' who 'whimpers under his silken eyelids'. Again a conflict emerges from the rift between human society (born of self-regulating technologies) and the colossomaniacal unbound (born of overabundant instincts to lash out and flow). But in this fabled context we see an injustice transpiring, a perverse inversion of hierarchy: a pathetically fragile humanity has appointed itself to some fabricated political superiority, while the beautifully lavish aristocracy of giants now finds itself 'walled-in' and deprived of its timeless 'whips'. Crucially, the new prison-house of the colossi is that of the 'ether': a fictitious upper air contrived by philosophical charlatans incapable of mastering the terrestrial plane. So it is that the once-plentiful colossal entities are now held captive in the ethereal smoke-and-mirror confluence of discourses, their ample tendons tied down, unable to flagellate the false king who cries in pitiful loathing for his own nudity and yet rules with phantom ornamentality over the world they built with coarsest hands. Nakedness (the human disgrace of Eden) versus Bareness (the ecstasy of titanic universes). And yet, given a fair chance, they would seize their right to punishment; they would flog the stark artificiality of the impostors.

Colossus and the belly; stirring; mud; the shower; bareness; the walls; the whip

5

The crow which flew over our heads
and descended into the disturbed thought
of a vagabond cloud
and the sound of which traversed
the breadth of the horizon
like a short spear
will carry the news of us to the city.
Everyone knows,
everyone knows
we have found our way
into the cold, quiet dream of phoenixes
we found truth in the garden
in the embarrassed look of a nameless flower,
and we found permanence
in an endless moment
when two suns stared at each other.

FORUGH FARROKHZAD[166]

We encounter our fifth colossomaniac amid a covert exchange of affection, as immensity appears through forbidden transactions in some secret garden. The colossus here, then, is the fugitive domain of lovers whose rendezvous occurs in a forgetting of the dialectic of

166 Farrokhzad, *A Lonely Woman*, 96.

judgment and sin (there is no world left to obstruct). And yet they are quickly detected, found out, and condemned by the arbiters of dogmatic custom—for the war between colossus and human is equivalent to a struggle between spontaneous affirmation (ethos of private desire) and systematic negation (ethos of public obedience).

The colossomaniacal lovers of this passage are in search of a runaway exteriority, somewhere they can garner measures of euphoric time-space apart from the otherwise stern keepers of social chronology (the orchard, the forest, the grove). Thus the remarkable significance of the statement that 'we have found our way' (i.e., an eloper's path), whereupon they expose themselves to the 'cold, quiet dream of phoenixes' (i.e., mythic creatures of immolation and regeneration). And yet the lovers' sanctuary is always under threat of incursion, incessantly stalked by the black-feathered 'crow' who punctures their 'vagabond cloud' and takes word of their prohibited meeting back to the sanctimonious jurisdiction of the temples. They are in fact betrayed by the explosive utterances of their own pleasure, the sonic incrimination of their sighing, moaning, and panting, which 'traversed the breadth of the horizon' to such a dire extent that now 'everyone knows, everyone knows'.

The colossomaniacal experience is hence defined across two intersecting axes: (1) the pandemonium of sound that escapes their throats/lips in the moment of erotic seclusion; (2) the vastness of the lush hideaway they construct. Note that, in either instance, their affective potency does not reside in some transgressive exhilaration; they are not enticed by their own unlawful disposition, nor does the looming possibility of rumour, stigma, and criminality intensify the affair. Quite the opposite: they do not revel in the status of being offenders, but rather perfect an alternative colossal technique of shielding—that is, they become temporarily neglectful and absent-minded in the illicit trade of 'embarrassed looks'; they effectively block out the numbing recitations of the social world and fall charmed beneath their own incantatory union. This is how they win a certain lyrical immunity, at least for a short while, stretching out like 'an endless moment'—and this stolen 'permanence' is of such delightful grandeur that it turns them both from mortal individuals into celestial bodies ('when two suns stared at each other'). The garden becomes a tiny shelter for an infinitizing passion, an amoral lair with antidotes to ward off the deadening non-solarity of the people left behind.

Colossus and the garden; the vagabond;
sound; traversal; horizon; knowing; permanence; solarity

6

In time he began calling the wadis and chasms and mountains by the names of the figures painted on their rocks. This was the Wadi of Gazelles, that the Path of the Hunters, that the Waddan Mountains, that, again, the Herdsmen's Plain; until, finally, he'd discovered the great jinni, the masked giant rising alongside [...] There a cluster of caves stood, crowned by mighty rocks; and these were flanked by that one towering rock that stood like a building soaring toward the sky, like a pagan statue fashioned by the gods. The masked jinni, with his sacred waddan, covered the colossal stone face from top to bottom. He stood long gazing at the tableau, then tried, vainly, to climb the rocks to touch the great jinni's mask.

IBRAHIM AL-KONI[167]

We encounter our sixth colossomaniac in a desert valley of representational images and vaulting iconic likenesses. It forms its own labyrinth of incredible caves, rock formations, painted aspects of an unknown nomadic mysticism—and at their centre a tremendously formidable, carved figure known as the *masked jinni*—an alarming shape, all stern and incomparable striations, which rises dreadfully upwards and watches over the gorge with eyes demanding

167 Al-Koni, *The Bleeding of the Stone*, 5.

veneration. A young tribesman is charged with the sacred duty of standing guard in the chasm's basin by day and by night, holding vigil before the perplexing statue to screen against the rancour of modern humanity and its destructive tendencies.

Here we have a literal colossus etched in elevated stone, and an intuitive youth, divorced from family and clan as he accepts the role of caretaker to this exquisite form (of which he knows almost nothing). His first initiation into its presence is an experience of ever-mounting bewilderment, as he stares obsessively, transfixed by its enigmatic quality (at once austere and riotous). This is the acrobatic tightrope of all idolatry, but here the idol is accentuated to overbearing levels. Nor is it incidental that all of this takes place in utter solitude, with no one to offer answers or doctrines that might correspond with the statue's initial purpose, for this compels the young man to draft his own totemic account. In the absence of any given chronicles, he is exempted from truth telling and proceeds unburdened to 'begin calling the wadis and chasms and mountains by the names of the figures painted on their rocks'. This discreet naming-act alone seals him into the alluring chamber of the valley and its many boulders, footholds, talismans, and granite inhabitants. He devises an esoteric storytelling and by extension a confidential relation to each manifestation, including the animals (*waddan*) believed to have hallowed ties to these revered plateaus of the herdsmen and the hunters. And yet it is the masked figure, above all others, that reigns over his perception with the harshest sway. In fact, so enamoured is the young guardian that he even brilliantly assumes the 'masked giant' to be an object 'fashioned by the gods' themselves, thus amplifying his task through the idea of a positive contamination: the statue has been directly forged by deities and hence itself carries the residual trace of godliness. From here, his thinking follows a path completely logical to mania: the increasing urge to 'climb the rocks to touch the great jinni's mask'. Beyond all conventional paradigms of prayer or pilgrimage, here we see the most strident fanaticism at work, the true summit of active supplication, as the youth begins (completely alone) to scale the rock face in quest of ephemeral contact with the colossus...though not to touch the face, but just the mask, for this layering is its own necessarily arcane mediation (pure immediacy would only bring instant annihilation). The colossus is thus even more threatening in its transparent obscurity, more mesmerizing in its impenetrable cloaking, for it is not the absence of an impossibly distant, unseen god sending messages but rather the inscrutability of a hyper-visible master who commands unconditional absorption and astonishment amid wordlessness. It is not surprising then that our young shepherd grows at once more tranquil and more paranoid throughout the tale, infused with an almost catastrophic calmness that signals his own inevitable martyrdom (jugular slit before the graven image). Colossal adoration demands colossal finality.

Colossus and the chasm; painting; stone; gazing; the statue; the mask

7

To search
to discover
and then
to choose of one's will
and to project the essence of oneself into a fortress

AHMAD SHAMLU[168]

We encounter our seventh colossomaniac engaged in a profound meditation upon death and its several prospective avenues. In the piece's first unquoted verse, the poetic interlocutor speaks of fearing not death itself (the indeterminate claws of the terminal) but dying in a homeland that is 'unworthy'—a damning epithet that he extends universally to encompass all nations. No human terrain holds sufficient nobility to meet death on the right terms—not that he holds the phenomenon of death itself in any great standing, for earlier in the same poem he proclaims that its 'hands are more brittle than banality itself'. Rather, bare life, in its obscene routinization, has grown so worthy of contempt that he despises the thought of 'dying in a land where the wages of the gravedigger are worth more than an individual's freedom'. The rebel poet therefore remains preoccupied with somehow ensuring

168 Shamlu, *Born Upon the Dark Spear*, 47.

an honourable negotiation of the end in an otherwise dishonourable world, and finds no alternative but to begin the journey toward a becoming-colossus.

Only the colossus dies well. The above is a seemingly unadorned stanza, and yet it lays out a meticulous formula, taking us from *searching* to *discovery* to *willed choice* to *projection* to *fortification*, that aspires to successfully prepare the manic individual for a superior perishing. More than a philosophical prescription, it is nothing short of a regimen of existential training to be decoded, internalized, and executed. We start with an injunction 'to search', a simple premise on the surface, but one that requires an often-agonizing self-realization that one's identity stands incomplete. To search is to confess the gaping hole of irresolution that leaves a blood trail wherever one walks. From this first step of extreme susceptibility, we then advance to the second degree—'to discover'—which would ostensibly quiet the anguish of the searcher's condition. But one must beware the misleading glow of a quick cure, for this writer often warns that most 'discoveries' are but ideological bait luring one down the well of further afflicted iterations of identity. To discover is hence to discover many prevailing forms, the majority of which entrap subjectivity in further binding quarters of weakness, alienation, or even enslavement. And so what is the protocol of differentiation? How does one proceed to sift through the garbage heap of possibility in order to find the diamond conviction? Maybe a clue resides in the next line, for one who survives this bitter phase of the trial will by right be one who correctly 'choose[s] of one's will'. At last, now we enter the landmine-ridden theoretical territory of the decision, for the author clearly does not mean some simple declaration of responsibility (only the most backbreaking measure will suffice). No, we are in the presence here of someone who himself literally stood before firing squads and torture chambers, thus pointing to a calibre of alertness that inscribes itself at often horrific costs. Not merely to die for the choice 'of one's will', but to guarantee that this willed death also produce a colossal illumination for the living; to somehow exploit nothingness as an incandescent missive to future sacrificial searchers, the base point of what might be called a death-in-free-form. This is what is meant by the final convulsive line—'and to project the essence of oneself into a fortress'—a colossomaniacal decree whereby one forfeits a single essence to launch upward the most elite citadel (against all centres). To die *colossally* is therefore to distribute an energetic ration: on the one side, to maim and paralyze with spectral impact those who live as if already dead; and on the other side, to rouse further those who have already learned how to turn their deaths into maximal instantiations of living, into sheer bastions, never more deliriously alive than when the blade falls upon them. Half-sabotage; half-propulsion.

The unparalleled laughter of those who build their camps in the borderlands of slaughter.

Colossus and searching; discovery; projection; the fortress

8

But in a flash we all understood the significance of what had happened. Some sniper had fired a shot at the rope and in doing so had demonstrated his prowess for everyone in the neighborhood to see. He'd said to us all: I'm capable of hitting any target, however tiny or delicate it may be. Every one of your hearts is within my range. I could put bullet holes through your arteries one by one. I could aim inside the very pupils of your eyes without missing the mark. I can aim my bullets at any part of your bodies I choose.

GHADA SAMMAN[169]

We encounter our eighth colossomaniac back in the throes of civil war, as the tenants of a sprawling city remain locked away in their apartments (Arabic *hisar*, meaning 'siege'). Their collective helplessness is palpable; they are each barricaded within the four walls of a home-turned-prison, with no assured release in store; they face either eventual starvation or grenades shattering through windows. The city itself is continually trampled by marauding sects who keep close and constant surveillance, making every street an incendiary battle-in-waiting. And poised above the rooftops stands a unique colossal force: the sniper.

169 Samman, *Beirut Nightmares*, 7.

In this passage, we are taken into the almost mechanical mindset of the gunman, an expert who understands time and space only through the crosshairs of a target and whose topographical vision of the metropolis is itself filtered through the black sights of a rifle. This colossus is anonymous; this colossus is brutal; this colossus is non-interchangeable; this colossus is infallibly accurate. They cannot go outside; they cannot test his aim, and are held hostage to the purgatorial sentence of an all-seeing firearm. The fact that the caged city-dwellers 'in a flash understood the significance of what had happened' illustrates the spine-rattling velocity with which the sniper makes his point, his ammunition conveying an ultra-awareness of their predicament (strandedness) with the blazing speed of near-instantaneity. Moreover, the fact that he seizes this occasion to 'demonstrate his prowess' transports us back to an epoch of marvellous performativity when shamans and soothsayers deigned to flaunt their might in competitive displays. To be somehow both esoteric and brazen, wearing one's prescience barefacedly (the sibyl, the telepathist). And like all cunning figures of divination, the gunman's message is delivered with unmistakable resonance: he is 'capable of hitting any target, however tiny or delicate it may be'. The sniper's dark exceptionalism rests in a double-edged talent: (1) the traversal of spatial distance, able to reach across the separation and the in-between to strike with invasive perfection; (2) the dominance of miniature entry points, able to navigate the thinnest, the frailest, and the narrowest straits of being. The colossal is therefore framed here as an occult endowment of both unmatched scope and precision, the peerlessness of a micro-focus culminating in a long record of perforated veins and sinew. This is what such a gifted inclination to piercing seems to tell us, and yet it is his next intrusive warning that stands out ('I could aim inside the very pupils of your eyes without missing the mark.'), for it suggests an ironic interplay of omniscience: the one who sees everything savours his ability to blind all others. Scrupulous; well trained; ghoulish. His clarity becomes their convolution.

Colossus and the city; flash; prowess; the target; the mark; aim; the sniper

9

> *On the slope, higher than the sea, higher than the cypresses,*
> *they slept.*
> *The iron sky erased their memories, and the dove flew away*
> *in the direction of their pointing fingers, east of their torn*
> *bodies* [...]
>
> *They sleep beyond the limits of space, on a slope where*
> *words turn to stone.*
> *They sleep on a stone carved from the bones of their*
> *phoenix.*
> *Our heart can celebrate their feast in nearly no time.*
>
> MAHMOUD DARWISH[170]

We encounter our ninth colossomaniac staring upward in the certainty that inestimably large beings take residence at high altitudes. Their immensity is experienced as a stratospheric phenomenon, aloft in the farthest astronomical space, their torsos cushioned in azure firmaments. And yet what is impressive about this descriptive rendering is the suspicion that such giants are in actuality forces of radical idleness, forever reclining or sleeping in states of forgetful resignation. They are anti-athletic sages whose restfulness and hush alone permeate the void, bereft of urgency or awakening...the colossus-in-cessation.

---

170 Darwish, *Unfortunately, It Was Paradise*, 16.

The poetic voice begins by situating us 'on the slope', where bases slide easily into disequilibrium, but why is this particular experience of the colossal accompanied by such imbalance? Even worse, might these slumbering figures soon drop unknowingly from their platforms, to come crashing down upon their counterparts below? The fact that they exist in spiral chambers 'higher than the sea, higher than the cypresses' only augments this danger, making an enemy of gravity's pressure as we imagine thc collisional shock of their impression striking the dust, or ourselves (the awful brunt of the fall). Furthermore, that they have lain themselves down in some unbreakable repose makes them intrinsically unreliable overseers; they have quit or renounced the game of creation itself, deserted the ever-rusting scales of Being. We cannot count on those who abide by a non-code of dormancy and irresponsibility, leaving us undefended amid their carelessness. Even more, the colossal ones have seemingly entered a condition of amnesiac tranquillity ('the iron sky erased their memories'). But why commission a metallic cosmos to purge all traces of our remembrance, and why order the dove (emissary of peace) to 'fly away'? What malice or detrimental wisdom is at work here, as they close their eyes gradually to our existential plight? No, this docility is purposeful; otherwise, they would not have selected for their bedroom a highly insular cocoon 'beyond the limits of space'. And the dove was clearly ordered to flee at the guidance 'of their pointing fingers'. This is a deliberative ejection, the retraction of the ceiling away from our breathing, restive forms; the colossal figures make their default a fatalistic matter of turning 'words [...] to stone'. It is a planned gesture of insensibility (elective unconsciousness), a conspiracy to blackout, whether vindictive or just weary; but this sound-proof limbo is purchased at highest cost. 'They sleep on a stone carved from the bones of their phoenix', making innocence their pillow—as the sacrificial mutilation of the phoenix (mirroring the gashes on their own 'torn bodies') in itself marks the extinction of all possibility for rebirth. The colossal ones will not allow their own revival (no embryonic return, no way back from their comatose slouch), thus consigning us to a hollow ritual 'to celebrate their feast in nearly no time'. Their stupor becomes our insomnia; their disregard consigns us to the desolation of the being-on-our-own, hailing seismic collapse, our last resort tied to the improbable chance that they might one day turn into sleepwalkers.

Colossus and the slope; height; sleep; memory erasure; celebration; the feast; the sleepwalker

10

> *The same dream recurs every night. There's a need for this ancient music, and yet how many of these timeless death stories have disappeared? What eternal naivety there is in tales about our beautiful death! These little stories that are pointed like a toothbrush. Why did we contrive to complicate these death stories? A giant shadow poses these questions to the man in the dream.*
>
> HASSAN BLASIM[171]

We encounter our tenth colossomaniac in an absurd scenario, waking one morning to find a soft smile etched across his face for no reason. It is uncontrollable; it overtakes the mouth and then his entire persona. A once-normal individual, this trivial supplement of the smile begins to cloak him in a deviant aura. It alienates those around him; it courts anger among the narcotized masses; it causes havoc in every communal setting (part provocation, part veil). His mad look offends a cinema audience as he grins through a tragic film; he is exiled from a bar of right-wing zealots, his beaming interpreted as a kind of partisan mockery. This lone impractical detail now ravages his interrelations with the whole external world, ending badly amid a barrage of concussive blows as a

171 Blasim, *The Madman of Freedom Square*, 86.

gang of bitter men leave him to die bleeding and beaten in a wooded clearing. And the source of this expressive contortion? A colossal shadow, we are told.

The excerpt above is taken from the night before the smile's emergence, a night which, like every other, is infested with a particular recurring dream: that of a woman brushing her teeth (set to die four years later) and a man tumbling down a well to the bottom of a staircase. When our narrator awakens, the smile that will later persist even into his autopsy introduces itself, as if surgically attached to the teeth. Does it stem from some serpentine continuation of this 'same dream [that] recurs every night', a waking vestige of its repetition-compulsion? The next line (seemingly disjointed) speaks of a 'need for this ancient music', as if the smile is the reactive remnant of a listening to some inaudible melody, a rustling in the nocturnal folds that then slinks into his daylight hours, though perhaps most important is this qualification of such primeval music-dreaming as a matter of lethal necessity. He continues in a strange lament over the disappearance of such 'timeless death stories' and the 'eternal naivety' they granted, castigating modern consciousness for its attempt to 'complicate' these otherwise 'beautiful' fatal narratives. But it is precisely here that we hit an abrupt dead-end, for we are told that these death-stream musings are not even comprised of his own self-spoken words but rather echo the interrogational questions posed by a 'giant shadow' to 'the man in the dream'. According to this accusation, the colossus is therefore a herald of inauspicious turns, one who creeps and scratches into sleeping minds to restore a different legend of the last breath. The vague smile, in turn, is the all-swathing emblem of this pact between death and dreaming, responding to the nightly whispers of some hulking form who creates a new gravitational field of doubt in the ears and across the mouth. And yet what is the exact intention of this giant shadow, its wrathful distrust and revenge against the decorated word/image of disaster? Why does it strive to maintain the simplicity of ancient death tales? Is there a sacred orthodoxy of finality that must be upheld, without embellishment or metaphor, failure to do so being punished by the imprinting of a frivolous smile that only draws hatred (its own mark of Cain)?

Colossus and the recurring dream; necessity; the ancient; music; the death story; the question; the shadow

* * *

We can picture the islands where the first colossal forms were sculpted: the Invictus, the unvanquished, the astral festivals and golden armour, the sun cults that forged a luminescent god with arrows, crown, torch, and chariot; his three children—dusk, night, and dawn; the halogen rays streaking from his hair. Many images flood the mind: the passenger arriving by boat who sails beneath its waist and kneels to gain safe passage; the metalsmith collecting endless bronze plates required to hammer out the abdomen alone; the caretaker responsible for polishing the broad shoulders, calves, and eyelids; the poets who harmonize their odes of frenzy and splendour; the earthquake that one day sent the legs crumbling into the ocean, and the sunken faces of the people watching the subsidence of their localized divinity. The incommensurate; the unequalled; fragile apotheosis. The will to immensity tempts immense wreckage.

Taking the colossus as a paragon of world thought leads us to seek out a paradoxical technique at once enveloping and yet highly acute, convinced and yet impermeable, sneaking and yet manifest, flagrant and yet unrelatable, iconic and yet iconoclastic, irrelevant and yet severe. It is to become unwavering though still emitting heretical waves; to simultaneously inflict possibility and intrigue. It is to situate the otherworldly concretely in the world, as a blank slate of both extreme power and atomized vulnerability, a prism of infinite superstition or an ideational minefield through which we rediscover epic, unrelenting notions. Stature that spellbinds, beguiles, frightens, agitates, and even possesses. Hardest trance; hardest enchantment. World thought as approximation of the unbearable (a return to giant idols).

Omnicide Returned: Endtime Visions

While combining mania and fatality might eventually generate an omnicidal conclusion (the killing of everything), we must also understand omnicide as the manic envisioning of all possible methods, atmospheres, complications, and experiences of this end (killing by every means imaginable). The many ways of the dream, and the dream of many ways.

The omnicidal mind wonders after all the potential times at which worlds could end: Should things cease at dawn, midnight, or twilight, at sunrise or sunset, in its early hours or later ages or middle passage? Should its relation to speed include accelerationist or slower tempos (or even racing between instantaneity and stillness)? Should its relation to death be considered a true accentuation of the mortal lot (absolute limit), an expansion of finality's core into a temporal beyond (aftermath, undead), or a supersession of deathliness altogether (eternality)?

The omnicidal mind wonders after all the potential spaces in which worlds could end: Should things cease in the terrestrial domains of the desert, the jungle, the forest, the sea, the mountain, the cave, or the garden, or should they cease in the designed zones of the library, the courtyard, the rooftop, the laboratory, the prison, alley, temple, or asylum? Should things cease in transitional spaces of the in-between (the archway, the corridor, the gate, the portal, the closet, the hotel room), or should they cease in the cosmological outer spaces (sky, constellation, ether, nebula, multiverse)?

The omnicidal mind wonders after all the potential objects through which worlds could end: Should things cease by sharpened or dull blade, curved or straight implement (dagger, razor, axe, spear, scythe), grasped by which metallic hilt (gold, silver, copper, steel, iron) or smooth material (wood, ivory, mother of pearl), and adorned with jewels of what colour (emerald, sapphire, turquoise), what pictorial etching (landscape, battle scene, calligraphic inscription)? What acute philosophical difference does it make to contemplate the world's end by fire (candle, torch, matchstick, chemical ignition, dragon-breath, lightning storm, nuclear blast), or by poison (cyanide, arsenic, anthrax, strychnine, ricin), weighing the gradients of paralytic agents or ecological pollutants that induce twitching, muscular constriction, asphyxiation, intoxication, and unconsciousness, and those serums delivered by syringe, inhalation, or random contact.

The omnicidal mind wonders after all the potential atmospheres in which worlds could end: Should things cease amid great marathons of fog (mist, blindness), heat (inferno), cold (ice age), or disappearance (avenged nothingness)? In a setting of open air or in confined quarters? And how does it radically alter the experience to consider the many geological disasters that could do omnicide's bidding: earthquake, flood, cyclone, meteor, famine, tidal wave, volcanic rupture? No doubt this atmospheric line of thought includes even the materiality of the end: its texture (smoothness or coarseness; manifestation across states of solidity, liquidity, or aeriality); its tactile form (like glass, cloth, or vapour); its proper colouration (blood reds, oceanic blues, diamond whites, smoke-like greys, pitch blacks).

The omnicidal mind wonders after all the potential impulses and motives through which worlds could end: Should things cease at the hands of human greed, envy, hatred, revenge, ambition, despair, adoration, reverence, seduction, rivalry, conquest, testing, surrender, excitement, splendour, misunderstanding, mercy, trance, or accident? Is the manic-fatal moment perceived as miracle, accomplishment, failure, necessity, or waste?

The omnicidal mind wonders after all the potential experiences emitted as worlds end: Should things cease in the face of pure fear (dread, anxiety, hysteria, horror, terror, pandemonium), or some particular typology of pain (abandonment, humiliation, sorrow, torment, agony, misery), or perhaps borne by pleasure (scintillation, ecstasy, rapture, delirium, euphoria)? Is it the eleventh hour of mourning (fallenness, loss), indifference (alienation, diabolical coldness) or celebration (festival, banquet, glory)? Is it experienced as something of intuition, destiny, disavowed knowledge, or pure surprise? Is it a performance sealing honour (overcoming, affirmation, vitality) or violation (defilement, condemnation, slavery)?

The omnicidal mind wonders after all the potential movements through which worlds end: Should things cease by trembling, writhing, running, kneeling, prostration, convulsion, swaying, dance, palpitation? Should its imminent process be one of erosion, decay, evaporation, fracture, evanescence, or devouring? A sacrificial token, or a tearing-apart by wolves?

The omnicidal mind wonders after all the potential utterances through which worlds end: Should things cease by some cruel spokenness (scream, gripe, outcry, panting, whisper, curse, howl, silence, echo), or by some chosen textual genre (religious scripture, philosophical tome, poetic verse, epic, play, short story, novel, aphorism, treatise, memoir, anthem, night-song, elegy, incantation, rant, nonsense)? In that vein, should the fatal password pursue a language of defamation, recitation, command, tragic lament, rageful vitiation, convoluted babbling, or toneless reckoning?

The omnicidal mind wonders after all the potential traces which ending worlds leave behind: Should things be wrought into debris, ash, smoke, dust, wasteland, artefact, ruin, image, tremor, fragment, shadow, virtual remnant, or total void? Should there be a single witness (sado-masochist, voyeur, messenger, chronicler, visionary) or a single architect (conspirator, doomsday prophet, seer, game-master, champion) to stand before the cherished erasure of all things?

There are countless stories we might tell ourselves at the world's bedtime (when putting to rest), though this is no simple narrative gesture: rather, each speculative horizon opens onto its being-fathomed, being-plotted, and being-fulfilled. The maniac is therefore the ultimate storyteller, and the storyteller is the ultimate closer of worlds (literally speaking: 'The End'). To visualize fatality through the maniacal looking glass is thus to bring forth the very time in which vision no longer happens: the close call; the supposed-to-lose. For every storyteller harbours a secret desire to be the one who tells the last story, just as every maniac wishes to inscribe the last fateful madness on earth.

Select Bibliography

ADONIS. *The Pages of Day and Night*, tr. S. Hazo. Evanston: Northwestern University Press, 2000.

— *A Time Between Ashes and Roses*, tr. S. Toorawa. Syracuse, NY: Syracuse University Press, 2004.

— 'Psalm', in *Victims of a Map*, tr. A. al-Udhari. London: Saqi Books, 2008.

— *Selected Poems*, tr. K. Mattawa. New Haven: Yale University Press, 2010.

BACHELARD, GASTON. *The Poetics of Reverie*, tr. D. Russell. Boston: Beacon Press, 1960.

BENSMAIA, RÉDA. *The Year of Passages*, tr. T. Conley. Minneapolis: University of Minnesota Press, 1995.

BLASIM, HASSAN. *The Madman of Freedom Square*, tr. J. Wright. Manchester: Carcanet Press, 2010.

— *Iraqi Christ*, tr. J. Wright. Manchester: Comma Press, 2013.

BURAIKAN, MAHMOUD AL-. 'The Bedouin Whose Face No One Saw', tr. A. Lawandow, in *Matahat Al-Farashah* (Labyrinth of the Moth), B. Al-Marabi (ed.). Cologne: Kamel Verlag, 2003.

DARWISH, MAHMOUD. *Unfortunately, It Was Paradise*, tr. M. Akash, C. Forche, S. Antoon, and A. El-Zein. Berkeley, CA: University of California Press, 2003.

— *The Butterfly's Burden*, tr. F. Joudah. Port Townsend, WA: Copper Canyon Press, 2007.

— 'I Am Yusuf', tr. A. Amireh, <http://www.naseeb.com/villages/journals/1-palestinian-poetry-oh-my-father-i-am-yusuf-68387>.

FARROKHZAD, FORUGH. *A Lonely Woman: Forugh Farrokhzad and Her Poetry*, tr. M. Hillmann. New York: Three Continents Press, 1987.

Green, T.A. (ed.). *Folklore: An Encyclopedia of Beliefs, Customs, Tales, Music, and Art*, vol. 1. Santa Barbara, CA: ABC-CLIO, 1997.

HEDAYAT, SADEQ. *The Blind Owl*, tr. D.P. Costello. New York: Grove Press, 1957.

— 'The Benedictions', in E. Yarshater (ed.), *Sadeq Hedayat: An Anthology*. Boulder, CO: Westview Press, 1979.

— *Three Drops of Blood*, tr. D. Miller Mostaghel. London: Alma Books, 2013.

KONI, IBRAHIM AL-. *The Bleeding of the Stone*, tr. M. Jayyusi and C. Tingley. Northampton, NY: Interlink, 2002.

— *The Seven Veils of Seth*, tr. W. M. Hutchins. Reading: Garnet Publishing, 2008.

— *The Puppet*, tr. W. M. Hutchins. Austin, TX: Center for Middle Eastern Studies, University of Texas, 2010.

— *Ibrahim al-Koni Interview: In the Desert We Visit Death*, interviewed by Anders Hastrup. Louisiana Channel, produced by Louisiana Museum of Modern Art, 2014.

— *A Sleepless Eye: Aphorisms from the Sahara*, tr. R. Allen. Syracuse, NY: Syracuse University Press, 2014.

MANSOUR, JOYCE. *Screams*, tr. S. Gavronsky. Sausalito, CA: Post Apollo, 1995.

— *Essential Poems and Writings*, tr. S. Gavronsky. Boston: Black Widow Press, 2008.

MICHAUX, HENRI. 'In the Land of Magic', in *Darkness Moves: An Henri Michaux Anthology, 1927–1984*, tr. D. Ball. Berkeley, CA: University of California Press, 1997.

MOHAGHEGH, JASON BAHBAK. *New Literature and Philosophy of the Middle East: The Chaotic Imagination*. New York: Palgrave Macmillan, 2010.

— *Inflictions: The Writing of Violence in the Middle East*. London: Continuum, 2012.

— 'The Captive and the Exile: Vulnerability, Sensation, Desire' and 'Paradox, Ecstasy and the Catastrophic Mind: Apocalyptic Writing', in *The Radical Unspoken: Silence in Middle Eastern and Western Thought*. New York: Routledge, 2013.

— *Insurgent, Poet, Mystic, Sectarian: The Four Masks of an Eastern Postmodernism*. New York: SUNY Press, 2015.

NEGARESTANI, REZA. 'The Militarization of Peace' and 'Solar Inferno and Earthbound Abyss', in *Abducting the Outside: Collected Writings 2003–2018*. Falmouth and New York: Urbanomic/Sequence Press, 2019.

SAMMAN, GHADA. *Beirut Nightmares*, tr. N. Roberts. London: Quartet Books, 1976.

— 'The Swan Genie', in *The Square Moon: Supernatural Tales*, tr. I. Boullata. Fayetteville, AR: University of Arkansas Press, 1999.

SHAMLU, AHMAD. 'The Road Past the Bridge', tr. J. Mohaghegh, from *Majmu'eh-ye Asar-e Ahmad Shamlu* (*The Collected Works of Ahmad Shamlu*). Tehran: Zamaneh Press, 1381/2002.

— *Born Upon the Dark Spear*, tr. J. Mohaghegh. New York: Contra Mundum Press, 2015.

URBANOMIC/SEQUENCE PRESS TITLES

The Concept of Non-Photography
François Laruelle

Fanged Noumena: Collected Writings 1987–2007
Nick Land

The Number and the Siren: A Decipherment of Mallarmé's Coup de Dés
Quentin Meillassoux

Synthetic Philosophy of Contemporary Mathematics
Fernando Zalamea

From Decision to Heresy: Experiments in Non-Standard Thought
François Laruelle

To Live and Think Like Pigs:
The Incitement of Envy and Boredom in Market Democracies
Gilles Châtelet

Intelligence and Spirit
Reza Negarestani

On Logic and the Theory of Science
Jean Cavaillès

Pleromatica, or Elsinore's Trance
Gabriel Catren

Omnicide II: Mania, Doom, and the Future-in-Deception
Jason Bahbak Mohaghegh

Post-Europe
Yuk Hui